Oliver Oldboy

George Bailey

A Tale of New York Mercantile Life

Oliver Oldboy

George Bailey
A Tale of New York Mercantile Life

ISBN/EAN: 9783337026714

Printed in Europe, USA, Canada, Australia, Japan

Cover: Foto ©Suzi / pixelio.de

More available books at **www.hansebooks.com**

GEORGE BAILEY

A Tale of

NEW YORK MERCANTILE LIFE

BY

OLIVER OLDBOY

NEW YORK

HARPER & BROTHERS, FRANKLIN SQUARE

1880

GEORGE BAILEY.

CHAPTER I.

"What's i' the air?
Some subtle spirit runs through all my veins.
Hope seems to ride this morning on the wind,
And joy outshines the sun."—PROCTER.

IT was a raw and gusty evening toward the end of March, 18—. The day had been cold, dreary, and sunless; great masses of leaden clouds had chased each other through the atmosphere; and the half-frozen snow of a late winter lay soiled on the streets and sidewalks of the city of New York. To the person whose business called him out-of-doors everything wore an aspect of indescribable gloom and discomfort.

At this period there existed in the central part of the city many rows of neat two-story houses with slanting roofs and dormer-windows, occupied by well-to-do citizens in the middle rank of life. Toward one of these houses a young man might have been seen walking with a quick, elastic step, his whole frame vibrating with perfect health, and his eye gleaming with hope and happiness. He was a little above the middle height, with great breadth of shoulder and depth of chest. His head was large, well set, and covered with masses of thick, dark hair. He strode along with the step of a young Titan, almost bounding in his eagerness to reach his home. He spurned the slush of the sidewalk, and he scorned the biting blast of the March wind.

"Oh Kate," said he, to the middle-aged domestic, who had answered his ring at the door-bell, "I am almost inclined to kiss you, I feel so happy."

"Oh fie, Mr. George! you ought to be ashamed of yourself!" replied the servant, with a smile which showed that she would not have been much hurt had he followed his inclinations.

"Where's mother—down-stairs or up?"

"She's up-stairs sewin' an' mendin', as usual."

The young man, having laid aside his overcoat and hat, ran up the stairs two steps at a time, gave an impatient knock at the door, and, without waiting for a reply, rushed into the room, seized his mother's head in both his hands, and showered a dozen kisses on her forehead and cheeks.

"Mother, congratulate me! mother, I'm in luck! No more poverty, no more struggling!"

"Why, George, what's the matter? Is the boy crazy? There, there, that will do. Tell me all about it."

"Mother, congratulate me; I almost ran home to tell you the good news. To-day I was promoted to be head-clerk, at a salary of three thousand dollars a year, in the house of Van Hess & Co. The old gentleman did it all. I am to be made junior partner at the end of the year; and — and he knows all about my feelings toward Grace, and he makes no objection."

"My son, we ought to thank our heavenly Father, who has been so good to the widow and orphan."

"Yes, my dear mother, I thank God always. But isn't it magnificent! When father died four years ago in debt, I was obliged to abandon my medical studies without a diploma, and most reluctantly enter a wholesale grocery store, in a subordinate position; and here I am on a fair way of becoming a merchant prince. After all, it is better than the life my poor father led, out late and early, curing the poor without profit, and leaving his wife and child to suffer for his easy good-nature."

"Hush, my dear! not one syllable against your good father. He was the best man I ever saw; and even you, George, are hardly as good as he."

"Now, mother mine, that's not exactly fair of you. You know that no son ever loved and respected a father more than I did mine; but that is no reason why he should have permitted hypocrites and impostors to ruin him, or why I should not condemn what I think was unwise. Every year since his death we have been pinched for money, and you have not been in the country for five years. But now, now, mother, during my holidays we shall go together to the mountains and the sea. The roses will come back to your cheeks, mother mine; and, do you know, you are a very good-looking young woman of forty, and who knows—"

"Hush, hush, you silly boy!"

It was a study to watch these two. The tears of pride and joy welled in the mother's eyes as she gazed at her strong, frank, and manly son, so like the husband she had lost; and the young man's deep blue eye was tender as he scanned the faded beauty of the delicate and fragile woman who had borne him. There was an indefinable expression of exquisite feeling in his face, such as good sons have for their mothers when they are still young and beautiful.

There was a ring at the door-bell; and Kate announced that Mr. Myron Finch desired to see Mr. George Bailey for a few minutes. Mrs. Bailey asked her son who Mr. Myron Finch was; for she had never heard his name before.

"Oh, he's a sort of friend of mine. I have a bowing acquaintance with him. We used to meet in the dissecting-room when I was studying medicine."

"Mr. Finch, I am glad to see you. What can I do for you?" were the words with which honest George Bailey accosted Myron Finch as he shook him cordially by the hand.

"Mr. Bailey, I have called to see you in relation to getting employment in some mercantile house. As you are already aware, I have been studying medicine and divinity, but to little purpose. I have pursued many callings since I came to New York, but have not succeeded in any. To-day I heard, by the merest accident, that there had been a general promotion in the house of Van Hess & Co., and that you (whom I cordially and sincerely congratulate on your good fortune) have been made head-clerk. This leaves a vacancy for which I would like to apply; and with your good word in my behalf, I think I might obtain it."

George Bailey was naturally a kind-hearted young man, and this evening, in particular, he felt unusually happy.

"My dear fellow," replied Bailey, "I shall do everything in my power to secure you the vacancy."

"Thank you, Mr. Bailey; I hope I shall merit your good opinion."

At this moment Mrs. Bailey entered the parlor on pretence of looking for something, but in reality to see what manner of man Myron Finch was. And what did she see? A young man somewhat below the middle height, with exceedingly light eyes, light hair, light eyebrows and light eyelashes. Were it not for this extreme light color, he might be called good-looking. His features were certainly regular. But there was a furtive restlessness in his pale blue eye which to the close observer imparted to his face a sinister expression.

Mr. Finch was introduced to Mrs. Bailey, and, after the usual salutations, the conversation was resumed by the latter.

"Suppose, then, Mr. Bailey, that I call at the store to-morrow; for I am very anxious to obtain permanent employment."

"Call to-morrow morning at 10 o'clock, and I shall take great pleasure in introducing you to Mr. Jacob Van Hess, the head of the firm, one of the kindest and gentlest of men."

In the conversation that followed George Bailey did nearly all the talking, and Myron Finch played the part of an attentive and respectful listener. George, in his present state of exaltation, excited by his promotion and his prospects, told his new friend a great deal more than was necessary; speaking of his father's debts, his own struggles, and his mother's patience. He even went so far as to state that all the debts were paid except one of $1500 to Mr. Wilde, of the firm of Warrenton, Wilde & Co. Several times his mother endeavored to catch his eye, but in vain. George rattled on. Bold, fearless, frank, and impulsive, and talking under the stimulus of success, and the gratification of using that success to help a former fellow-student, he spoke of private affairs which he had no right to mention to any one save his mother.

Myron Finch was cautiously measuring his man, and treasuring up every sentence that he uttered. Mrs. Bailey kept her gaze fastened on Mr. Finch with an air of suspicious watchfulness, as is the habit of all mothers, feline, canine, or human, when they instinctively feel that their offspring are in danger. Finch felt the mother's eye penetrating through and through him, and he became, under her glance, restless and uneasy. Mrs. Bailey's pale face became flushed, and her blue eye brilliant, as her maternal instinct became aroused.

With George's repeated promise that he would do all in his power to help him to obtain the vacancy in the house of Jacob Van Hess & Co., Myron Finch took his leave, obsequiously polite to the mother, and profuse in his expressions of thanks to the son. When he had left the house, Mrs. Bailey, in a very excited tone, exclaimed,

"George, George, why did you talk of our affairs to that young man? That man is a snake, and I know it—I feel it! Don't trust him, my son. Have nothing to do with him. Take my advice, and do not urge his appointment to the vacancy. If you do, you will be sorry for it. While you were talking I watched him. George, he is a snake—a snake—a snake!"

"Why, mother, this is really unlike you. I have never before seen you so excited. I have never heard you speak ill of any human being before to-night—not even of the people who robbed and plundered my poor father. Surely Mr. Finch did not say or do anything to cause you to speak so unkindly of him."

"I warn you, my son; you must drop this man. I am not mistaken. I do not reason with my intellect; I reason with my mother's heart, and that heart makes me feel him a venomous, poisonous snake."

"Mother," said the son, with a measured dignity of speech and manner, "my word has been given, and I cannot go back on my word. I am your only child—all that is left you— and you dream dreams and see visions. Your great love for me causes you to fancy danger where no danger exists. Come, cheer up, mother; here's a kiss for you, and another, and another. Why, mother, the excitement has brought back the roses to your cheek. Good-bye! I'm off to see Grace Van Hess;" and away strode the young man, hopeful, gallant, affectionate, and overflowing with good-will toward all mankind.

What sixth sense is this maternal instinct? Is it not some higher attribute given to good mothers, as to good angels, to warn them of the approach of danger?

CHAPTER II.

"How silver sweet sound lovers' tongues by night,
Like softest music to attending ears."—SHAKSPEARE.

THE house of Jacob Van Hess, to which George Bailey was now hastening with rapid strides, was one of the finest and most costly in the city. All that wealth could purchase in the way of painting, of statuary, and of bric-à-brac, rare, dainty, and delicate, were placed here and there in seemingly careless profusion; and yet there was unmistakable taste in all the arrangements. Indeed, it would have been very difficult for the most fastidious artist in form and color to have changed the position of a figure, or altered the shade of a single article of furniture, without detriment to the effect of the whole. Everywhere the eye fell on evidence of wealth without gaudiness or ostentation. The ceilings were lofty, the halls were wide, and the materials were of the best. Many of the paintings were by the old masters, and had been purchased by Mr. Van Hess during his last trip to Europe.

Jacob Van Hess had risen from a humble position to be one of the great merchant-princes of a metropolitan city.

His education was limited, his views narrow and circumscribed, and his opinions formed by his newspaper and his minister. His business, his politics, and his religion engrossed his time and attention. In his mercantile pursuits, in which he relied on his own sagacity, he was clear, simple, and direct, and governed by a strong sense of justice; but in other matters he was intensely prejudiced and bigoted. His panacea for all the evils of society was Total Abstinence, based upon Methodism. Two charities were almost entirely supported by his means; and it is needless to say that both belonged to his creed and accorded with his views on temperance. He did not believe in the higher education of the common people, nor in universal suffrage. The former he considered the parent of discontent, and the latter of license to do evil. Yet, withal, he was kind-hearted and generous, ready to relieve the afflicted, and sympathetic with all suffering.

It must have cost him thousands of dollars annually to support temperance lecturers and to issue temperance tracts. He waged unrelenting war against the liquor dealers; and year after year his agents were presenting bills to the Legislature which never had the least chance of being passed, and which were used by unscrupulous men for the purpose of extorting money out of the honest fanatic.

He had one other object of devotion—an only child, a daughter nineteen years old, on whom he bestowed a love boundless as the ocean. He had been long a widower; and all the treasures of his affections were reserved for his darling Grace, on whom he showered every favor and every luxury that money could purchase.

In the library of the beautiful home which has just been imperfectly described sat Grace Van Hess, a girl of rare loveliness of face and figure. Her complexion was smooth, soft, and white—that rare Knickerbocker complexion found only among pure Americans of Dutch descent. Her hair and eyes were in harmony with the color and texture of her skin. She would have been beautiful, but for an expression of weakness; and yet it was difficult to say where that weakness lay. Perhaps it was in the small, delicate mouth; perhaps in the eye, which was large, and slightly projecting. But no matter where it was, the expression of want of firmness was unmistakably stamped upon her otherwise charming face; reminding one of a fairly painted ship constructed of soft wood, which may safely sail in fine weather, but will assuredly founder in the first tempest that overtakes her.

Indulged by her father, her every want was not only gratified but anticipated; with domestics and teachers at command from infancy, she had nothing to think about, nothing to fear, nothing to struggle against. It is the hopes, and fears, and struggles, the high thoughts and noble aspirations, and, above all, the victory over ourselves, which chisel homeliness into beauty, and beat character into every lineament of the face. It was this beauty of character which was singularly lacking in the countenance of Grace Van Hess.

Dr. George Bailey had been the family physician of Jacob Van Hess. When the doctor had died involved in debt, his son had, as before mentioned, abandoned his medical studies, and sought mercantile employment as the easiest channel in which to earn a support for himself and his mother, and, in time, sufficient money to liquidate his heritage of debt. George Bailey very naturally applied to Mr. Van Hess, who gladly gave him a subordinate position in his counting-house. The young man's vigor, cheerfulness, intelligence, and aptitude for business attracted the notice of his employers, and led to his promotion from step to step, until he had reached the place of head-clerk and prospective partner in one of the most flourishing houses in New York.

George Bailey became a great favorite with the head of the firm. About one year before the opening of our story, he had been invited by Mr. Van Hess to accompany him to his church to hear some celebrated preacher from the Old World; and after the services were over he had been asked to an early Sunday dinner. Thus began his acquaintance with his employer's daughter and sole heiress, the lovely Grace Van Hess. Her position, her surroundings, her fragile beauty, and her very weakness, made her an object of attraction to the energetic and ambitious young clerk, whose family was superior to hers, and whose education and training made him the equal of any woman in a republican country; and Grace admired, from the first interview, the strong, manly, dashing young fellow, quick of repartee and frank of speech. These two young people were singularly suited to each other. He was dark, strong, courageous; she fair, fragile, timid; he was the larger segment, she the smaller complement which completed the circle. Her affectionate, dependent disposition would have soothed him; his manly strength and determined will would have sustained her in all the trials and troubles of life.

Mr. Van Hess was worth millions; and money was no object to him when weighed in the balance against his daughter's happiness. He had, from the commencement, perceived the sterling character of his young clerk; had seen that he was the soul of truth, honesty, and honor; and had observed the kindness of his heart, and the love and veneration which he felt for his widowed mother. Mr. Van Hess was growing old, and his daughter's establishment in life was a matter of great concern to him. He dreaded seeing her the wife of one of the idle rich young men of the city, and much preferred to have her wed a self-made man like himself, who would feel grateful for the position which Grace's fortune would bestow. He had thought of George Bailey as a son-in-law long before the invitation to dinner; and, indeed, he had designedly brought the young couple together, and had furtively watched and condoned their meetings and love-makings.

While George Bailey had been patronizing Myron Finch, Grace was reading, or trying to read, one of the Idyls of the King by Alfred Tennyson, and wondering why her lover was so late in keeping his engagement. Every minute or two she raised her eyes from the handsomely bound volume, and seemed to be lost in reverie. It was evident that her mind was far away from Arthur and the Knights of the Round-table. Her father had told her at dinner of George Bailey's promotion and prospects, and had whisper-

ed a few words in her ear which had brought the roses to
her cheek. She was expecting her lover, and, therefore,
could fasten her mind on nothing else. "I wonder what
detains him; he cannot be ill," she said, in a low tone, as
she closed the volume and passed in front of a large mirror.
As she stood there, with the rosy tinge of the light caused
by the crimson curtains giving a richer color to her face and
neck, she did, indeed, look beautiful; and the evident admiration of her own charms was excusable. As she gave
the finishing touch to her light brown hair, she murmured,
"Will he never come? It is now past nine o'clock, and he
promised to be here at eight." The words were hardly spoken when the loud, clear ring of the front-door bell caused
her to start, and she had scarcely taken her seat, book in
hand, when the servant announced Mr. Bailey.

"Good-evening, Grace; excuse me for being tardy; but
an old acquaintance called to see me on business and de-
tained me beyond the usual time."

"No excuse is necessary: I have been so absorbed in
Tennyson's new poem that I have taken no note of time."

"Then you did not miss me?" said Bailey, in a tone of
slight vexation.

"Why should I miss you? I saw you on Sunday, and
this is only Wednesday."

The young lady seemed to take a kind of cat-like pleasure
in annoying her lover, and found it a very easy matter to
utter many little fibs to prove to Mr. Bailey that she could
live very well without his company. Of course our simple,
impulsive George believed every word she had spoken; and,
disappointed that she had not missed him, or at least manifested more pleasure at seeing him, he lifted the volume
which she had laid on the table, and, to change the subject,
asked her if she were fond of Tennyson.

"Very; I admire him very much."

"I don't," said the young man; "he is too artificial—too
strained; his figures are far-fetched, and smell of the parlor
and the hot-house.

> "'The little rift within the lute,
> That by-and-by will make the music mute!'

I wonder how long it took him to think that out. His poetry is full of fine filagree."

"Why, George, you are severe; your tone is harsh. Come over here, and read for me these lines from Locksley Hall. You know how I love to listen to your reading."

Grace's voice, as she made this request, was low, loving, and persuasive. George opened the volume, and read in a deep, grave tone, and with much feeling, one of the very best of the poet's productions. If Bailey could have seen the expression of her eyes while he read, he would have been perfectly satisfied that she, at least, admired his manly beauty.

"What do you think of that?" she asked, as George closed the volume.

"I think it exquisite art, but nothing more—art of the highest order, which is, in some respects, superior to genius, because genius is not always understood, while art is. Art, for example, is never ambiguous, while genius often is. Compare this with that about the lute:

> "'Pleasures are like poppies spread;
> You touch the flower, the bloom is shed;
> Or, like the snow-flake on the river,
> A moment white, then lost forever.'

Here a natural poet looks over the fields, or scans the winter's sky, and finds the material for the best of figures. He does not search the parlor for a lute, nor the cellar for a barrel of apples."

"George, you must have read everything. I am ashamed of my ignorance. Except the fashionable books of the day, I have read nothing. Tennyson happens to be the fashion now, and so I must be prepared to hold my own in society."

Grace uttered this in a tone of sadness, which smote the loving heart of George Bailey.

"Never mind, my darling, it is all the better. After our marriage we shall have the exquisite pleasure of reading together;" and George took her little hand in both his and tenderly caressed it. "We shall begin with old Geoffrey

Chaucer, and we shall read the poets down to that prince of poets and king of novelists, Walter Scott."

The young girl placed the disengaged hand fondly on his shoulder, and, looking lovingly into his tender eyes, said,

"George, you will have to teach me a great deal. You will have to bear with my weaknesses, and train me to be strong."

George's reply to this sealed her lips, but in a physical way.

"Train you, darling! of course I will, on condition that you train me; for you see I am the quickest and most impulsive sort of fellow you ever saw, and I trust everybody. Even this evening my dear mother gave me what would be, from any other person, a severe scolding for promising to assist an old college acquaintance, Myron Finch. Yes, darling, you must train me to be sedate, calm, cool; you must make me a sort of human refrigerator, so that I may repel people who come to prey on my good-nature."

"George, I am so weak, and you are so strong! It always seems to me as if you must be victorious, triumphant over all difficulties. My education has cost enormous sums of money, and I know literally nothing. Where were you educated?"

"Chiefly at home," replied Bailey. "My mother taught me until I was eleven years of age, and taught me most admirably; then she sent me to a good day-school, but still superintended my studies during the evening. This continued until I was prepared for college. During these years my mother selected my general reading matter, marked the portions of the great poets that I was to commit to memory, and even chose the best novels for me, as she said, to cultivate my imagination. I graduated from Columbia College at the age of twenty; ranked among the honor-men of my class; might have been head, only mother thought it was not good for me—might make me conceited, and spoil me. Grace, I tell you my mother is a wonderful woman! Wait until you know her as I do! Well, my course in the medical college was nearly finished, when my father died, and I had to earn money to support mother and myself. My mother, Grace, was my best teacher."

"And I have had no mother," said Grace, sadly; "but—but—won't your mother love me as—as—a daughter, and won't she teach me many things that I ought to know?"

"Of course she will; she will be as much your mother as mine. But that brings me to the point. Grace, my sweet love"—and he took her hand again in both his—"I have good news for you. I have been promoted to the position of head-clerk, and have been promised a partnership in the firm at the end of this year. Seeing I stood well with your father, I asked—for—for what, think you? for you! Ha, ha, ha!" and the enraptured Bailey snatched a kiss. "Yes, for you, Grace; and the old gentleman gave me a very diplomatic answer. Give me a kiss, love, and I'll tell you what it was. He said, 'You must apply to the party concerned, for she had passed out of his jurisdiction long ago.' The 'party concerned!' That was good, Grace, wasn't it?"

Grace Van Hess laughed a low laugh, which annoyed Bailey, for he could not understand its meaning. With considerable anxiety in his tone, he said,

"Grace, what do you mean by that laugh?"

"Oh! nothing, nothing. It was so pleasant to be lovers under difficulties! It was so romantic, and all that! 'The course of true-love,' you know, and so forth. But now that you and my father have made the course run so smoothly, I have a good mind to run off into the rough places, among the briers and the bowlders, just for the fun of the thing."

"Why, my love, what means this change in a moment?"

"It means — ha! ha! ha!" and the low laugh again smote discordantly on the heart of George Bailey — "it means that you have taken the very life out of our romance; our romantic engagement has been spoiled. Let me see how it ran: 'you were to gain a commanding position before you sought my hand in marriage, and I my father's permission before I consented.' Now both have been accomplished, and me—whither shall I fly?"

Here the very weakness of character which she herself had deplored but a few minutes previously manifested itself. The spoiled darling of fortune had obtained her heart's desire too easily. She would, perhaps, have preferred her father's opposition and an elopement. But to be won in this easy, prosaic fashion was almost unbearable. And yet, in her way, she loved George Bailey; she would not have lost him for the world; she valued his love beyond everything else in the universe. But there was a vein of romantic coquetry in Grace Van Hess, born of the exciting French novels which had fallen into her hands at the plastic age of fifteen years, and this coquetry caused her to play, cat-like, with the truest heart that ever beat in human breast.

"Grace, my own darling, you love me, I know you love me; and surely you ought to be glad that your good father has removed every obstacle from our path."

Bailey had seized her hand, and was sadly, earnestly, lovingly gazing on the beautiful face before him. Her mood changed once more, as she said,

"Will you answer me truthfully" (and the word "truthfully" grated on George's ear) one question? Would you have married me had I been the daughter of Timothy Quin, father's porter?"

Bailey hesitated to answer this question. He was in the strictest sense of the word a man of truth. He knew that he was ambitious; he knew that he could never have loved the daughter of Timothy Quin had she been as beautiful as Venus. He now recalled his feelings and thoughts on that Sunday when first asked to dine with Jacob Van Hess; and he recollected too well that one of the factors that caused him to seek the daughter was that, by this means, he might become a partner in the firm.

Grace noticed his hesitation, and had she been a girl of a higher order of intellect and of moral nature she would have respected and loved him all the more for it. She would have seen that had he been a man of less integrity, he would have promptly replied that, "Of course, he would have loved her for her goodness and her beauty had she been the daughter of a felon or a convict."

Grace repeated her question.

"Your question, Grace, is a difficult one to answer. In the first place, the daughter of Timothy Quin could never be like you—could never have your education or your man-

ners, even if she had your beauty. In the second place, I
cannot truthfully say how far your father's kindness mould-
ed my feelings for his daughter. I cannot say how far the
aroma which wealth breathes on all it touches may have
turned my thoughts in your direction. This is the naked
truth. I can now say as a man of honor that I have never
loved any woman but you, and that now I would marry
you were you as poor as a pauper of the streets."

"That will do, George—that will do. You know that
no woman likes to be married for her wealth. Pardon me.
I am wilful; I ought not to wound your loyal heart."

"Now, Grace, my darling, you talk like your own sweet
self: you were only joking a moment ago; but, dear, you
must not do it again; it is too serious a matter to joke
about. If I lost respect for you, I would tear your image
out of my heart even at the cost of my life. I could not
continue, I would not continue, to love the woman whom I
had ceased to respect."

It seemed as if a ray of light had fallen on Grace Van
Hess's character, and had caused George Bailey an invol-
untary shudder. She perceived her error, and, to make
amends, grew caressing in her manner, and tried to soothe
him with a tone of tenderness. She asked him about his
duties and financial affairs, of which she understood as
much as she did of the Binomial Theorem. After she had
smoothed the temper of her lover, he took his leave not
quite so elated as when he left his mother.

Chapter III.

"I do not think a braver gentleman,
  More active valiant, or more valiant-young,
  More daring, or more bold, is now alive,
  To grace this latter age with noble deeds."
                                        SHAKSPEARE.

THE next morning, according to his promise, Bailey introduced Myron Finch to the head of the firm, and recommended him for the vacancy caused by a general promotion

of the clerks.   Mr. Van Hess asked Finch a few questions
concerning his qualifications and testimonials, and, chiefly
on the strength of Bailey's recommendation, appointed him
to the position.

Myron Finch performed his duties in a quiet, orderly
manner, which gave entire satisfaction to his employers.
Toward George Bailey his manner was that of a profoundly
grateful man; he was lavish in his praises of the goodness,
the ability, and the industry of the head-clerk, and sought
occasion to flatter him as a paragon of perfection.   Bailey
was not naturally a vain man, for he had too many excellent
qualities for vanity to find a home in his heart.   Men are
usually vain of what they are not; seldom of what they really are.   Nevertheless, the adroit flatteries of Myron Finch
pleased him, and day after day George found that the society of his new friend became dearer and dearer to him.   On
several occasions he had invited Finch to dine with him,
and on every occasion his mother had warned him to beware.   These warnings George scouted as the offspring of
maternal fancy, slightly out of tune in consequence of too
much lonely meditation on the past.   He told her to go
out every day and take the air; that the fresh air of heaven
would quickly blow away these foolish, morbid fancies.
Mrs. Bailey would reply by saying, "I hope you are right,
George, and I wrong.   But some feeling — perhaps indescribable — I might describe it to a woman, but not to a
man—tells me that this Myron Finch is your evil genius,
and that he will yet sting you like an adder.   George, seeing this ineradicable dislike and terror of Finch, soon ceased
to invite him to his home, and found means to meet and
talk with him elsewhere.

Finch was a close, keen observer, and quickly fathomed
the best and worst characteristics of Mr. Van Hess; and,
resolved to please his principal employer, he assumed a tone
and bearing of profound piety.   He bought religious newspapers and books, and ostentatiously placed them where
they could be noticed; and he became a strong advocate of
total abstinence from intoxicating drinks.   He even went so
far as to reprove the cartmen and laborers, in the presence

of Mr. Van Hess, for using profane language, and found fault with Timothy Quin, the porter, for using tobacco, which was only an incitement to strong drink. Myron Finch regularly but unobtrusively attended Mr. Van Hess's church; and on one occasion he had the honor of an introduction to his daughter Grace.

One Sunday afternoon the two young men were slowly walking up Broadway toward their homes, when they were attracted by a crowd at the City Hall steps listening to a man declaiming.

"Let's see what's up. Come, Finch, let's see the crowd and hear the preacher."

"No, no," replied Finch, "it is only that vulgar fellow, Grady, ranting on temperance. He is one of Van Hess's reformed drunkards, now telling his experience, and denouncing the liquor-dealers and the rum-shops."

"Come—come on, Finch; I really wish to see and hear this Grady. I have heard so much about him, I am anxious to see what manner of man he is."

The two young men drew toward the outer line of the crowd, and saw a curious sea of human faces turned toward a man furiously declaiming, roaring, screaming, pounding one hand with the other, and gesticulating in the wildest and most uncouth manner. He was a stout-built, bull-necked Irishman, apparently about forty years old. His head was large and round, the hair closely cropped, and the face cleanly shaven; his complexion was sallow, his eyes keen, small, black, and round, and, like the eyes of most born orators, slightly protuberant; his mouth was large, though the lips were mobile and well chiselled. At the present moment his eye was gleaming with a fiery zeal that seemed to consume him. Legs and arms were wildly tossed about, after the manner of some Western speakers, whose trick he seemed to have acquired. In spite of the man's rasping brogue, in spite of many violations of the rules of grammar, rhetoric, and logic, there was in his composition no small share of the divine afflatus which makes men poets and orators.

"Fellow-citizens, fellow-countrymen! why do ye throw

away your money for the diabolic poisons which destroys
yer lives and ruins yer families? Alcohol—alcohol has been
the bane of our nationality; and here ye come and plant
a low groggery on every corner of this noble city; and
the miserable, degraded reptiles who make money on yer
misfortunes dress in purple and fine linen, and leave ye and
your children to starve. There will never be peace, law, order, quiet happiness, and prosperity among ye, until ye rise
as one man and gut out the rum-holes. When men drank
whiskey in Ireland or Scotland, it was whiskey in reality;
it was not poisoned colored alcohol, which maddened ye
and sent ye home to beat and abuse your wives. Did one
of ye ever hear of an Irishman kicking and killing his wife
in old Ireland? Never! (Cheers) Ye may well cheer!
Did ye ever hear of an Irishman beating, and killing, and
murdering his wife in New York? Ah! ye may well hang
yer heads for shame. Well, fellow-countrymen, I tell ye no
Irishman in America, in his right senses, ever laid his hand
on his wife, except in kindness, unless he was maddened
with poisoned rum. So down with the rum-holes! exter-
minate them—root them out forever! Rum is our enemy;
rum has done us more injury than all the Saxons ever born
across the water. Down with the liquor-sellers!"

While Grady was denouncing the men who fatten on the
folly of their neighbors, a band of about twenty men were
edging their way slowly and together up to the step from
which the orator was addressing the crowd. For the time
being the declaimer seemed carried away by the very fierceness of his rage; for he did not see, or, if he saw, did not
notice, the angry scowls of that part of his audience directly in front of him. "Liar!" "ranter!" "hound!" "let us
duck him in the river!" were some of the expressions that
fell on the ears of Bailey and Finch. Both saw the danger
to which Grady was exposed, as the angry crowd surged
nearer and nearer.

"Madman! fool!" exclaimed Finch, "you'll be torn in
pieces!"

"By Jove, he's a brave fellow! He no more fears them
than he does the marble steps on which he stands!" rejoin-

ed Bailey, with a gleam of admiration at the speaker's audacity.

In one of the pauses in the oration, Grady caught the expressions, "liar" and "thief," and, turning quickly around, said, in a tone clear, distinct, and ringing, penetrating far beyond the place where the young men were standing, in a tone, too, quite natural, for the oratorical voice had been dropped, "Will the coward that called me names just step up here and repeat them?"

But no man in the crowd accepted the invitation.

"Cowards!" continued Grady—"you, who make widows and orphans by the hundred, may slink behind your companions, and cry 'liar' from a safe distance; but not a villain among ye dares to meet this carnal weapon;" and the orator raised an arm that might well make the bravest of them think twice before he encountered its full force. "I am not talking," said he, "to the corner rum-sellers; I am talking to and advising their poor dupes. Oh, my fellow-citizens, why will ye spend your money for that which not only maddens but poisons ye, which reduces you to a state lower than the brutes, which destroys yer bodies and yer souls?"

The compact crowd of about twenty men continued to press closer and closer to the speaker; and Bailey saw, to his dismay, that they now completely surrounded him. Some one struck Grady on the forehead with a stone, which made an ugly gash, and caused the blood to flow quite freely. This was the signal for the angry mass to close in on him, and twenty arms were raised to strike him down.

"Come away, Bailey—come away," said Finch; "we'll get into trouble."

"See! see!" exclaimed Bailey, "the crowd have attacked him—one brave man against twenty cowards! By Jove, that will never do; that is not American!" and, in spite of Finch's effort to detain him, George Bailey rushed up the steps, and struck right and left, knocking down a man at every blow. One villain had drawn a knife, and in another moment would have plunged it into Grady's back, had not

Bailey observed the action, and felled him to the marble pavement like a log of wood. With every well-directed blow he shouted, "Stand back! stand back! shame on you! One man against twenty!" The very fury of George Bailey's attack, for a minute or two, caused Grady's assailants to pause. During the lull he shouted, at the top of his voice, "This is a free country, of free speech; and if you don't like the speaker's language, you need not listen to him; you can go away about your business."

But the cowardly mob soon recovered from the panic caused by Bailey's sudden attack; and one of their number cried out, "Come on, boys! there are only two of 'em—let us lick 'em both!" But the words were hardly out of his mouth when Bailey struck him a terrific blow, which sent him spinning down the steps, and stretched him on the gravel-walk below. Grady and Bailey were now in deadly peril; and had not the noise and uproar brought the police to their rescue, it is more than likely that both would have been murdered on the spot. The whole affair had taken place in less time than we have taken to describe it. Mr. Myron Finch had kept himself carefully in the rear of the fracas; but, now that it was over and all personal danger at an end, he rejoined his companion, and pretended that he had been endeavoring to come to his rescue, but was unable to reach him owing to the compactness of the crowd.

As soon as the mob was dispersed, Mr. John Grady approached his preserver, grasped him by the hand, and requested the name of the man who had saved his life.

"My name is George Bailey. But that was nothing; I would have done the same thing for the meanest thief, if that thief were assailed by twenty other thieves."

"Mr. Bailey," replied Grady, "you are a brave man—a fine, courageous gentleman; and you strike with the arm of a gladiator. You have saved my life this day, and the life you have saved is henceforth at your service."

This was spoken by Grady in a rich Celtic brogue, which we take the liberty of omitting, as his language otherwise was not bad, and in a tone of deep feeling indicative of his gratitude toward his preserver.

"Mr. Grady," said Bailey, "instead of thanking me for such a trifle, you had better come over with us to the drug store and have that ugly wound on your forehead attended to. It bleeds quite freely."

"It's only a scratch," rejoined Grady, as he wiped the blood off his face with his pocket-handkerchief.

All this time Mr. Myron Finch was a silent spectator— fidgety, uneasy, and anxious to get away. Bailey had not introduced him, and so he acted with Grady as if he had known him all his life, his object being to avoid the mention of his name; for, though John Grady did not know Myron Finch, Myron Finch knew John Grady well, and had been anxious to avoid a meeting from the moment that Bailey had made the proposition to enter the park to see and hear the notorious temperance lecturer. We shall show very shortly why Mr. Grady was the last man on earth whose acquaintance would be desired by Mr. Myron Finch.

The two young men left Grady in the drug store to have his wound attended to, and then resumed their walk, arm-in-arm, up Broadway. Ah, upon what a slight thread does our future destiny hang! Had George Bailey mentioned the name of Myron Finch to John Grady, he, Bailey, might have saved years of misery. But it was not to be.

Chapter IV.

"This world to me is like a lasting storm,
Whirring me from my friends."—SHAKSPEARE.

THE day was rapidly approaching when George Bailey and Grace Van Hess were to be joined together in holy wedlock. Everywhere among the wealthy connections of Mr. Van Hess, George was cordially received as the accepted suitor, as the engaged husband, of the young and lovely heiress. She was proud of his manly bearing, his good looks, his physical strength, and of that reckless courage so dear to timid women. One thing only she regretted, and that was that he was not a soldier. She often reflected how well he would appear in a military uniform, and what a fine officer he would make. Like many daughters of successful merchants, she was ashamed of her father's business; and she had acquired the aristocratic idea that trade is plebeian, and that the army and navy are the proper places for young gentlemen of means. Grace had a sensuous eye for color, and hence the scarlet or blue of a military uniform for her possessed a peculiar charm. The brightest intellect, the purest moral nature, dressed in a sober suit of black, stood no chance with Grace Van Hess, as against the most insipid youth, if that youth were only adorned with the gay glitter of a regimental uniform. Had George Bailey been an army officer, her happiness would have been complete. When the newspapers described how boldly, how gallantly, Bailey had rescued John Grady from the mob, the tears of joy and pride welled up in her eyes, and she inwardly called him "her hero." Her father was almost as proud of him as the daughter. Jacob Van Hess had but one fault to find with his future son-in-law: he did not take sufficient interest in the temperance movement; and worse than this, instead of being a Methodist, he was a High-Church Episcopalian.

After discussing the rescue of Grady and praising George for his conduct, the old gentleman remarked to Grace, " I am sorry that George does not take any interest in any of the revivals, nor in the grand work of the temperance people to overthrow the reign of Rum. He is keen and intelligent enough in the performance of every duty connected with business; scrupulously honest and conscientious in all the relations of life; and he is an excellent son, and, Grace, you know the old adage, 'A good son makes a good husband.' But yet—yet, I wish with all my heart he had a little more religious piety."

"But, father, is not George as good a Christian as most people? He goes to church, and believes in God, in the Saviour, and in the Bible. What more can we ask? He is not at all bigoted, for you know he goes to church with me every Sunday."

"Yes, yes, I know all that. He is as good as the general

run of professing Christians; but—but," and the old gentleman seemed to reflect—" now, there's his friend, Finch,
just as sharp and clear-headed in business as Bailey, but so
truly religious! He is never without a pious book or a
religious newspaper. He always carries a little copy of the
New Testament in his pocket, and during lunch hour I have
often surprised him in the act of reading the Gospels. He
told me, one day, that when he was leaving his home in
Vermont his dear mother gave him that pocket edition,
with strict injunctions to read it night and morning; and
the tears came to the poor fellow's eyes as he told me that
his mother had died quite recently, and that the little Testament was a great comfort to him. I have heard him reprove Quin for using tobacco, and the draymen for swearing. Ah! Grace, young Finch is a marvel of religious piety for one of his years. It is truly a good old head on
very young shoulders."

"Finch—Mr. Myron Finch? Do you mean the young
man with pale face, pale eyes, pale hair, and with paleness
all over him, whom George introduced to me one Sunday
coming out of church? He looks so good, so mild, so innocent! Now, father, George Bailey is worth forty thousand such wishy-washy young men."

"Don't understand me, my dear, as uttering one word
against your affianced husband. On the contrary, George
is a noble fellow; only—only—I wish he was as devout a
Christian as his friend Finch."

In truth, Jacob Van Hess was one of those well-meaning
men, of limited and narrow vision, who found it difficult
to trust the honor of any man who was not a professing
Christian of his own denomination. He could hardly admit that a pagan like Cato could be a man of the highest
integrity; and he doubted the honesty of the most conscientious Roman Catholics. If a clerk seeking employment produced a testimonial from a Methodist minister,
that testimonial outweighed a hundred recommendations
from merchants of the highest standing. It will be readily seen, from this alloy in a character otherwise good and
noble, what an influence, in so short a time, Myron Finch

had gained over the mind of his employer. This influence
Finch carefully concealed from Bailey. Perhaps he was
afraid of rousing the latter's jealousy, or perhaps he had a
more sinister motive. The pious books and papers which
Mr. Van Hess had mentioned to Grace, Bailey was never
permitted to see.

It was observed that a singular intimacy had sprung up
between Myron Finch and Timothy Quin; and when Bailey jokingly rallied his friend concerning this incongruous
friendship, it was explained by the remark, "·I am trying
to make a convert of him!" Timothy's duties were very
miscellaneous, if not multitudinous. He went on errands;
he swept out the store and the offices; he put away the
books; he lighted the fires; in fact, he was the servant of
all. He was a cunning, ignorant, sycophantic Irishman, with
a vulgar face deeply marked by the small-pox, and a quick,
furtive eye, which never permitted the slightest thing to escape
it. Being himself devoid of every semblance of a conscience,
and a thorough rogue at heart, he had no faith in human
goodness, and was suspicious of all who approached him.

One evening George Bailey was obliged to return to the
counting-house for something which he had forgotten, and
what was his astonishment to find Finch and Quin with
their heads close together and engaged in earnest conversation! It was after eight o'clock. They were in the inner
private office, a place sacred to the members of the firm
and the head-clerk. For a moment Finch was confused,
but, quickly recovering—for he was a young man of rare
coolness and self-possession—he said that "he had lost his
pocket-book somewhere during the day, and, thinking that
it might have been in the store, he had come down to look
for it. He knew that Quin did not usually finish the
sweeping until nearly nine o'clock; and so it was just as
he had surmised, honest Timothy Quin had found and returned it." To this honest Timothy nodded his head with
an affirmative nod, as much as to say, honesty is but another
name for Quin. Bailey was the most unsuspicious of men.
He took Finch by the arm, and both walked up Broadway,
the best and most cordial of friends.

About a month after the time when Bailey had found Finch and Quin together in the private office of the counting-house at such an unseasonable hour, Mr. Vanderbilt, the junior partner, returned from the South, whither he had gone in search of health very much impaired by too close an application to business. This gentleman had had charge of the financial affairs of the firm before his departure, and during his absence this duty had been assigned to George Bailey. No one, however, had power to draw checks except Mr. Jacob Van Hess.

Mr. Vanderbilt called Mr. Van Hess into the inner office, and carefully closing the door, said,

"Mr. Van Hess, do you know anything of this check? It struck me yesterday as somewhat singular. It was returned among twenty or twenty-five cancelled checks, and in looking over the books I could find no business transactions with the banking-house of Warrenton, Wilde & Co. In fact, I could find no record of it anywhere."

Mr. Van Hess scrutinized the check very carefully, and with an anxious and troubled expression of face, and then replied that neither the firm nor himself, individually, had ever owed William Wilde one cent, and that he had never signed that check.

"Your signature is well copied, is it not?"

"Admirably. No wonder the paying-teller of the bank was deceived."

Mr. Van Hess continued to scrutinize the check, and his face became more and more troubled. Mr. Vanderbilt, a keen, cold man of business, watched his senior closely, and waited patiently for him to continue.

"That's not what troubles me: it is the handwriting in the body of the check which alarms me."

"Ah, indeed! whose handwriting is it?"·

"You know as well as I do."

"You neither wrote nor signed this check? Then, sir, IT IS A FORGERY!"

"I fear it is. Surely, surely George Bailey could not have committed so clumsy a crime as this. He must have known that it would be detected."

"Not so clumsy, after all, Mr. Van Hess; for during my absence he had charge of the finances, and I was not expected to return until May next. He had ample time to cover up a paltry sum of fifteen hundred dollars; and perhaps he may have thought that my lung trouble was fatal, and that he might remain permanently in charge of the finances."

Mr. Van Hess was greatly distressed. He was sorry for Bailey himself; but for his daughter, as the affianced of a forger, and for the social position of this daughter and himself, he was in a state of agony. He had little doubt that Bailey, taking advantage of his position, and of his partner's absence, had been tempted to pay off an old debt previous to his marriage with Grace. He was always suspicious of a man who did not make strong professions of piety. With all his narrow bigotry, Mr. Van Hess was a moral, upright man, and he could not lie against the truth.

"Mr. Vanderbilt, I recognized Bailey's handwriting in a moment. Yet I can hardly believe in his guilt. Some expert may have imitated his writing. Perhaps Mr. Wilde never received the money. We ought not to condemn him too hastily."

"I hope he is innocent," said Mr. Vanderbilt; "but we can easily ascertain. We can learn if Mr. Wilde has received the money; if Bailey owed him fifteen hundred dollars; and how he, Wilde, received the check."

"There is no necessity for haste," pleaded Mr. Van Hess; "hitherto we have found the young man honest, and there may be a mistake. I trust that the matter will come out all right for him."

The partners discussed the matter *pro* and *con* all the afternoon; and then agreed to request an interview with Mr. William Wilde, and to examine Bailey on the following morning.

A messenger was sent with a note requesting Mr. Wilde, if convenient, to call at the counting-house of Van Hess & Co. between twelve and one o'clock. George Bailey was informed by Timothy Quin that he was wanted in the inner office. Mr. Van Hess handed Bailey the check to read, and as he read he turned first scarlet and then deadly pale.

"Mr. Bailey, whose handwriting is that?" asked Mr. Vanderbilt.

"It looks like mine and Mr. Van Hess's; but — but I never wrote it. *This is a forgery!*"

"So we thought, Mr. Bailey," replied Mr. Vanderbilt, in a slight tone of irony.

"Bailey," asked Mr. Van Hess, "did you owe Mr. William Wilde fifteen hundred dollars?"

"Yes, sir, I did."

Mr. Vanderbilt, at this confession, gave Mr. Van Hess a knowing look, as much as to say, "I told you so." Poor Mr. Van Hess was bewildered and dumfounded.

"Mr. Bailey, you had charge of the financial affairs of the house during my absence in the South. Were you not under the impression that I would not return before May?" asked Mr. Vanderbilt.

"Certainly, certainly," replied Bailey, who had no more idea of prevaricating than he had of flying out of the window. "But, gentlemen, surely, surely you do not suspect me of forging this check?" This was uttered by Bailey in a tone of astonishment, as the idea slowly entered his mind that he was suspected by both the partners.

"The handwriting is yours—at least, like yours, by your own confession; and you admit that you owed this amount —this exact amount—to William Wilde. To be frank with you, Mr. Bailey," said Mr. Vanderbilt, "we are forced to think, after deliberate consideration, that you forged this check. We may, however, be mistaken, and I trust that you will be able to prove your innocence."

"Prove my innocence!" said Bailey, in a tone of indignation and surprise. "Do you mean to say, gentlemen, that you suspect me of this clumsy crime, which was sure to be detected?" The thought of "doctoring" the accounts, to cover his presumed guilt, never once entered Bailey's mind. "Mr. Van Hess, do you think that I could commit such a crime?"

"The matter looks serious, Bailey; and I don't know what to think," replied Mr. Van Hess, in a tone of deep distress.

Mr. Van Hess motioned Mr. Vanderbilt to come over to the window, and whispered in his ear, "Mr. Vanderbilt, I fear he is guilty. Did you notice his face change from scarlet to white the moment he looked at the check? The amount, to me, is a trifle; but Bailey is engaged to my daughter, and the scandal will kill her. I will see that you are no loser. If he confesses to the crime, will you agree to let him escape?"

"Well, I don't care to condone a crime like this. He was trusted, esteemed, promoted; and to take advantage of my absence and your kindness and confidence was incomparably mean as well as criminal. But, my old friend, to save your daughter's name from the tongue of scandal, I will agree not to prosecute, provided he makes a clean breast of it."

"Mr. Bailey," said Mr. Vanderbilt, approaching him, "Mr. Van Hess and I have agreed, for several reasons, not to prosecute you, provided you confess your crime and make restitution to the best of your ability. Otherwise, the law must take its course."

"Confess! Confess what? That I committed a forgery for the purpose of robbing my benefactor? That I committed a shallow crime like this? That I was a fool as well as a knave? Confess a lie? Never, sir! never! You and Mr. Van Hess ought to know me better."

"Bailey, for my daughter's sake, for my sake, for your mother's sake, if not for your own sake, confess, and make all the restitution you can; and then you may commence the world anew in some other State or country."

"Sir," replied Bailey, with great dignity, "you have had my answer. I cannot confess to a crime which I never committed. You ought to know, gentlemen, that the same hand which forged the signature of Jacob Van Hess could as easily forge the handwriting of George Bailey."

"True, Mr. Bailey, we admit that; but whose interest was it to pay a debt of fifteen hundred dollars to William Wilde? You admit the debt."

"Bailey," pleaded Mr. Van Hess, "we have sent for Mr. Wilde. He will be here in a few minutes. If you did this deed, confess it before he arrives; for if he state that he has been paid by means of this false check, nothing can save you. There is just one chance for you—and that, I fear, is but one chance in a thousand—and that is, that Mr. Wilde did not receive the money."

"Gentlemen," said Bailey, "I am really astonished at you. To think that I could possibly commit such a crime!"

"All criminals talk this way," said Vanderbilt, in a cold tone of voice. "I do not say that you are a criminal; the law will decide that point."

"Very well, Mr. Vanderbilt," replied Bailey, "let the law take its course. 'The law is the friend of the accused.' I'll prove my innocence in a court of justice. Abscond!" continued Bailey, "why, to abscond is to admit the crime."

"George Bailey," pleaded Mr. Van Hess once more, "my partner and I are willing to let you go, provided you confess. Confess, and I shall make good my partner's loss."

"Mr. Van Hess," said Bailey, "I swear before my Creator, by the bones of my dead father, by the honor of my widowed mother, that I have never seen that check until called into this office this morning! Gentlemen, gentlemen, I am innocent—indeed, I am innocent!"

Jacob Van Hess possessed the characteristic of narrow and bigoted minds—an immense fund of stubborn tenacity. His Dutch blood was now up, and he was resolved to make Bailey confess or take the consequences.

"Bailey, are you mad?" said Van Hess. "You have admitted the debt of fifteen hundred dollars. The handwriting can be sworn to by a dozen clerks in this house. Be warned in time!"

"My mind, sir, is made up. I shall either be acquitted or convicted in a court of justice. I shall not abscond; for life and liberty, with such a stain on my character, are not worth the possession."

"Come, Bailey," said Mr. Vanderbilt, "you have confessed enough already—provided Mr. Wilde has received the money—to send you to State-prison. You owed money; it was paid for by means of this forged check. Have you a receipt? But, of course, the question is useless; the receipt would be destroyed."

By some singular fatality Bailey involuntarily put his hand into the pocket of his business-coat—a light summer-coat, worn only in the counting-house—and drew out a paper. Why he did so, or what prompted him to perform this mechanical action, he could never tell. It seemed as if, when the misfortune of the check was brought home to him, every other misfortune must follow in its track. He opened the paper, and, as his eyes took in its meaning, they almost started from their sockets with amazement and terror. Bailey was a brave man, as we have already seen, but this was too much for him. He turned deadly pale; his lips were drawn back until the exposure of his white teeth imparted a ghastly expression to his countenance; his face and form assumed a look of premature age, as if some invisible power had suddenly dried up the sap of his youth. Never again could George Bailey wear the gay and joyous look of the young and the light-hearted. He threw himself down on the nearest seat, covered his face with his hands, and wept silently. It was a pitiable sight to see this young Titan bowed to the earth beneath such a load of misery. The great round tears slowly trickled through the fingers that hid his eyes. "O God! my God!" he murmured, in a voice scarcely audible, "why hast thou permitted this? I am lost, lost, lost—ruined! Oh, my poor mother! oh, my poor mother! What is to become of her?"

The two partners looked at Bailey and pitied his misery. There was now no doubt of his guilt, for the paper which he had taken out of his pocket was the fatal receipt.

"Warrenton, Wilde & Co., Wall Street,
"New York, November 20th, 18—.

"Received from George Bailey the sum of Fifteen Hundred Dollars ($1500), the amount in full for all claims against the estate of his late father.   WILLIAM WILDE."

"Bailey, I have, as I told you, sent a messenger to request Mr. Wilde to come round to our office," said Mr. Van

Hess; "but if you will confess, now that the very receipt has been found on your person, it is not yet too late. I will make some business excuse to send Mr. Wilde away. For my daughter's sake, for your mother's sake, confess, and you may go away unharmed."

In a broken tone, and with great humility, George Bailey replied, "I thank you, sir, for your kindness and humanity; but I cannot confess to what I never did."

"Bailey, remember that the penalty is ten years' hard labor in State-prison. I would save you, if you would let me; but, if you will not confess, the law must take its course."

"Mr. Van Hess, I thank you from the bottom of my heart; but, I repeat, I cannot, will not confess. What is liberty to me with the stain of this great crime on my character? Unless I am cleared, I prefer to be imprisoned."

Mr. William Wilde, of the banking-house of Warrenton, Wilde & Co., entered the office. He was a handsome, vigorous gentleman, about fifty-five years of age. His hair and beard, which were long, gray, and silky, gave him the appearance of being older than he really was. His eye was clear and shrewd, his form erect, and his movements energetic.

Mr. Vanderbilt handed him the forged check and the receipt, and asked him if he remembered the person who had paid him.

"Very well, indeed. It was just before the closing of the bank. I was in the inner office, writing. It was growing dark, and I was thinking of lighting the gas, when a man entered somewhat hastily and said, 'Mr. Wilde, I am George Bailey, head-clerk with Van Hess & Co., and I have called to pay the last instalment of the debt which my father owed you.' He handed me a check for fifteen hundred dollars—the very check now in my hand—and I gave him this receipt."

Mr. Van Hess asked, "Did you notice the man's appearance?"

"As I told you before, it was growing dark, and therefore I could not swear to the man's face."

"Did you notice anything peculiar about the man?" asked Mr. Vanderbilt.

"I certainly noticed a subdued excitement in his tone of voice, and a rapidity of utterance, like one who has committed his speech to memory. But I was struck with astonishment that the head-clerk of your house should walk nearly half a mile, on a raw, chilly day in November, without an overcoat, and with nothing on him heavier than a light summer business-coat. I observed, too, that though the words were correct, the tone of voice was not that of a gentleman."

George was an attentive listener to Mr. Wilde's statement. Mr. Van Hess turned to Mr. Wilde, and then pointing to Bailey, asked,

"Is that the man who gave you the check, and to whom you handed the receipt?"

Mr. Wilde carefully scanned George Bailey from head to foot. "That is the coat, certainly. The man was about his height; but I don't think that is the face. It seems to me (as well as I can remember) that the face of the man who paid me was older and coarser. I could swear to the coat; and even that would hardly be safe, for doubtless there are thousands of coats of the same cut and material."

"Mr. Wilde," said Bailey, "may I ask you one or two questions?"

"Certainly, sir: I will answer them as far as I am able."

"This is the second of December. It is now nearly two weeks since some person presented you this check and received your receipt. Can you remember the voice of the man who spoke to you? These gentlemen know that I am not now disguising my voice. Does my voice resemble the voice of that man?"

"Not in the least. Your voice is clear and distinct; his was thick, rough, and, if I may use the word, muffled. I remember that I noticed at the time the rapidity of his utterance."

"Mr. Wilde, you noticed what you considered an attempt on the part of this person to disguise his tone; in your opinion, could my voice be made to sound like that of the man who gave you the check on that fatal day?"

"No, sir; not unless you are an admirable mimic."

"My friends here, and also at home, know that my strong individuality has always prevented my imitating anything. Mr. Wilde, you have twice unconsciously addressed me with the epithet, *sir:* pardon me if I ask you if you could have so addressed the man who personated me in your office?"

"I think not; for though the man was dressed as you are now, had hair and mustache like you, I could not help thinking at the time that he was not a *gentleman*, as—excuse the compliment—you evidently are."

"Thank you, Mr. Wilde. One question more: Did you ever press me to pay you that debt of fifteen hundred dollars?"

"As long as you regularly paid the interest I was satisfied. I never asked payment."

Mr. William Wilde retired without asking a single question concerning the check, for he was a thorough gentleman, and, as such, seemed to manifest no interest in the private affairs of a mercantile firm. He saw that there was something wrong, and that the head-clerk was suspected, perhaps, of forgery, but it was none of his business, and so he bowed himself out of the counting-house.

After the first shock, and especially after the copious flow of tears, all Bailey's courage and clear common-sense returned. He realized the diabolic cunning of the plot, the masterly ability with which it was concocted, and the almost impossibility of proving his innocence. Nevertheless, like a strong swimmer against wind and wave and tide, he would struggle for life while life lasted.

"Gentlemen," said Bailey, "this matter is now very clear to my mind. Some villain, who has learned to imitate my handwriting, and yours too, Mr. Van Hess, has forged this check and given it to Mr. Wilde, and received his receipt. The man who committed this crime belongs to your house; he is one of the fifteen clerks employed by your firm. This scoundrel wore my business-coat, and at the proper time placed the receipt in my pocket. The daze caused by the first shock of the calamity is over. Perhaps my counsel will be able to sift it all out and detect the wily forger.

That is my only chance. I admit that, as I now see it, the evidence is greatly against me. But I must be acquitted, I repeat, or convicted in a court of justice. To fly is a confession of guilt, and that is worse than State-prison. I can scarcely blame you for thinking me guilty. Still, Mr. Van Hess, who has known me and my family so long, should, I think, have had more confidence in my integrity. I now surrender myself for trial, in the hope that I may receive that justice which I can scarcely blame you for denying me."

Had George Bailey carried a pious book in his pocket, read a religious newspaper during lunch-hour, or condemned the poor workmen for drinking liquor or using tobacco, Mr. Jacob Van Hess could never have been brought to believe in his guilt. Had Bailey paraded the religion of Christ, and ranted about it from the lip out, without one scintilla of it in his heart, this night he would not have slept a prisoner in the Tombs.

CHAPTER V.

"Alas! the breast that inly bleeds
    Hath naught to dread from outward blow:
Who falls from all he knows of bliss
    Cares little into what abyss."—MOORE.

MRS. BAILEY sold her little homestead for about two-thirds of its value, for the purpose of raising money with which to employ able counsel to defend her son, and to liquidate the debt of fifteen hundred dollars to William Wilde, of the house of Warrenton, Wilde & Co. Van Hess & Co. sustained no loss on account of the forged check.

Day after day the poor delicate mother visited her son in his cell, consoled him, comforted him, and endeavored, with her grand maternal love, to induce him to put his trust in the goodness, mercy, and justice of the Father who does all things for the best. From the prison cell she went to the lawyers who were engaged to defend him; from the law-offices she went to the teachers, professors, and ministers who had known her boy from childhood, for testimonials as to conduct and character; and from the residences of these people she went to the business men who had known him during the past four years, for letters recommending him for honesty and integrity. The energy of this weak, fragile lady was something wonderful. She left no stone unturned to save him from his impending fate. She employed detectives, by advice of her counsel, to follow the clerks employed by Van Hess & Co., and to discover, if possible, the criminal who had perpetrated the forgery.

The day of trial came at last. Experts in penmanship swore that the writing in the body of the forged check was, to the best of their belief, the handwriting of the accused. Mr. William Wilde gave his evidence, the substance of which has been already stated. The business-coat and the debt of fifteen hundred dollars were very damaging. The finding of the receipt in the presence of the two partners was testified to. The district-attorney dwelt upon the motive and the opportunity; that opportunity being the absence of the junior partner in the South. Against all this Bailey's counsel could only insinuate, without a particle of proof, that some enemy in the counting-house had committed the forgery for the purpose of ruining the prosperous head-clerk. But when asked for the name of a single enemy, they had none to give. They used Mr. Wilde's evidence concerning the man who presented the check with great skill. They presented at least a score of recommendations from the best and purest men of the city; but all to no purpose. The evidence of guilt was too clear to the minds of the jury; and after retiring for ten minutes they brought in a verdict of guilty. The judge passed sentence in the following words:

"George Bailey, you have had a fair and impartial trial before an intelligent jury of your countrymen, and have been convicted of robbing your employer under circumstances the most aggravating. You are a man of more than ordinary education, culture, and refinement; you have been the trusted clerk, the almost adopted son, of the head of one of the oldest and most respectable firms in the city, and hence for you there was no possible excuse. About to become a partner in the house, with prospects the brightest, in order to pay off a paltry debt you take advantage of the absence of the junior partner, and, relying on the confidence of the senior, you deliberately commit the crime of forgery. Notwithstanding that experts have declared the writing to be yours, your own admission when the forged check was first shown to you, and notwithstanding that the receipt for the fifteen hundred dollars was found on your person, you have persisted in pleading not guilty. In the teeth of evidence the most convincing, you have steadily insisted on your innocence. No jury, no matter what their sympathies might have been, could have done otherwise than bring in a verdict of guilty. In that verdict I cordially concur. You have been defended by able counsel. The highest testimonials as to your previous good character were received and duly weighed. The witnesses against you were as tender as the nature of their oaths would permit. I can see nothing in the testimony to mitigate, but on the contrary a great deal to aggravate, your crime. I, therefore, sentence you to confinement at hard labor in the State-prison for the period of ten years. This is the highest punishment that the law allows, and in my opinion you deserve it."

George Bailey was quickly removed to his cell. He sat on the side of his cot-bed, his eyes gazing away into vacancy: his mother sat on the solitary wooden chair beside him. Their hands were clasped, but neither uttered a word. Sorrow, anxiety, and confinement had driven the ruddy glow from the young man's face, never again to return to it. There was a sort of sad relief, now that anxiety was at an end, and that the worst had come. Mrs. Bailey squeezed his hand and wept silently. It was a blessing that the tears came to soften her nameless grief.

At length she said, "George, darling, do not give way to despair. God is good and just; and your innocence will yet be proved before the world. I will go to the governor, and on my bended knees obtain your pardon."

"Pardon, mother? That means that I have committed a crime. No, no, no! I must be proved an innocent man; I must be released from an unjust imprisonment—released, not pardoned."

"Released, then—you must be released. Your father's friends and my own will work day and night until you are released, my son."

George seized both his mother's hands and kissed her on the forehead. His voice trembled as he said, "Mother, if it were not for you I could bear this unjust punishment; but the thought of you drives me nearly mad. What will become of you during these long, weary ten years? The punishment is more than doubled, for you receive by far the greater part of it. Oh, God! I could bear all, being young and innocent, but my mother, my mother!" and the young man ran his hands through his hair with a movement of despair.

"George, George! you break my heart by your despair! Be humble and trust in God, and he will prove your innocence."

"Ah! if I alone were concerned, I could wait, wait—ay, wait thirty years—until the foul, dark plot that has ruined me comes to light; for God were not a God of justice if he permitted this crime to go unpunished. Mother, it is worse than murder; for it is disgrace, and the loss of all that made life and liberty dear to me. It is a double murder, for it destroys you as well as me."

"George, darling, don't think of these things. You will soon be released, and then we shall leave New York, and go away to some strange city, where you can begin life anew."

Bailey had relapsed into a state of abstraction, and after a long pause he said,

"Mother, are you still of the opinion that Myron Finch was the cunning devil who planned and compassed my destruction?"

"I am, most assuredly. I warned you against him at the very beginning. I well remember being very much annoy-

ed at your mentioning family affairs to him the first evening he called at our house. You saw that I instinctively
feared and disliked him, as though he were a poisonous
reptile."

"The proof, mother? What proof have you beyond
this instinct?"

"Remember Mr. Wilde's testimony. That man with the
coarse, thick voice—that man about your height—that man
with the dark hair and mustache was Timothy Quin. The
man who forged the check and sent him on his criminal
errand was Myron Finch. Proof! I need no other proof
than my mother's heart. I watched every witness closely."

Still, Bailey could not believe that the man whom he
had befriended, the man whom he had made a companion,
could concoct and execute so foul an act of fraud and
treachery; and yet there were circumstances that pointed
to Myron Finch as the perpetrator of the crime. He alone,
of all the employés in the firm, knew of the debt of fifteen
hundred dollars, and he remembered the peculiar intimacy
between him and Quin. But the proof was wanting, and
Bailey was too just a man to condemn another on evidence
so slight. He took his mother's feminine instinct for what
it was worth, and quietly assumed that her mind had been
always prejudiced against Finch.

After another long pause—for great grief, like great happiness, is apt to engender silence—Bailey asked, not without reluctance and embarrassment,

"Mother, have you heard anything of Miss Van Hess?
Has she ever called on you? She has never sent me a
single syllable in reply to my note. Does she believe me
guilty, or has her father put her under restraint?"

"I do not know," replied Mrs. Bailey; "I have never
seen her, never heard from her. Her father evidently believes that you committed forgery, and doubtless he has
imparted his own belief to his daughter. It can hardly be
otherwise."

"This indifference to my fate relieves my mind of half
its trouble. Had she believed in my innocence like you,
had she sympathized with me in my misfortune, the

thought of her love and her misery, added to my anxiety about you, would have driven me crazy—I could not have borne it. Whatever feeling she had for me will soon die, if it has not already died out, under the belief that I am a forger and a robber!"

This thought caused the young man to compress his lips and clinch his hands, in an effort to suppress any outward emotion which might add aught to his mother's trouble. He forced himself into a state of mental calm, as he continued, "I am sorry, very sorry for the misery she must have endured. Her pride, which is her principal characteristic, must have been dreadfully wounded. But this dream is ended! I have you only, my dear mother, to think of now. You had a great deal of money to pay to lawyers, and you had many expenses besides: how much money have you left? When the house was sold you paid the bank the fifteen hundred dollars?"

"Of course I did. Had I died of starvation the next hour I would have cancelled that debt. That man, Mr. Van Hess, had the indecency to offer to pay the money. I indignantly refused. He begged me to retain a portion of it. I told him that I would not accept one cent to save my life: that, had it been necessary, I would have sold your father's grave to procure the money to pay the bank. With all his goodness and piety, Jacob Van Hess is a coarse-minded, stubborn bigot. Had his nature been of a higher order, had his mind been comprehensive, he would have trusted your honesty and integrity, in spite of appearances against you. Mr. Wilde, who never saw you but once before the trial, told me that in his opinion you were innocent as the child unborn. He promised me that he would use all his influence to procure your par— I mean, your release."

" Mother, if ever you see Mr. Wilde, give him my grateful thanks, and tell him that the time will come when my innocence will be known to the world. But, mother, how much money have you left, after paying all expenses?"

"No matter about that, my son; you will soon be released, and then all will be right. We shall go West and begin the world anew."

"Mother, mother, my heart is aching for you! Let me know the worst at once; anything is better than suspense."

"Well, if you must know, I have just sixty-five dollars and fifty-two cents remaining."

Again Bailey compressed his lips, and clinched his hands until the finger-nails cut his palms. His face writhed with suppressed agony. No longer able to contain himself, he exclaimed, "Mother, mother, I shall go mad! mad! mad! Why does God permit such deeds?"

"Hush, hush, my son! do not blaspheme! Trust in God, and he will deliver you at the last."

Mrs. Bailey gently laid her thin white hand over the young man's mouth, to prevent his revilings against that Being who did all things for the best.

While mother and son were talking in this sad way, the jailer announced that a gentleman desired to see the prisoner. The announcement had scarcely been made when in stalked Mr. John Grady, the temperance lecturer, and editor of the *Weekly Reformer*, the man whom Bailey had rescued from the mob on the City Hall steps. He seized George Bailey by both his hands, and gave them such a squeeze as ought to have pressed the blood through the tips of his fingers. "And how are ye, my boy? Don't be cast down: we'll have ye out in no time. It's only a matter of a few weeks, or a few months at the most. The governor must pardon —I mean, release you." Grady's quick black eye had caught the cloud on Bailey's brow at the mention of the word pardon, and with a presence of mind alike creditable to his head and his heart, had changed it to the word release. "I'd like to see the governor keep an innocent man in State-prison! I'll go myself to Albany and get you out. So don't be cast down, my brave boy."

When Grady became very much excited his rich brogue predominated, and gave a heartiness to his words of good cheer that caused mother and son to smile for the first time since their trouble commenced.

"So, Mr. Grady, notwithstanding the weight of evidence against me, and notwithstanding my conviction, you believe me an innocent man, do you?"

"Do I? You insult me by the question! Weight of evidence? Weight of humbug! I am an impulsive Irishman, and I jump at a conclusion like a woman. I cannot exactly give my reasons, neither can a woman; but in nine cases out of ten we are right; aren't we, Mrs. Bailey?" and he turned to the lady and spoke to her as if he had known her all his life, when the fact is he had never seen her until this moment. "The man who was brave enough to face an angry, howling mob of twenty or thirty men to save a perfect stranger from being murdered, could never be base or mean enough to commit a forgery or robbery. That may not be logic, according to the books, but it's reason, according to common-sense; isn't it, Mrs. Bailey?"

John Grady was a man of strong animal magnetism, of extremely sanguine temperament, and of hope so very large that the phrenologists ought to have marked him eight plus. To the sad, weary mother, to the hopeless, miserable son, there was something really comforting and consoling in the emphasis and manner of this man's words. It lay not in the words themselves: the consolation came from the man himself.

"Of course you are innocent," he continued. "Let any one say anything to the contrary, and, provided that person is not an old man, a small boy, or a woman, he will feel the weight of John Grady's carnal weapon;" and at the words "carnal weapon" he raised an arm and clinched fist that might well have inspired an enemy with terror. "Besides, were you guilty ten times over—or, to be scriptural, seventy times seven—do you think that John Grady would ever forget or forsake the man who saved his life? I repeat, you are innocent; but if you were as bad as I used to be— Mrs. Bailey, I beg pardon; but I must tell you that I have been a very wicked man. I was flogged several times in the army and navy; I killed a man once, but in self-defence. So, if my friend here had committed murder, I would stand by him to the last."

Grady, like Lord Byron and some others, gratified a peculiar kind of vanity by boasting of his past wickedness; nay, even took a strange pleasure in exaggerating his former sins. Now, the truth is, John Grady was a warm-hearted, honest, brave fellow, whose gratitude for the slightest favor was boundless.

"Mr. Grady," said Bailey, taking him by the hand, "do you truly believe in my innocence? or do you talk in this manner for the purpose of comforting me in my misfortune?"

"I really and truly believe you innocent."

"Thank you, Mr. Grady; you do not know what consolation this belief gives me."

"I not only believe you an innocent man, but I think I know the criminal who planned this diabolical plot and had it executed. I am convinced it was a scoundrel whose name begins with F."

Bailey looked at his mother, and his mother returned the look with a significant expression, as much as to say, "Did I not tell you?"

"What proof have you," asked Bailey, "that Myron Finch committed this crime against his best friend? It is too horrible for belief!"

"Proof! proof! I have no mathematical proof; I have only my convictions, as your mother has. I put this and that together, and, woman fashion, I jump to a conclusion. Proof! If I had proof, do you think that I would not have the villain arrested within one hour? Ah, Mr. Bailey, the mischief of it is that he has covered his tracks so carefully that I can obtain no proof. Why in the name of Heaven did you not name his name that Sunday when you saved my life from the mob? If you had done so, you would never have fallen into this trouble. I knew the scoundrel's reputation; I knew that he was a black-hearted hypocrite; but I had never set eyes on him until that day, and of course did not know him personally. Had you but mentioned his name to me—"

"Mr. Grady," said Bailey, "please tell me all you know about Myron Finch; for, if he has done this deed"—and at the very thought of it George Bailey's eyes assumed an expression never before seen in them, and his jaw and face became as set, as rigid as iron—"if he has done this deed, the memory of it would keep me alive amidst scenes of the most sickening misery, not only for ten years but for fifty. But I want to be sure."

"What I know of his life prior to the time that you met him is the secret of another, and therefore sacred. Suffice it that I know him to be the most hard-hearted villain on the face of the earth. You are aware that Mr. Van Hess is one of the principal managers of the society that employs me to advocate the cause of temperance among my countrymen, and hence I have a slight acquaintance with him, but only at the rooms of the society. Until your arrest I do not believe that I had been three times at his place of business, and then only for a minute or two. Latterly I have tried to warn Mr. Van Hess against Finch; but the old American-Dutchman is as stubborn as a mule. He replies to my statements of fact by saying that Finch has confessed with tears of repentance that these sins were committed in his time of darkness; but now, since his conversion, he is another man. Finch has the old gentleman securely in his clutches; pretends to be a paragon of piety and a preacher of total abstinence; goes to church with him and Grace twice every Sunday; attends their weekly prayer-meetings; calls himself a 'brand plucked from the burning;' has been made head-clerk; and, in a word, my dear Bailey, he has just shoved you, by means of a forged check, out of your shoes, and stepped into them himself. It will be my business to ferret this out; for among my many employments I was once a detective on the Dublin force. I would not annoy you now with this information, only for the hope I have that it may be a relief to both of you to know that I shall follow this matter up until Finch is detected and convicted, and you are released from unjust imprisonment."

Bailey and his mother listened attentively to all that Grady had said. The former, with a concentrated look of wrath and a movement of despair, exclaimed,

"Dotard! Fool! Mother, forgive me! You were right. You knew this man by instinct, while I, relying on my superior judgment, have proved myself the veriest sim-

pleton that ever breathed. I see it all. I told Finch about
the debt of fifteen hundred dollars to William Wilde. I
remember what a remarkable penman the villain is. It was
one of the points on which I recommended him to Mr. Van
Hess. I remember wondering at his intimacy with Quin.
I found them one evening in the inner office long after
all the other employés had left. He had waited until he
had heard that Mr. Vanderbilt was coming home. He
took care to commit the act at the fittest time. Quin is
dark-complexioned like me, and about my height. When
all was ready, he sent this wretch to personate me during
the uncertain light of a winter's afternoon. Oh! oh! oh!
this is too horrible!"

Until now George Bailey had resisted all his mother's
attempts to show that it was Finch, and no one else, who
had forged the check; but in the light of John Grady's
statement, and of his own memory of facts, the conviction
was irresistible that Myron Finch and Timothy Quin had
wrought his ruin. He became calm, stern, fearful to look
at; he became the very embodiment of the spirit of revenge. There was no more groaning; tears could never
again come to those eyes. His mother seemed to know his
thoughts, and they filled her heart with a vague terror.

"My son—my dear, dear son!" she said, as she took one
of his strong hands in both of hers and fondly stroked and
caressed it; "be patient; trust in the All-Wise, who does
everything for the best. Do not give way to vindictive
feelings; do not let them destroy your better nature : what
is the loss of reputation compared to the loss of character?
The leaves may be blown to the four winds of heaven, but
while the roots are sound the tree will live and bring forth
fruit. My son, my son! this storm has only blown away
the leaves of reputation ; take care that you keep the roots
of character untouched by the viler passions; and revenge
is among the vilest of them."

But while his mother was weeping and pleading, and trying to save what was dearer to her than liberty or life—
her son's character as a Christian gentleman—Bailey sat
rigid as a statue of marble, and made no response whatever

to anything that she said. The tears came to the round black eyes of Grady, as he placed his hand on Bailey's shoulder and said, "Cheer up, my boy ! you'll soon be free to punish the guilty rascal." If Mr. Myron Finch had heard the Irish burr of the *r* in the word rascal, it would have caused him to tremble in every limb. But Grady's attempts were as futile as Mrs. Bailey's. The young man was in a kind of mental stupor, and, as the enormity of Finch's treachery was realized, he seemed to forget everything else, even his own condition. At length John Grady, as if to arouse him, said,

"You saved my life, Mr. Bailey, and the Gradys never forget a friend. While I live, and can earn a dollar, your mother will never want for a home."

George Bailey silently pressed the hand of his friend in token of the gratitude he felt but could not express. The next morning he was to be escorted to State-prison by two deputy-sheriffs. At length the hour came when mother and son were compelled to part ; and Grady, after bidding his friend farewell for the present, retired into the corridor in order not to disturb the privacy of their parting. We draw the curtain over the scene—a scene perhaps harder to bear than death itself—and leave Bailey to his sad and lonely meditation on all that had happened to him during the past few months. Since his mind had slowly arrived at the conclusion that Finch had accomplished his ruin, a thirst for revenge had arisen in his heart which the villain's blood could not suffice to quench. Nothing short of a slow, lingering death by inches and in torture could satisfy his vindictive feelings. A new and fearful passion had entered Bailey's heart, and, like Aaron's rod swallowing the rods of the magi, it devoured the last remnant of the passion he had felt for Grace Van Hess. His last thoughts on the first night of his conviction as a felon were, "My passion for revenge will keep me alive by filling me with hope, and the ten years will quickly pass away."

John Grady had kindly given his arm to the poor stricken lady, and, without a word, had escorted her to his home. She had passively accompanied him, without knowing or inquiring whither. He quietly introduced her to his wife with the simple remark, "My dear, this is the mother of the young man who saved my life, and she is tired, and sorely needs rest." Mrs. Grady, without uttering a syllable, took her hat and shawl, and tried to make her comfortable in her own rocking-chair.

Chapter VI.

"My hair is gray, but not with years,
    Nor grew it white
    In a single night,
As men's have grown from sudden fears.
    *   *   *   *   *
I suffered chains and courted death."—BYRON.

BAILEY entered the prison resolved to do his duty, and to submit patiently to his lot; to conform to all the rules and regulations, and, if possible, to merit the approbation of the prison authorities. The putting on of the striped clothing caused a shiver to pass through his frame; the prison fare he found coarse and bad; but this he did not mind much, for he had never been very fastidious about his eating, provided the food was clean; the small narrow cell seemed at first to stifle him, but he soon got used to it; the manual "hard labor" in the stone-quarry he felt was good for him, because it produced that weariness of body which enabled him to sleep. He seldom spoke to any one. He appeared always brooding over his great wrong. His first month in prison was passed quietly enough. The thing that most troubled him was the indifference of the warden, who paid no attention whatever to the convicts. His authority was exercised by the keepers, the most of whom were utterly ignorant and extremely brutal. The chaplain performed his duties in a perfunctory manner—preached his sermons, drew his salary, and never once condescended to mingle personally among the criminals, to touch their hearts and reform their morals. The higher officials were always very busy preparing the cells, the workshops, the dining-hall, the beds, the food, the very walls with whitewash, for a few days prior to the visit of the State-prison inspector. That visit once safely over, they all relapsed into their chronic state of self-indulgence. The reform of the prisoner was a matter of no consequence; the maintenance of rigid discipline was the one thing needful. Hence the slightest, the most careless or thoughtless infraction of rule was punished with exceeding severity. During the second month of his imprisonment Bailey found himself working beside a sickly youth, who was suffering from a severe cold which had settled on his lungs. The fact is, Williams—for that was the name of the youth—should have been sent to the hospital, for he was totally unfit to do the heavy work assigned him. In making some heavy lifts Bailey had frequently assisted him. The keeper, one Tinan, a low, burly, brutal fellow, who seemed to take pleasure in inflicting pain, observing this, swore at Williams, and struck him with his whip. George Bailey said,

"Don't you see that the lad is sick? and as long as I do his work and my own, you have no right to strike him."

"Haven't I?" replied the ruffian; "you are insubordinate, and by —— I'll strike you too!" He gave Bailey a lash across the cheek. In a moment George felled him to the earth with a single blow, which would, perhaps, have killed him had not his skull been of more than ordinary thickness. The fellow, though stunned and dazed, began groping for his pistol, while Bailey, standing over him, said,

"If you draw that pistol I shall kill you in self-defence. I call these men to witness that you were the aggressor, without the shadow of a cause."

The cowardly brute arose and approached Bailey with a manner which was meant to overawe him; but the latter kept his eye on him in such a manner that he did not dare to strike or shoot.

"By —— I'll pay you off for this! I'll have your life for this, as sure as my name is Michael Tinan!"

For this offence the warden sent Bailey to the cold shower-bath—a horrible punishment—and to a dark cell, on bread-and-water, for thirty days. The cell was underground, damp, and unwholesome. He had a little dirty straw, without blanket or other covering, for a bed. But, thanks to his excellent constitution, he survived this barbarous treatment. In the mockery of a trial that had preceded his punishment, some of the convicts, through fear or in the hope of shortening their terms of confinement, had absolutely endorsed the falsehoods of Tinan the keeper, and made it to appear that Bailey was the aggressor. After the expiration of the thirty days Bailey went to work again in the stone-quarry. He saw that Tinan was seeking an opportunity to insult him, and an occasion to have him punished. He observed that all the keepers had imbibed a strong prejudice against him. A keeper named Ronan, who relieved Tinan, approached Bailey one day at work, and asked him for what he had been sent up?

"Nothing," replied Bailey.

"You are a liar!" said Ronan.

"You are a coward and a bully!" said Bailey.

The keeper struck him with his whip. George seized a billet of wood which happened to be near and chased the brute for his life.

Again there was the mockery of a trial. Again there was the false evidence of cowardly convicts. This time Bailey defended himself with great skill. He said,

"Mr. Warden, there is a conspiracy to murder me among your brutal keepers. Tinan and Ronan have sought to take my life. They have so frightened the miserable convicts under their care that they perjure themselves through fear. When you inflicted your punishment of the shower-bath, and the thirty days' confinement on bread-and-water in a dark cell, I committed no offence except to expostulate against whipping a sick youth who was unable to work. When the inspector comes here again I shall demand an investigation, and I shall show forth your negligence and your inhumanity. If you imprison me you cannot cover the facts, for they are in the hands of my friend, who is the editor of a weekly paper."

At the word editor the warden grew pale, for of all things he most feared the Press. He was extremely anxious to hold his position, which to him was a sinecure. Bailey continued:

"You will have to murder me before you subdue me. Your legal punishments cannot kill me, for, thank Heaven, I am strong, and mean to live out my ten years. But remember this, Mr. Warden, I mean to obey all the rules and regulations, and you must order your brutes to let me alone. My friend, the editor, is now in Albany seeking my release, and when I am free I shall thoroughly expose the horrible treatment given the helpless convicts in this prison."

If these words frightened the warden, who was simply an indolent coward, and saved George Bailey from a severe punishment, they were the means of preventing his release before the expiration of the full term of ten years; for every inquiry concerning his conduct received an unfavorable reply, and the adjectives placed opposite his name were " proud," " stubborn," " disobedient," " quarrelsome," and " dangerous."

The only punishment for the second " offence " was that he should wear a ball and chain for fifteen days. His speech showed him an educated, humane gentleman; and so the vulgar brutes of keepers christened him " Gentleman George," by way of ridicule. But they all mightily feared him; for they soon saw that, valuing his own life little, he valued theirs much less. He conformed to the rules, and treated the officials with contemptuous indifference.

One day the prison inspector sent for Bailey, and told him he was very sorry to find such bad reports concerning his conduct, "for, as Mr. John Grady, the editor of the *Weekly Reformer*, had been for weeks in Albany begging the governor to pardon you, I have been requested by his Excellency to inquire into your case, and I am very sorry to find that you are considered incorrigible."

"I am deeply grateful to Mr. Grady, but, sir, I desire no pardon, for I committed no crime. Had I been a hypocrite, or pretended to a piety I did not feel; had I been an inhuman brute, and allowed a sick boy to be beaten to death, then you would have received glowing accounts of me, and the governor would have graciously pardoned me. Why, sir, the worst thieves and burglars shorten their terms by playing what they vulgarly term and meanly boast of as 'the pious dodge.'"

"Bailey, you talk like a man of education. For what crime were you sent here?"

"For no crime whatever."

The inspector shook his head, as much as to say, "Truly he is a hopeless case." Then he and the warden exchanged meaning looks, and Bailey was informed that he might retire.

"Mr. Inspector," said Bailey, "you know nothing, nor are you allowed to know anything, of the inhuman cruelties perpetrated within these walls. From the warden down to the lowest watchman—"

"Silence, sir, and go to your work!" said the warden. "You are the most dangerous convict in the prison."

That night, after the inspector had left to visit and look into the condition of other prisons in a like able and searching manner, George Bailey received the punishment of the shower-bath, and was sent to a dark cell for thirty days, to be fed on bread - and - water administered once each day. When the period of his solitary confinement had expired, he was compelled to wear a ball and chain for two months. The chaplain, a neat, genteel, and very decorous kind of young man, who went through his duties in a perfunctory fashion, but who had no feeling of charity, like his MASTER, for the poor fallen sinner, approached Bailey one day as he was returning from the stone-quarry, dragging the ball and chain, and attempted to utter some words of pious but superficial condolence. Bailey waived him off with the remark, "I don't believe in your God: your God is a time-server and a condoner of lies and cruelties: your God stands silent, and allows falsehoods to be poured into the ears of prison inspectors." The neat young chaplain colored, either with anger or shame, perhaps with both, as he raised his soft white hands, of which he was very proud, and uttered the one word, "Incorrigible!"

No one was now allowed to see Bailey. Letters from

his mother and Grady were intercepted. He was completely shut out from the world beyond his prison walls. He
conformed to all the rules; being strong and healthy, he
performed the hard labor assigned him. The warden, the
chaplain, the physician, all the officials, from the lowest to
the highest, hated and feared him; but, as long as he vio-
lated no law, they let him severely alone. Although the
better class of convicts respected him on account of his rescue of the sick lad, he held no communion with them.
Bailey was called by some "George the Silent," and by the
keepers, by way of irony, "The Gentleman."

With brutality, profanity, obscenity, and licentiousness
everywhere about him and above him, Bailey began to fear
for his moral nature; and a nameless dread took possession
of him, that long before the expiration of his ten years of
confinement he might become degraded and brutalized by
the very force of association. His aim became to preserve
his self-respect; and so he longed for darkness and his solitary cell. Here he formed the habit of talking in a low
tone to himself. He reviewed his past life; wondered for
what offence of his own, or for what sin of his father's, he
had been doomed to such a terrible fate; questioned the
justice and mercy of God, though he was too intelligent to
doubt his existence. He arrived at the conclusion that
God paid no more attention to the struggles of men than
to the battles of ants. The ants make fellow-ants slaves;
and have their captains and governors, their palaces and
prisons, their wardens and keepers (no doubt brutal ones
like our own), and inspectors just as sagacious as ours. "I
wonder," soliloquized Bailey, "how many ants are immured like me for no crime, only to make way for the promotion of other ants like Finch and Quin. God's laws
govern the universe, and men and ants are governed by
their own passions and propensities. The days of miracles
passed away with the apostles. 'Vengeance is mine, I will
repay, saith the Lord.' Very well; when I get out of this
prison I shall assuredly help the Lord, and in this thing I
shall certainly do the Lord's work. I shall be an instrument of retribution in his hands. All I ask is patience—

patience, and the retention of my self-respect and my reason."

He laid out a course of study by review. He demon-
strated mentally all the propositions of Euclid. The intellectual effort to recall the order of the theorems and problems strengthened his memory, and the demonstrations dis-
ciplined his reasoning faculty and improved his power of
expression. He solved algebraic problems in the darkness
of the night. The mental pictures of the equations, by
practice, became as clear to his conception as though they
were written on paper. He reviewed all the history he had
ever studied or read. The empires of the East, the repub-
lics of Greece and Rome, the Roman and Mohammedan empires of the West and of the East, with their capitals, their
laws, their civilization, and their geography, were all carefully and systematically traced. Naturally his mind dwelt
on all the noted State prisoners. Duke Robert of Norman-
dy, Richard of the Lion Heart, Richard II., Edward II.,
Henry VI., Charles I., Louis XVI., Napoleon, Toussaint
l'Ouverture—all the prisoners, great and small, had a special fascination for him. The fate of the "Man in the Iron
Mask" was peculiarly interesting to him. His mind, however, always reverted to the brave Italian, the study of
whose life had inspired him (Bailey) to preserve his mental faculties by constant exercise—to that truly courageous
patriot who, immured for many years in an Austrian dungeon, deep and damp, kept himself alive, in spite of his
jailer's attempts to destroy his life, by composing poetry,
without pen, ink, or paper, and treasuring whole cantos in
his memory, so that he was able to print them when at last
released. Bailey was not a poet; he was rather a practical
man with a scientific turn of mind, caused, perhaps, by his
medical studies. His knowledge of physiology and hy-
giene enabled him to take good care of his physical health ;
and his acquaintance with psychology, though limited,
showed him the danger of "evil communications," and
warned him to beware of wicked associations. He reflected ; he talked to his favorites ; he would say, in a tone half
of pity and half of scorn, "Robert, my poor fellow, how did

you feel in your prison when your learned brother had your eyes plucked out—a trick that the Crusaders had brought back from that highly civilized capital of the Roman empire of the East?" "Good Marquis Lafayette, you had a hard time of it, no doubt, in your Austrian dungeon of Olmutz—you, who had been the friend and companion of our own Washington; and your term was just the same as mine." When Bailey reflected on the punishment of the shower-bath, whose severity always caused him to shudder, he would recall the case of Jugurtha, captured by Marius, and kept alive for nine days up to his neck in cold water. "Ha! those Romans knew how to punish as well as to reward."

It may be easily understood that, under an enforced simplicity of diet, regular habits, and constant reviews, the young man grew physically and intellectually a Titan. All the impetuosity, all the frankness, all the sunshine of his nature, which had made him, before his imprisonment, so lovable a companion, were forever gone; and instead of the impulsive, light-hearted youth whom we introduced in the first chapter of this story, we find a keen, cold, calculating, vindictive man, whose long, weary term of imprisonment has at last drawn to a close. He is only thirty-three years old, but looks at least ten years older, for his face is clear, pale, and strongly marked, and his hair and beard are an iron-gray.

CHAPTER VII.

"Sick in the world's regard, wretched and low."—SHAKSPEARE.

"A soul exasperated in ills, falls out
With everything."—ADDISON.

AFTER his release from prison Bailey sought employment as a day-laborer, and worked sometimes for farmers and sometimes on the railroads. In the first place, he desired to accustom himself to freedom; and in the second place, to earn money enough to enable him to obtain em-

ployment congenial to his taste and his education. He
wished, also, to enter the great city of New York in the
garb of a gentleman. He was resolved to bend every energy to the acquisition of money; for without money it
would be out of his power to wreak vengeance on Finch
and Quin. Visions of revenge occupied his thoughts by
day and his dreams by night; in the field, in the cellar, on
the railroad, wherever he toiled for his dollar a day, while
his great strength enabled him to perform the work of two
men, his thoughts never wandered from his settled purpose
to destroy the two fiends who had caused his ruin and his
sufferings. He lived upon the coarsest fare; he slept on
the meanest bed; he had no expenses, for he had no little
vices. His first impulse on leaving the prison was to seek
his mother; but, on reflection, he hesitated to return to her
in his poverty, and become, perhaps, a pensioner on her
bounty. Bailey had learned the lesson of patience, and
had wisely concluded that a few months could make little
difference. At present a return to the city could not improve, but very likely injure, his mother's condition in life,
whatever it might be. For years he had not heard anything concerning her or John Grady, for the prison officials,
with a refinement of cruelty, had intercepted and destroyed
their letters.

For four months after his release he had toiled and saved,
until now, at the close of an August day, he found himself
with fifty dollars in his pocket and a respectable suit of
clothes on his back. He stood alone on the heights of
Weehawken, overlooking the city of his birth, which lay
before him, long and low, like some huge monster of the
deep, endeavoring to make its way out to the ocean beyond. The smoke lazily arose from a thousand chimneys,
and a thousand vessels of every description speckled the
lordly Hudson and the magnificent bay below it, from
Yonkers to Staten Island; for, from his elevated position,
his eye swept over a distance of twenty miles. Behind
him the blood-red sun of a sultry day was slowly sinking
toward the horizon, and casting his crimson rays over the
swampy plains that stretch away toward the Orange Moun-

tains. All was silent save the song of bird and the hum of the countless insects bred of the torrid heat.

This was Bailey's first sight of the city since he left it ten and a half years ago. The time now appeared short; but oh, how long in passing! Perhaps the very vividness of his recollection of the events that occurred at his trial and conviction made it to appear as if all had happened yesterday. He looked long and intently at the city; his brow became corrugated with thought and passion; he clinched his hands and stamped his feet as though he were treading an adder to death, and the look of his face was fearful in its rage—dark as the thick clouds which portend a thunder-storm. Gradually the expression changed to one more sinister and dangerous, whose only outward symbol was a laugh—a laugh which would cause the listener to shudder, so fierce, so malignant, and so vindictive was it. Finally he shook his head, and, as was his wont, commenced to talk to himself. "No, no, none of this. There must be no outward sign. All feelings, all emotions, all passions must be subservient to this one master-passion. Hatred and anger must be subject to revenge. Time, toil, money, must minister to the sole purpose of my life. God and man forsook me. I would have died but for my hope. I must not let meaner passions betray their monarch. Foolish trust, and still more foolish talk, put the weapons into the hands of my foes which they used against me to my destruction. Silence, reticence — ah! I have received excellent training in prison—a face of adamant, a heart dead, dead to all the world save my dear mother and my good friend Grady—these be my armor; while skill, cunning, and courage shall be my offensive arms." Again Bailey shook his head and his frame, as if trying to shake off some hideous dream. As he turned to plod his weary way toward Hoboken, he murmured, in a tone tender and loving, "My mother, my sweet, gentle mother, how it will gladden your heart to see me!"

As he strode along the public highway, past the Elysian Fields toward the ferry, with the firm, elastic, graceful step of perfect health, many a man and many a woman too turned to look again at the youthful face and form, so handsome and so strong, and wondered to see the iron-gray hair of middle-age. Bailey had the introspective expression which solitude always imparts, and an appearance of patient dignity which long suffering invariably gives. There was also the air of the cell about him—a nameless, indescribable air, which once seen can never be forgotten, and which a detective can always recognize in a moment.

When George Bailey had reached the city, he sought the nearest drug store to examine a directory. He searched in vain for the name of his mother. He turned to the word Grady, and took down the addresses of four John Gradys. He took down the residence of Myron Finch, merchant, and of Timothy Quin, liquor dealer. He first endeavored to find his friend Grady; but the particular John Grady whom he desired to see had evidently left New York. He remembered the residence of his old pastor, and thither he hastened, to obtain, if possible, information concerning his mother. Relying on the change that time and trouble had made in his appearance, he resolved to leave the good old man in ignorance as to who he was. The Rev. Caleb Smith, Bailey knew, was well acquainted with his mother, with Mr. Jacob Van Hess, and perhaps with Grady.

"Mr. Smith, excuse a stranger's intrusion; but being a stranger in the city, and anxious for information concerning a lady who was formerly a member of your church, I have taken the liberty to call on you."

"Pray be seated, sir," said the pastor; "it is no intrusion, and I shall be happy to give you any information that it may be in my power to give."

"You were acquainted, Mr. Smith, with a lady, the widow of the late Dr. George Bailey?"

"Certainly, sir; I knew the lady intimately."

"Can you tell me," said George, "where she now lives?"

"The lady you speak of is now no more: she died about four years ago."

The young man turned the color of the dead; he almost fell from the chair. He turned on the seat and grasped the back with both hands, as he groaned,

"Dead! dead! My God! is she dead?"

The good clergyman arose, and bending over Bailey, said, "Young man, you appear strangely affected; was the lady a relation of yours?"

Bailey, by a superhuman effort, repressed his emotion, arose, and confronting Mr. Smith with an expression which was fiercely savage, demanded,

"Of what did she die? Was she alone? Was she neglected? Was she starved to death?"

"No, sir; Mrs. Bailey died a natural death. She was matron of a half-orphan asylum: she was gently and tenderly nursed by Miss Edith Wilde, the daughter of William Wilde, the banker."

"William Wilde, of the banking-house of Warrenton, Wilde & Co.?"

"The same. Miss Wilde obtained for Mrs. Bailey this excellent position soon after her son's conviction as a forger. But, sir, may I ask if you are any relation? Do you know anything of that wicked son of hers, who brought her gray hairs with sorrow to the grave?"

"Enough, enough! Mr. Smith, I am a near relation. You are mistaken about that wicked son of hers. He never committed an act of forgery."

"All I know is," replied Mr. Smith, "that he was tried and convicted; that I read the evidence at the time, and that this evidence proved him guilty. Mother and son being members of my church, I very naturally took a deep interest in the trial, and I could not resist the conclusion that in a moment of weakness he fell."

Bailey's iron-gray hair prevented the pastor from forming the least suspicion that the man he was condemning was then standing before him.

"Well, let that pass," said Bailey. "When did you last see Mr. Jacob Van Hess?"

"I met him only two weeks ago," replied Mr. Smith, "at a meeting of the Temperance Alliance. He is getting very old and very infirm. The business is carried on now chiefly by his son-in-law, Mr. Myron Finch."

"Finch married his daughter Grace?" gasped, rather than spoke, Bailey.

"Yes; soon after the conviction of young Bailey, My-ron Finch was made a partner in the house, and married Miss Van Hess."

"Are you acquainted with a temperance writer and lect-urer named John Grady?" inquired Bailey.

"I knew him slightly," replied the pastor, "but for some years back I have lost sight of him. It seems to me that he has left the city."

"Thank you, Mr. Smith; that is all. I will go now. I am only tired."

Bailey uttered the last sentence to cover the state of his feelings; for he had observed an expression of anxiety and pity in the good clergyman's face, and he did not care to submit to any close questioning as to the cause of his trou-ble. When he had reached the sidewalk his head became dizzy, and for a minute or two he staggered like a drunken man. Ever and anon he groaned, "Oh, my poor mother! my poor mother! Could I but have seen you once before you died! Could I have had your blessing! Dead! dead! dead! Alone! alone! Now for Finch and Quin, her murderers!" Had either of those worthies crossed his path at that moment he would certainly have strangled him to death. Gradually he recovered his equanimity, for the passion of revenge had again absorbed every other emo-tion; and this feeling had been nursed so long, and he was so accustomed to it, that it usually calmed him. He pray-ed for patience. He was actually afraid that in his present mood he would be in danger of abandoning his carefully prepared plans, and of so acting that, instead of being able to wreak vengeance on his mother's murderers, they might be able once more to work him infinite injury—for Bailey knew that the scoundrels hated him because they had wronged him.

And what were those plans? Simply to obtain employ-ment and to earn money. "Money is the sinews of war." Money buys everything, because it represents labor; or, in fact, it is accumulated labor. Twenty thousand dollars com-mands the labor of sixty men for one year. The labor of these sixty men would destroy Finch and Quin as readily

as it would blast a rock forty feet high.   Thus Bailey had
reasoned in his solitary cell, and while toiling on a farm as
a day-laborer.   Money became an absolute necessity to him,
and he must have it.   But how was he to get his foot on
the first round of the ladder?   When once the ladder is
found, and grasped with both hands, the ascent is easy
enough; indeed, those below us will either shove us up or
off.   It is often hard enough for a man with the best of
testimonials to obtain employment suitable to his tastes
and his education; how much more so for a convict without a friend in the world.   Bailey wandered all over the
city, from early in the morning until late at night, seeking
a position but finding none.   He boarded in a mechanics'
eating-house; he slept in a little hall bedroom; he paid for
his meals as he ate them.   In short, he lived on twenty-five
cents a day.   But he was hardy, and suffered little.   He
suffered more from a sense of utter loneliness than from all
else combined.   After his imprisonment the terrible solitude amidst thousands and thousands of people appalled
him.   His solitary cell in State-prison did not appear to
him half so oppressive as the unknown sea of faces on
Broadway and other streets of the huge city.   The crowd
chatting and laughing, not one of whom he knew, appeared
to him so weird and strange—as strange as though he had
found himself among the inhabitants of Sodom, raised by
a miracle out of the depths of the Dead Sea.   He found
himself repeating a line from Byron, "Solitary as a lonely
cloud in a summer sky," and confessed to himself that
"Lonely as a stranger in a great city" would have convey-
ed a much better idea of that loneliness which, worse than
"Hope deferred, maketh the heart sick."

Wherever he sought employment Bailey was asked for
a city reference.   A large store advertised for a clerk
and book-keeper at a moderate salary.   The proprietor
was pleased with Bailey's appearance, liked his handwriting, and was satisfied that he was a man of business
ability.   About to employ him, he was asked for his references.

"I have no city reference, sir; I am a stranger."

"Then you have a country reference?" asked the proprietor.

"I have not, sir; I have no reference of any kind."

"What, no reference from your last employer?"

"No, sir."

"Who was your last employer?"

"I decline to answer," replied Bailey.

"You decline to answer, eh? So that's it, is it? Why, man, you know that no merchant of any business capacity could possibly employ you. I am really sorry, for, having taken rather a fancy to you, I would have liked very much to have given you the position."

"Sir, sir, you can trust me; you can, indeed! I have been very unfortunate, but never criminal."

"My dear fellow," replied the merchant, "it is madness to expect employment of this kind without testimonials as to character. Why, for aught I know, you may have been in the State-prison. Of course I do not say this to insult you, for I do not believe that you ever were. But if we employed men without proper testimonials, we might fill our stores with thieves and returned convicts."

"Yes, yes; doubtless, very true, sir," said Bailey, in an absent kind of way; "you are right; it is only just. I, in your place, would very likely act in the same way. Good-day, sir, and thank you;" and George Bailey sadly left the store.

He now resolved to seek meaner work. He saw very clearly that all the higher sort of labor was closed against men who could not produce the very best testimonials. But even this lower work was not so easily obtained as he had fancied. Bailey answered, in person, an advertisement for a young man to open oysters. The man scanned George from head to foot, and asked him if he had ever opened oysters. He replied that he had not. The rough owner of the oyster-cellar burst out laughing in his face, and told him that he would not suit, and that he was too old to learn the trade. He applied for a place as waiter in a hotel, but found that the colored race had a monopoly of the business. He sought employment to blast rocks in the upper part of the city; but there he found the Irish in full possession, and the "Boss" opposed to the amalgamation of the different races.

His little store of money, notwithstanding the utmost frugality, was almost consumed, and work of some kind he must find or starve. He could return to the country and obtain employment as a farm hand, but that would have interfered with his plans for vengeance on Myron Finch. Bailey found the position of returned convict anything but a pleasant one. If he had confessed what he was—a much-injured man—no one would believe him, no one would trust him. Every convict told the same story of the miscarriage of justice and of conviction on perjured evidence. Bailey could not enlist as a private soldier, nor could he seek a new career in another land, because, for the reason already stated, he must be near his enemies.

He walked mile after mile of the streets of the city. He ran after this advertisement and then after that, but to no purpose. The shoes were nearly worn off his feet, and he could not afford to expend money for their repair. He was fast becoming seedy in his appearance, nor could he any longer pay for his washing. He toiled on and on, reminding one of the last man in a six-day's walking-match, who has not one chance in fifty of succeeding, but who, nevertheless, plods on almost hopelessly, determined to persevere to the very last moment. A publishing-house advertised for book canvassers; but Bailey had not the necessary sum of money to deposit as security. For six weeks he had thus sought an opportunity to earn an honest livelihood. Everywhere he had been refused. It seemed as if State-prison and forger must be written on his face, for no one would trust him. In his long walks he had met many persons whom he had known before his conviction; he recognized them, but they failed to know him, and Bailey was too proud to make himself known. He saw and recognized Finch and Quin, for he had a great curiosity to see the two men whom he intended to destroy, and so he went purposely near their places of business. His sufferings and privations were very severe, but he never groaned, he never

whined, he never complained. With a patience and a fortitude born of the solitary cell and the single meal in the
twenty-four hours, he bore all without a murmur, and made
up his mind to succeed or die in the attempt. He never
went to church; he never prayed. He had no faith in the
justice or mercy of God; indeed, as previously stated, he
had arrived at the conclusion that God did not meddle in
human affairs. All Sunday he lay in his bed, resting, and
reflecting on the past, and thinking of some way of getting
work.

One day he read an advertisement stating that for one
dollar, paid in advance, situations as clerks, book-keepers,
railroad conductors, etc., could be procured. Bailey had resolved to try this as a sort of forlorn-hope. After paying
the dollar, he had just fifty cents left in the world. The
name of the advertiser was Sphinx—truly an appropriate
name; but even a better name for him would have been
Shark. Two days had passed, and Bailey had heard not a
word from the benevolent Sphinx. The fifty cents were
nearly gone, and the young man was well-nigh desperate.
He called several times on this Mr. Sphinx, but could never obtain a satisfactory interview with him. Bailey found
others like himself anxiously waiting; and, on inquiry, discovered that they had been coming to Sphinx's office for
several weeks, and that he had never been known to procure
a single position for a single individual. It was clearly a
hoax, and Sphinx was a rascal and the meanest kind of robber. He was the very carrion of thieves, because he fat-
tened on the miseries of helpless and impoverished immi-
grants, and on the misfortunes of his own countrymen.
Bailey needed his dollar too badly to allow himself to submit to the swindle. He entered Sphinx's shabby office and
demanded his money; but that worthy tried to put him
off, as he had done hundreds of others, and threatened the
police. Bailey quietly went to the door, turned the key in
the lock, and then put it in his pocket. "Now, give me
my dollar, or I'll knock you down and take it from you.
I have no money to go to law, nor have the others who
come here, and, you scoundrel, you know it. You worse

than highway robber, you worse than burglar, you rob the
starving, knowing that they have no redress! Come, foul
carrion, give me my dollar, or—"

"What?" asked Sphinx, shaking all over.

"I'll knock you down, take my dollar, pass out to the
nearest station-house and give myself up to the authorities,
and thereby expose your nefarious traffic."

The shark Sphinx, seeing that he had not an ignorant
immigrant to deal with, handed Bailey his money, and told
him to clear out of his office—an act which Bailey was not
slow in performing, for he was afraid that he might be
tempted to give the rascal personal chastisement.

CHAPTER VIII.

"Our time is fixed, and all our days are numbered;
How long, how short, we know not: this we know,
Duty requires we calmly wait the summons,
Nor dare to stir till Heaven shall give permission."

BLAIR.

BAILEY made his last dollar support him for eight days
longer. He abandoned his lodgings in the mechanics'
boarding-house, and slept sometimes in the Park, and sometimes in vacant lots in the upper part of the city. He
lived on a single loaf of bread a day, which he moistened
with water obtained from a hydrant; and still he did not
give up the idea of procuring employment in the city.
Hardships and privations were not new to him. All these
and more he was resolved to bear, in the hope that he
would finally succeed, and be in a position to re-establish
his reputation in the very place where it had been lost.
His rehabilitation presupposed the exposure and ruin of
Finch and his base confederate.

Finally his last cent had been expended for a penny
newspaper — not for the news, or the crimes, or the politics, but for the sake of the column headed "Wanted."
Foot-sore, weary, hungry, he plodded on, visiting the store
or the office of every advertiser, but the inevitable demand

5

for a city reference drove him into the street again. Sick, almost in despair, he sank on a bench in Washington Parade-ground, and stretched himself out at full length to snatch a few hours' rest, perhaps sleep, ere he started out to renew his search for work. He was gazing at the stars, and bitterly thinking of all the abundance around him, while he was suffering the pangs of hunger. His reflections were bitter in the extreme. Here was Myron Finch with his palatial residence, his country-seat, his club, his horses, and his yacht; nay, with his dogs better fed and housed than he, George Bailey. Here was that other villain, Quin, with his many liquor stores, his abundance of money, and his horses and carriages, while he, Bailey, was starving — he, a man who had never done the slightest wrong to any human being. "There is a God," muttered Bailey, "who made those stars and this round world of ours, but he permits the wicked to 'flourish like a green bay tree.' 'I am old,' saith the false psalmist, 'yet have I never seen the righteous begging their bread,' or something of this sort. Oh, mother, mother! I hope you cannot see your wretched son to-night. If you are in one of those many mansions, I trust you are not permitted to know what takes place on this accursed earth !"

Gradually his reflections grew darker and darker. Thoughts of suicide took possession of his mind. Had it not been for the desire of vengeance, which absorbed his every fibre, it is more than likely that he would have walked down to the Hudson River that night and ended his miseries, as thousands had done before him. His eyes closed at last, and he fell into an uneasy slumber. In a few hours the chill of a cold, damp October morning awoke him, and he shivered. It was the hour before dawn: the cold had penetrated to the marrow of his bones, so that his teeth fairly chattered. He arose and staggered toward the river, in the vague hope that he might find employment as a stevedore. He was weak from hunger, and dizzy from cold and sickness. He staggered on like a drunken man; he reached the brink of the river, and gazed long and intently at the dark waters temptingly inviting him to make one plunge and all would be over. As the river flowed past him, his feverish imagination saw eyes, and mouth, and face; and he fancied that the moving monster said, "Come, one plunge, and all is over! I'll give you rest in my soft bosom!" By a superhuman effort Bailey turned, saying to himself, "This is madness: I must leave before my reason is completely lost." Daylight had come, and with it the desire to make one more struggle, and, if he failed, to lie down and die. He would not commit suicide, he would not beg, nor would he, above all, steal. Either suicide or theft would help to confirm the justice of the sentence that sent him to State-prison.

As Bailey was passing one of the low dens, half eating-house, half groggery, and wholly a rendezvous for thieves, he was astonished to hear himself accosted by his prison title of "Gentleman George."

"Why, Gentleman George, as I live!" said a well-dressed man, two or three years younger than Bailey.

"Can I believe my eyes?" replied Bailey. "Is this the weak, sickly boy whom I used to know ten years ago?"

"The very same lad for whom you got the cold shower-bath and thirty days' solitary confinement. See how strong I have grown! But for you the rascally keeper would have killed me. But—but you look sick and seedy. No luck, no 'swag,' I suppose. Come, come, I'll share with you; I am 'flush;' made a haul a week ago."

"I am afraid, my friend, that I do not quite understand you. I am glad to see you look strong and well, but if you have obtained money in any improper way I want none of it."

"Come and have a glass of something warm—have some breakfast with me."

"No, no; I have vowed to live an honest life, and I shall not accept a portion of what was stolen from another. I am glad to see you so well and so strong. Good-morning. I must go."

But Bill Williams (for that was the name, real or fictitious, by which he was known) placed himself in front of Bailey, and said,

"See here, Gentleman George, I understand your feelings and respect 'em; and I'd be the last man to wish to see you one of us; for, since the day you knocked that there scoundrel of a keeper down, I've loved you as I used to love my mother: that is, the loves was alike. It was respect for goodness and tenderness, and tenderness particularly for the weak and sick. I may not explain myself clear, but I've respected and loved you since then. I always knowed you was an innocent, injured man; leastways I believed it. Now, what are you agoin' for to do? Are you agoin' to try to git work, and be honest, as I did? Then take my word for it, you won't succeed. Why, man, them fellows ask you for city references, and for the name of your last employer; and when you have none to give except the name of the State-prison, they suspects you direct to be a thief."

"You must have had my own experience," said Bailey, "after your release."

"Oh yes, your experience is my experience, and my experience is the experience of all. No matter how innocent we may be when we go to prison, when we are discharged we must become criminals for life. Nobody will trust us; nobody will employ us. We are driven to either steal or starve!—a nice choice, ain't it?"

"Yes, yes; I know, poor fellow. Did you suffer much?"

"Much? Now see here, Gentleman George, I really did try, for my dead mother's sake—and maybe for yours, for I believed you good, like my mother—to lead an honest life; but they wouldn't let me: they wouldn't give me work; and when I was nigh dying of hunger one of the 'boys' met me and introduced me to the 'fraternity.' I took a fever, from cold and hunger and worry, and the 'boys' was kind to me, and nursed me and pulled me through; and of course I've stuck to 'em ever since."

"These returned convicts were very kind to you."

"Kind! you may say that—far kinder than any one I ever saw, exceptin' mother and you."

"They poured oil and wine into your wounds, poor fellow," said Bailey, "while the priest and the Levite passed by on the other side."

"I don't quite take your meaning. I only know that they poured oil on my wittals, and wine down my throat, as I was a-gettin' better of the fever; and as for priests and parsons, I hate 'em all ever since that dapper little feller used to preach humbug to us on Sundays, and then stand by and see us punished for nauthin' on week-days."

"Have you tried, since your recovery, to find honest work?" asked Bailey.

"No; I have not, and never intend to. I made the effort once and nearly died in the attempt. The 'boys' was good and kind to me, and I'll stick to 'em through thick and thin. But see here, Gentleman George, you want to lead an honest life, I know you do. Here's five hundred dollars; you can have it as a gift—you can have it as a loan: you may pay me when you are able. I'll never trouble you about it."

The tears came to George's eyes as he waved the money aside, and said,

"No, no; I cannot, indeed I cannot. I am very grateful, so grateful that I cannot put my gratitude in words."

The thief quickly divined his reason.

"Gentleman George, here is a watch that was never bought with stolen money: this here watch was left me by my mother. You are hungry, and you won't eat with me; you have not a cent, and you won't take a dollar to oblige me, to relieve my feelin's; now take this here honest watch and pawn it. You'll get enough on it from your 'uncle' to keep you a week or two. But mark my words," continued the thief, as Bailey waved the watch aside, "you must come to it or starve. Why, a man of your abilities would soon be chief; and then you need do no 'work' yourself; you need run no risk. All you would have to do would be to sit in a cosy parlor and plan the 'work' for the 'boys.'"

George Bailey smiled, for the first time in a week, as he replied,

"Thank you, my friend, for the honor; but really I must decline it. If I die, I shall die in my integrity. I have never yet committed a single crime, and I am not going to commence now."

As the two men approached Broadway, Williams, the burglar, well known as such to the police, saw two of the officers closely eying Bailey, and wondering who was the new recruit. Williams paused and said, "I am very sorry that you won't take the watch; but I must leave you here or I may get you into trouble. Here's my number: if ever you think better on it, inquire for Bill Williams, and all that a man can do for another I will do for you." The two men, whom a strange chain of circumstances had brought together, shook hands and parted.

Bailey plodded on, weary, oh, how weary! his limbs were so tired and weak! He desired to lie down and sleep. His head ached, and his whole body burned with a feverish heat. His hunger was gone, but a quenchless thirst had taken its place. Almost intuitively, for he was well-nigh dazed, he paused at every hydrant and drank copious draughts of water, and freely bathed his burning temples. Still he mechanically staggered on, with the vague hope of the morning dispelling all other thoughts—that he would find rest or comfort near the river. Once or twice he overheard, in a dim, indistinct way, a policeman say, "That fellow's pretty drunk; but he's quiet, and I'll let him go home." His senses were nearly gone; and yet the river had for him a strange, unaccountable fascination. He had overcome the desire for self-destruction while his will was active and under command; but now the fever was fast destroying the vigor of his mind and driving him to the fatal river. "A cold bath in the soft water—the fire consumes me!" Bailey, with glazed eye and tottering step, stumbled rather than walked onward through Grand Street, determined on one thing only—not to fall down and die in the streets, but to hide himself and his miseries in the bosom of the deep waters. He had almost reached the river when he began to reel. By a superhuman effort he supported himself against a lamp-post; ran his hand across his brow, as if to sweep away the mists that obscured his mind and his sight; and steadied himself by force of will for one more severe struggle by clinching his hands and bracing his whole body, and saying to himself, "God has forsaken me: I must not die in the streets like a dog. I will drown myself! This act at least will be my own." These thoughts, vague and shadowy, flitted through his mind, already poisoned by malarial fever and weakened by starvation. He had advanced about one hundred feet nearer the grave he had been so resolutely seeking, when all his exhausted energy suddenly gave way, and he plunged forward head-foremost on the sidewalk. In a moment a crowd of men, women, and children had collected around the fallen and unconscious man. It was a marvel how quickly that crowd had sprung into existence. No man could tell whence it came or whither it would go.

There they stood, looking at the prostrate form before them with that strange pleasure which mankind seems to take in watching human suffering. One said he was drunk, another that he was in a fit, and a third person announced that he was dead as Julius Cæsar or a door-nail. [Though why Julius Cæsar or a door-nail is deader than anything else, it would be difficult to say.]

A burly police-officer approached and unceremoniously made a lane in the crowd, and when he had glanced wisely for the space of twenty seconds at Bailey's face, now as pale as that of the dead, he sagaciously muttered, rather to himself than the mob, whom he despised, "Dead drunk!" He rapped for assistance, told the crowd to make room for the officers, and repeated the statement, "The man is only dead drunk."

The people accepted this decision without demur, for great is the force of authority, and were slowly retiring, when a strong, dark man of middle-age and with clean-shaven face, elbowed his way through the crowd, and said,

"Stand back, and give the man a breath of fresh air! Stand back, I say, or you'll tempt me to use the carnal weapon!"

At sight of that carnal weapon, and the shoulder from which it grew, and, above all, at the ominous burr of the *r* in carnal, even the very police-officer drew back.

"Why, ye fools," said the new-comer, "the man's no more drunk than I am! Don't I know a drunken man when

I see him? What have I been lecturing on these fifteen years?"

While he was talking to the crowd he had been loosening Bailey's cravat and sprinkling his face with cold water. "Here, officer, hold up his head: some of you fetch me a little brandy and peppermint."

While the policeman was raising the head and shoulders of the dying man, his hat fell off and exposed his entire face and head to view. The middle-aged gentleman who had interposed so opportunely now looked as if he saw a ghost; his eyes stood out like two round black beads, and his whole face manifested the deepest astonishment; but he quickly recovered.

"Hurry up with that brandy!" It was quickly poured down Bailey's throat. It acted like magic, for Bailey had always been a very temperate man. He opened his eyes and gazed wildly around.

"Where am I?" he asked. "Why, Grady, my good friend, is that you? I've been searching for you for a long time."

"Don't talk, my boy—don't talk. Some of you fellows fetch a cab. Ha! it was lucky I came along, or these intelligent gentlemen would have locked you up as a drunken man, and you would have been found dead in your cell to-morrow!"

Chapter IX.

"Hol. He draweth out the thread of his verbosity finer than the staple of his argument.

"Moth. They have been at a great feast of languages and stolen the scraps."—Shakspeare.

We shall now trace the fortuitous circumstances that led Mr. John Grady to discover his friend, Mr. George Bailey, in the hands of the police, ready to be locked up in a cell for the crime of starvation, translated by those sapient and sagacious guardians of society into the word "drunkenness." What "over-study" or "malaria" is to the stupid physician who fails to diagnose a disease, "drunkenness" is to the ignorant policeman; it is a handy term to which he can apply everything beyond his comprehension. While Bailey is being tenderly nursed at Grady's home, we shall give an outline of the career of the latter since the two friends had parted at the prison door.

It will be remembered that Grady tried to explain to Jacob Van Hess what manner of man Myron Finch was, and to warn him to beware of the villany of his future son-in-law, but to no purpose. Finch's professions of religion completely blinded Van Hess. Just as soon as the wedding between Finch and Grace had taken place, and as the young man was assured of his partnership, he retaliated by demanding the removal of Grady from his salaried position as lecturer for the Temperance Alliance. The removal was accomplished. The weekly temperance paper which Grady edited produced but a very small income, and consequently he had been obliged to wander about from city to city seeking more profitable employment. He had purchased a little home in Williamsburgh, which, no matter where he travelled, was always his head-quarters. Latterly he had "drummed" the States South and West for a manufacturing firm in Brooklyn. During his periodic returns to his wife (he had no children), and to look after the interests of his newspaper, now almost entirely edited and managed by a printer, he often hankered for his old business of lecturer. He knew that he was a natural-born orator; but latterly his voice had failed him, and this failure was a sore trouble to him. If his throat could be cured, he might again gain fame and money as a public speaker.

One morning he saw in a daily paper an advertisement which ran as follows:

"WASHINGTON SCROGGS, M.D., Office — Broome Street, by his world-renowned vacuum method cures all congestions, liver complaint, diseases of the throat and lungs, of the kidneys, apoplexy, paralysis, erysipelas, clergyman's sore throat, and all inflammations whatsoever. Office hours from 9 to 12 and from 2 to 5 o'clock."

"Clergyman's sore throat!" thought Grady. "That's my man!" To resolve and to execute were with John Grady almost simultaneous actions. He seized his hat, on the impulse of the moment, and rushed over to New York, to try the effects of the "world-renowned vacuum cure."

"Are you the vacuum doctor?" demanded Grady, in a stern, rasping tone, which rather startled the quiet little man of the "receiver and air-pump."

"I am Doctor Washington Scroggs, sir, the inventor of the world-renowned vacuum treatment, the greatest blessing to the human race, not excepting Harvey's discovery of the circulation of the blood, or Jenner's method of inoculation with vaccine (from *vacca*, a cow) for the varioloid, vulgarly called the small-pox."

Words would be inadequate to express the self-satisfied unction with which this exordium had been uttered. Suffice it to say that it completely fascinated John Grady; for John, being an orator, loved learned words of ponderous sound, and, not being a scholar, failed to detect the pedantry of the little quack.

"My dear doctor, I have clergyman's sore throat. I have been a lecturer. I am now editor of a paper entitled the *Weekly Reformer*. I wish to return to a congenial employment. Can you cure me, doctor?"

The little quack eyed John Grady with his mild, furtive blue eye, while he smiled placidly and said, "Take a seat, sir: may I ask your name?"

"John Grady, at your service."

"Well, Mr. Grady," said the little man, as he gently crossed one little leg over the other, and embraced the upper limb with both his hands in a manner remarkable for its self-complacency, and with a smile so bland that it would take a poet to find something in heaven to which he could compare it, "Well, Mr. Grady, suppose *we* explain *our* system." To whom else the "we" and the "our" referred no person ever yet has discovered. Perhaps in his own line he was a king of quacks, and therefore entitled to use the plural pronoun. "Let me premise by saying that I have explored all the systems of medicine—allopathic, homœopathic, hydropathic, eclectic, and the system by manipulation; this is by rubbing, and kneading, and pinching with the hand (*manus*, a hand). They have all their excellent points, Mr. Grady—excellent points, but points only; and points were defined, when I went to school, as things that have position but no magnitude. These systems, sir, are nothing, nothing but empty wind;" and the little man waved them off with his thin white hand. "These things, these systems just impinge (you know the root, sir), just impinge the truth. Each doth only touch it, as doth the tangent of a circle at one point. When we diagnose a disease, sir (diagnose from the Greek), that is more than half the battle. We first ascertain the nature of the disease; secondly, its cause; and lastly, the proper remedy to remove it."

John Grady was lost in wonder at the fluency and learning of the quiet little quack, with the thin gray hair and shabby suit of black. He listened in rapt attention to every word he uttered—a fact which was not lost by the watchful eye of Washington Scroggs, M.D.

"All disease," continued the quack, gently lowering the right limb and lifting up the left with both hands, and giving it its fair share of nursing—"all disease, Mr. Grady, is in the blood. Apoplexy (another word from the Greek: the Greek, sir, is prolific in scientific terms)—apoplexy is caused by an afflux of blood or serum (both Latin, sir), on the brain. What then? Death or paralysis. The cerebellum ceases to perform its proper function; that is to say, the little brain, which is the seat of movement, doth not, by means of the outcarrying nerves, convey intelligence to the extremities, and the patient is unable to move his limbs. According to the size of the clot, or the amount of serum diffused, the paralysis is partial or complete. The nerve is a telegraphic wire, and when the brain is injured, intelligent communication is cut off. You follow me, Mr. Grady?" said the little man, with the blandest and most complacent of smiles.

"Follow you? Doctor, I drink it all in. This is the most cogent reasoning I ever heard. Other doctors feel your pulse, look at your tongue, ask a few questions, look profoundly wise, write a prescription in bad Latin, take their fee, and then leave Nature to cure you; but you, doctor, explain everything so that even a child could understand you."

The mild little man, evidently pleased with this recognition of his lucidity, proceeded:

"All disease, I repeat, is in the circulation. Propel the life-giving, the life-preserving sanguineous fluid in healthy currents (from *curro*, I run) to the diseased part, and congestions are removed. I do not pretend to cure all fevers, as you may have observed, for fevers are of two classes— the one caused by congestion, the other by poison. Malaria, for example, is a poison, vegetable in its nature, which enters into the circulation, and causes several kinds of fever that my system will not cure. You perceive, sir, that there is nothing of the empiric in me, for I make no claims to infallibility. But when the fever is congestive, as in the case of your throat, my remedy is absolutely certain. There are, sir, millions of small, delicate vessels called capillaries (from *capillus*, a hair), as fine as the hairs of your head, scattered throughout the human system. A congestion, a clot, can only be removed by forcing these little vessels, or rather the sanguineous fluid in these little vessels, to ebb and flow like the tides of the mighty ocean. Constantly repeated— for great is the power of repetition—these minute vessels will fritter away, so to say, the hardest clot, the worst congestion. Now, Mr. Grady, your case is one of chronic (from *chronos*, time) inflammation of the throat. The blood in the capillaries (the root I have already given) is congested, clogged, clotted. You take my meaning? Your disease had its origin in this manner: You had talked long and loud, peradventure in the open air; the exercise inflamed the blood-vessels; in this condition a stream of cold air struck them; and as cold contracts everything but water when it turns to ice, this cold contracted or congested the blood, and hence your acute inflammation (from *flamma*, a flame) of the throat. Neglect, or probably bad treatment, converted an acute into a chronic attack, and you have consequently suffered for years. This, Mr. Grady, is, I trust, a correct diagnosis of your disease."

"Most assuredly it is, doctor. You could not have described it better had my case been your own."

"The cause and the disease I have explained to your satisfaction, and now we must seek the cure. When I was a boy, the old women—no bad physicians, some of them—used mustard, blisters, cupping, poultices, and blood-letting; and leeching was also a favorite remedy. These things were in the right direction, like the astrology which preceded the science of astronomy, but ineffectual and partial in their results. The old women aforesaid were wiser than they knew. The regular faculty of medicine (the most conservative men in the world, by-the-way) called it counter-irritation. They desired to draw the blood from the congested part; but their plasters, and blisters, and blood-letting were usually ineffective, because the work was only half done; because the means employed were necessarily insufficient and imperfect. The desideratum was to discover, or rather invent, a plan which would be gentle, constant, and harmonious, and which would not exhaust by depletion nor endanger by cold. This desideratum I have invented."

The gentle, complacent expression on the face of Washington Scroggs was a beautiful thing to behold. The benevolent little quack perceived that his fish was securely hooked, and so he thought he might as well play with him for a little while before he landed him in his bag.

"You are aware, Mr. Grady, for I perceive you are yourself a scholar, that air presses on the human body in every direction at the rate of fifteen pounds to the square inch."

"Then there must be four hundred and sixty pounds of air pressing on my hand this minute!" said Grady, with an expression of amazement on his strongly-marked features.

"Yes," said the little philanthropist, with his customary smile, "but the same number of pounds is pressing on the other side of your hand, the one balancing the other; otherwise, sir, the weight of air would crush us. You can readily imagine that if the air under the cranium did not press upward with the same force that it presses downward, the superincumbent (Latin, *incumbo* and *super*) weight would crush us. Why, sir," continued the little quack, with all a teacher's loquacity who has found an attentive scholar who will pay him the honor of listening— "why, sir, the air, to a certain appreciable extent, penetrates through these brick walls, lath, plaster, and all."

The observant little quack did not fail to note the effect of this last statement on Mr. Grady, and running his white, thin fingers through his white, thin hair, he continued:

"These philosophic truths I taught many years ago, Mr. Grady, in my high-school of Vermont. I had been an unremitting student of science and nature in those days, and, although I lost my position as a teacher, owing to the treachery of a young man whom I instructed with great care, yet the knowledge was of paramount importance in the study of therapeutics (that is, the science of cure). By-the-way, let me say, in passing, that I received a prize of one thousand francs from the Academy of France for my essay on counter-irritants. But to the point, Mr. Grady. The air, as I have just enunciated, presses on all sides at the rate of fifteen pounds to the square inch. You may remember, at some period of your life, applying mustard to relieve a pain in some part of the body. Well, sir, the heat causes an expansion of the air; the blood in the little capillaries is pressed by the air within endeavoring to force its way to the surface, to fill the vacuum caused by the expansion. This rush of blood to the surface relieves the congestion which occasioned the pain. Mustard-plasters and cupping were great remedies some fifteen years ago in my native State; and having a great taste for the study of medicine, I inquired into the causes of cure, for to a certain extent cures were effected. The noble profession of Galen and Hippocrates had charms for me; and, therefore, having excellent opportunities, I pursued carefully my botanical studies, oftentimes accompanied by my favorite pupil, Myron Finch—"

"Who? Myron Finch, did you say? Myron Finch, from Vermont?" interrupted Grady, in a tone of great surprise.

"Yes; Myron Finch, from Vermont. Do you know him?"

"Had he weak, pale eyes, that looked washed out, a flabby, pale face, and thin, pale hair?"

"The youth of whom I speak," replied Scroggs, "had very light eyes and hair, and a pale, fleshy face. He was silent and reserved, and as bad a young man as ever lived since the days of Cain."

"It is the same. There cannot be two men in the whole universe who could answer that description," said Grady, "and be so abominably wicked at the same time."

"You seem to be acquainted with the youth; but I trust you have no dealings or intercourse of any sort with him. If you have any, cease at once, for he is a consummate liar and hypocrite, and capable of perpetrating any crime. But to return: One day, while ruminating in the woods, a thought flashed through my mind like inspiration. Could I but make the body *blush* all over; could I drive this blood back from the surface, and could I force it in and out at pleasure, I would make the greatest discovery that mortal man ever made. To make a long story short, I invented that instrument" (pointing to an air-tight wooden vessel, curiously constructed). "If you will go into it, I shall cover you all over, except your mouth, nose, and eyes, with India-rubber. I shall then exhaust the air by means of that powerful air-pump. I can withdraw from the surface of your body one hundred, five hundred, or fifteen hundred pounds of air. The air within rushes out to fill the vacuum, and, in doing so, propels the blood before it until it reaches the surface, which then blushes all over. The air is allowed to rush back again, and thus the blood is propelled (*pello*, I drive) backward and forward until the attrition removes the clot, or congestion. You comprehend me, sir?"

"Certainly, certainly, doctor," replied Grady, who had been a somewhat inattentive listener ever since the name of Myron Finch had been mentioned. But he saw that it was useless to try to stop the mild old man when once he was mounted on his hobby. Scroggs had formerly taught etymology in the high-school, and the habit which he had contracted of giving the roots of words to his pupils he could never abandon. His pedantry was simply prodigious. He was fond of teaching his patients; and, until he introduced the name of Finch, Grady was a splendid subject on which to practise his art of teaching.

"Certainly, I comprehend you, doctor. But what about Myron Finch, your former pupil?"

"Let us eschew him for the present. When we shall have finished our business, I shall tell you all about Myron Finch."

The little quack, though a great "benefactor" to the race—in point of fact, a "philanthropist" of the highest order—had to eat, drink, and be housed like ordinary mortals; and hence he had his mild blue eye fixed on his fee of four dollars. He had a curious peculiarity of having folded up, in small neat squares about an inch in size, several one-dollar bills, and placed carefully in his vest pocket, so that when the patient handed him a five-dollar bill (four being the first retainer), the single bill was all ready to be handed back as change.

"Mr. Grady, take off your coat and vest, step into the 'receiver,' and see if *it* does not diagnose your disease with unerring accuracy."

Grady did as he was told, stepped in, and was encased except his eyes, mouth, and nose, in India-rubber. He sat, for all the world, like a cowled monk of the Middle Ages. The little quack placed one leg over the other, which was his favorite attitude, smiled most blandly, and pumped out one hundred pounds of air, which was marked off on a graduated scale with a clock-shaped face, attached to the "receiver."

"Do you feel any pain?" asked the quack.

"No, sir; none in the least," replied Grady.

The quack then turned off two hundred pounds of air, and asked,

"Do you feel any pain now?"

"Yes, doctor; I feel a slight crawling sensation in the lower part of my throat."

"Ah! very good," said the little man, with his customary benignant smile; "the instrument begins to locate the exact position of your disease."

He then turned off two hundred and fifty pounds of air, and said,

"How now, Mr. Grady ?"

"The crawling sensation is increasing."

"Very well, very well, sir; let us see if you can bear three hundred pounds. How do you feel now ?"

"I think, doctor, that that's about as much as I can stand."

"Very good. We shall now go back to two fifty. Do you feel it now, Mr. Grady ?"

"Scarcely."

"All right. How now ? This is three hundred."

"Just a little crawling," replied Grady, "but not as much as before."

"Now we shall try three fifty and four hundred. How do you feel ?—can you stand any more ? You can ? Here is five hundred. How does that affect you ?"

"I can bear it, doctor."

Thus backward and forward, from two fifty to five hundred, the little quack pumped the air out and allowed it to rush in again for about half an hour, all the time smiling and chatting with the air of a man performing a most meritorious action.

As Grady stepped out of the "receiver," his first words were, "Doctor, what is your charge ?"

"Only four dollars for the first *operation*. My usual charge is forty dollars for twelve *operations;* and if any more are necessary, which is not often the case, the charge is reduced."

Grady promptly handed the mild philanthropist his fee, and then took his seat to listen to all he could learn of the antecedents of Myron Finch.

Washington Scroggs, M.D., feeling in the best possible humor, took a seat opposite Grady, lifted the right leg with both hands and gently laid it over the left—a position without which it would have been impossible for him to expatiate on the wonders of his system, or to narrate even the youthful history of Mr. Myron Finch—and taking out an antiquated snuffbox, and first offering Mr. Grady a pinch,

6

which that gentleman politely declined, filled both nostrils
with the pungent powder, as a sort of awakener of his re-
tentive faculties, and thus began the story which John Grady was so anxious to hear:

"About fifteen years ago I was a quiet, industrious teacher of a high-school in the State of Vermont. I was addict-
ed to scientific studies, particularly to botany, mineralogy,
and geology; and during the pleasant afternoons of the
summer and autumn it was my custom and pleasure to se-
lect certain of my pupils remarkable for docility and intelligence to accompany me in my researches. Among these,
the most docile, the most orderly, the most apprehensive,
was my favorite scholar, Myron Finch. The lad was about
nineteen, fair to look at, and with an intellect clever beyond
his years. He was the son of a well-to-do farmer, and was
completing his education under my careful supervision, for
the purpose of engaging in the teacher's profession. To
me he appeared extremely grateful and deferential—qualities which, combined with his unquestioned natural abilities,
commended him to my favor."

Scroggs always endeavored, except when working at his
machine, to "talk like a book," and never failed to inter-
lard his conversation with the Latin and Greek roots of
the big words which he was in the habit of using. These
roots we take the liberty of suppressing, for doubtless they
would be as annoying to the reader as they were to honest
John Grady.

"The school board," continued Scroggs, "was composed
of the clergyman, the physician, and the lawyer of the town.
I use the definite article 'the,' Mr. Grady, not because there
were not other clergymen, physicians, and lawyers, but because these three were the orthodox Presbyterian gentlemen whose congregation, patients, and clients constituted
more than seventy-five per centum of the population. This
was a period when the writings of certain scientists of Europe began to make a deep impression on many ardent and
enthusiastic minds; and not a few of the scholarly youths
of the town, whom I had trained to a love of Nature and
her operations, gave expression to opinions, especially in

regard to the science of geology, which were considered by
the elderly conservative people at war with revealed religion. Myron Finch was a reticent lad, kept his own counsel,
and attended the Presbyterian church most regularly, in
which he taught a Sunday-school class. Shortly it came to
pass that there were whisperings regarding *my* orthodoxy—
whisperings that *my* unconscious teaching was in the direction of the advanced thinkers, and that I was a propagand-
ist of dangerous heresies. In truth, I was made responsible
for all the infidelity and indifference to religion of which
the orthodox complained. It is true, I was a nominal Christian, was regular enough at church, and had never wittingly
uttered one syllable not in accordance with Divine revelation. Of course I was the last man in the town to hear a
whisper concerning my own wickedness. In this connection, bear in mind, Mr. Grady, that Finch was a capital penman, and excelled in drawing. He could imitate my signature with ease, and so thoroughly that an expert would
fail to detect the forgery."

" What! imitate your signature with ease?"

" Yes, perfectly, Mr. Grady."

" Poor Bailey! poor Bailey!" exclaimed Grady, in a tone
of deep pity. " But go on."

" Many a time, for mere amusement, he had signed my
name to passes granting permission for some of the schol-
ars to leave school before the hour of dismission. One Saturday morning there appeared in the little weekly journal
of the county an article entitled, ' The Efficacy of Prayer,'
said by the editor to be written by one of the ablest men
in town. Certain words and phrases, certain turns of expression—for every scholar has his own peculiarities—and
certain scientific terms, which I was known to use quite frequently, clearly indicated that I, and not another, was the
writer of the article in question. It was a most laughable
imitation of my style; in fact, I laughed at it myself as a
good joke. But, on a closer inspection and perusal, I perceived that it might damage me exceedingly; for the article turned out to be an attack on religion. When the
clerical member of the board of trustees afterward taxed

me with being the writer, of course I stoutly denied the authorship, and volunteered to go with him to the office of the paper and prove, by the handwriting of the manuscript, that I had nothing to do with it. Accompanied by the other two trustees, we called upon the editor; but, though the manuscript had been destroyed, the little note giving the real name of the author was preserved. What was my astonishment to find the name of Washington Scroggs appended to this note! The forgery was so perfect that all three trustees looked at me in amazement at my audacious falsehood. I was horror-stricken. There was but one man living who had the ability to thoroughly imitate my words, my turns of expression, and my chirography, and that man was Myron Finch. I immediately charged him with the forgery; but, with a refinement of subtle hypocrisy remarkable in one of his tender years, he simply smiled a denial, and said it was a hallucination of his good old teacher. The villain even condoled with me, and expressed his sincere regrets at my misfortune. He even went so far as to say, in my presence, that, like Paul, 'too much learning had made me mad!'

"But why dwell upon this rascality? I was removed; Finch was appointed to my place."

"Good God!" ejaculated Grady, "the forgery that sent my friend Bailey to prison for ten years was but a worse repetition of his treatment of you."

"I am not astonished," said the placid little quack, "to hear that the villany which he practised on me he repeated, on a larger scale, on another. But the clergyman, who was mainly instrumental in my removal, and in promoting this pious youth, paid a very dear price for his zeal in the cause of true religion. The minister had a niece, his companion and house-keeper (for he had no family of his own), who was the very apple of his eye. She was his only sister's child, and an orphan. Finch became an inmate of the pastor's house, a teacher of the high-school, as I have said, superintendent of the Sunday-school, and a very paragon of piety. Under a promise of marriage he ruined this niece, and fled to New York. She followed him, partly in the hope of making him fulfil his promise, and partly to hide her shame in a great city. Her uncle, the minister, died a few months afterward of a broken heart. So now you know the early history of Myron Finch."

Grady thanked Scroggs, and took his departure.

Chapter X.

"She is of so free, so kind, so apt, so blessed a disposition, she holds it a vice, in her goodness, not to do more than she is requested."
                                                                SHAKSPEARE.

WILLIAM WILDE, the banker, whose evidence helped to consign Bailey to State-prison, had always been of the opinion that the whole trial had been, in some inexplicable way, a miscarriage of justice. He had spoken of it at the time; and his conversation concerning it had made a deep impression on the minds of his two children, Walter and Edith. So much was this the case, that, two years after the conviction of George Bailey, Edith Wilde had been instrumental, through the influence of her father and several of her wealthy relatives, in procuring for Mrs. Bailey the position of matron of a half-orphan asylum, for which she was admirably fitted by education and high moral and religious feeling.

As Edith advanced in years she became the secretary of the board of managers, and in this capacity spent many hours with the sad and stately matron, between whom and herself one of those singular but permanent friendships arose, somewhat unusual between two persons so dissimilar in age, in social position, and in all the circumstances of life. Each knew instinctively that the other was good; and this goodness was a sort of free-masonry that bound them together. It gladdened the heart of the lonely and stricken mother to see this bright, witty, clever girl, with her clear, pale, healthy face, and large, frank, wide-open, gray eye, come gracefully and affectionately to her private room in the asylum to have a "private chat." And the motherless girl loved Mrs. Bailey as though she were in reality her mother. Many and many a time the old lady spoke of her darling George—how brave, how strong, how good, how tender he was—until the tears would trickle down Edith Wilde's cheeks in sympathy for the lonely, bereaved woman. She was never tired talking of her son. The young girl would kiss and soothe the matron, and tell her that she would be to her a daughter. In every way possible Edith made Mrs. Bailey's home in the asylum comfortable. Not a week passed that she did not visit her once or twice, and these visits were to her a source of sweet consolation.

But Mrs. Bailey was broken in health. At no period of her life had she been a strong woman, and the death of her husband, followed so soon by the terrible misfortune of her son, hastened the consumption which was hereditary in her family. During the last three or four years of her life she could hear no account of George, for, as already stated, her letters to him were intercepted and destroyed. Shortly after her appointment as matron John Grady ceased to call upon her, for the very good reason that he had left the city, owing to the machinations of Myron Finch.

Mrs. Bailey grew weaker and weaker day by day, until at last she was confined to her room, unable to attend to her duties; and every day Edith Wilde called, and spent two or three hours with the invalid, either in arranging the duties of the subordinates of the asylum, or conversing and reading aloud to amuse and comfort her.

"How do you feel to-day, Mrs. Bailey? Is your cough easier? Let me just raise that pillow a little—so: now you feel more comfortable," were the words with which Edith accosted the sick lady.

"Yes, darling, I am easier to-day. The cough is leaving me and my feet are swelling. I know what that means; but God's will be done. You have been such a comfort to me, Edith! It seems—it seems—as if He" (raising her eyes to heaven) "had sent you to be to me a daughter, when for some inscrutable purpose he allowed my son to be torn from me."

"Don't talk, dear Mrs. Bailey; you will only tire and distress yourself;" and the sweet girl pressed her beautiful lips against the pale, wan forehead of her friend. "I will read this charming book, and you can fall asleep as I read."

"No, no, my pet; I must talk to you to-day, for the end is approaching. I shall never see my son—my good, noble son, who has suffered so much unjustly. Oh! if I could but see him; if I could but press his hand once—only once; if I could but give him one parting kiss with my blessing—oh! if I could, I would die happy. But it cannot, cannot be;" and the poor lady wrung her thin hands in an agony indescribable.

"Mrs. Bailey—dear, dear Mrs. Bailey—please don't distress yourself;" and Edith took the worn hand in both of hers and stroked it soothingly.

"God's will be done! But, Edith, remember this—my son will be proved innocent before the world. I know it. With the shadow of death before me, I know it, I feel it; and this, too, is a great comfort."

"To be sure he will; the wicked cannot always go unpunished. Let me lift up your head a little, Mrs. Bailey; it is too low, and interferes with your breathing."

Edith Wilde read—not the charming book which she had brought—but, at Mrs. Bailey's request, that portion of the Gospel of St. John which described the sufferings and death of the Saviour. Edith had a low, sweet, penetrating voice, perfectly musical and soothing in its cadences; and the grand event which atoned for the sins of the world was read with a dramatic pathos that went to the heart of the sick lady.

"And so his mother saw him die on the cross! Alas! her grief was greater than mine, for she had greater reason." This was slowly and musingly spoken by Mrs. Bailey, but more in the tone of soliloquy than of conversation. "My darling child," continued Mrs. Bailey, turning toward Miss Wilde, "all my clothes, papers, all George's things—in a word, all our little family plate and trinkets are in those two trunks. Might I leave them in your charge? for sooner or later he will come to inquire for me, and he will come to you."

"Certainly; I will take charge of them with pleasure."

"And, my precious darling, if you find my George hardened and vindictive, owing to his wrongs and his sufferings, will you, for my sake, try— No, no—this is too much!"

But the true friend bent over the dying woman, and said, "Say no more; I understand you. I will be a sister to your son;" and, as if to seal the pledge, she bent down and kissed her cheek.

"May God reward you, my blessed darling!"

*　　　*　　　*　　　*　　　*　　　*

Two days after the conversation just recorded Mrs. Bailey died in the arms of her young friend. This event occurred about three years before George Bailey was released from prison.

On the death of the matron, Edith Wilde continued to take a deep interest in the asylum. Being the only daughter of a very wealthy banker, she had the means of adding to the comforts of the orphans, and also the time at her disposal to personally see that the children were kindly treated, and provided with everything which the board of managers had allowed them. For the past three years Edith had been constant in her attendance, and had devoted her time to the reorganization of the school.

Mr. William Wilde had received a very superior education. He had been a distinguished graduate of the university; and he had been in doubt, for some months after his graduation, whether he would pursue the profession of law or medicine, or enter the banking-house of which his maternal uncle was then the head. After mature deliberation he had resolved to be a merchant and banker. His talents and acquirements were such that he would have succeeded in any calling; and bending the energies of his trained faculties to business, a few years had placed him at the head of the banking-house in New York. The house had had argosies on every sea; and their mercantile and banking affairs had extended over most of the civilized countries of the Old and the New World. And yet, notwithstanding the pressure of the enormous business which he had to direct and control, Mr. Wilde had found time to review the studies of his youth, and to keep himself abreast of the current literature of the period. He was passionately fond of good poetry, and the "Lake Poets" were his especial favorites. To this splendid education were joined a sound common-sense and a native craft (in its best sense) which gave to his varied attainments a pungency and crispness that made him a delightful companion in every society. He was truly pious, without ostentation or bigotry, and really deserved the character which had been accorded to him by all who knew him, of a kind, Christian gentleman. He had always been fearless in the discharge of every duty, and as long as he satisfied the promptings of his own conscience he cared little for the opinion of the world. He had been a widower since Edith was ten and Walter eight years of age. The value of a good education had been so thoroughly appreciated by himself that he took special care of the education of his two children. Walter had graduated with high honor from Columbia College, and had been for the past year managing a branch house in California. Edith had been instructed by the best governesses, native and foreign. She was a fine Latin and French scholar, and knew a great deal more of mathematics and the natural sciences than ladies know in general. Her father had taken care to cultivate, from her earliest years, a love of literature and history. In Mr. Wilde's old age Edith was not only his beloved daughter but his friend and companion.

After dinner one day Mr. Wilde and Edith were sitting alone in the library, she working with worsted, and he reading his favorite Wordsworth. With his clear eye and clear complexion, and flowing, snowy beard, he was certainly a handsome old gentleman; for vice had not left a single bad line on his face, and exercise of mind and body had preserved that wholesomeness of countenance and elasticity of frame so beautiful to behold in those who have reached the allotted threescore and ten. Edith was rather below the medium height, delicately and beautifully formed, with a clear, pale, patrician face, and large, wide-open gray eyes, indicative of the highest order of intelligence. But there was a nameless grace and charm in her whole person, which can only be accounted for by the pure and lofty soul that dwelt within a faultless body.

Mr. Wilde, raising his eyes from his book and looking over his glasses, said,

"Edith, do you know that this is your twenty-third birthday?"

"Yes, father, of course I do."

"What would my Edith like for a birthday present?" and Mr. Wilde took out of his pocket a little velvet box and held it out before her eyes, as he said, "Guess what is in it."

"I cannot guess—how could I?" and there was the slightest possible shade of disappointment in her tone, which her father's quick perception failed not to observe.

"Then you wanted something else. I might have known that you cared very little about jewellery," remarked Mr. Wilde, in a tone even of greater disappointment than that of Edith.

But Edith arose, kissed her father's forehead, and said, "Forgive me! I am afraid I am growing selfish. I fear you have spoiled me with too much kindness."

"Hush, little one! I have nothing to forgive. I am only disappointed that I have failed to divine your taste or your wishes. But last Saturday I saw you admire this diamond star; and, as you are fond of wearing black, it struck me that it would look well on you. I perceive, however, that I have no taste in matters of this kind."

"You have excellent taste. The pin is a perfect beauty, and I do admire it very much; but—but—"

"But what?" interrupted Mr. Wilde.

"Nothing worth mentioning," replied Edith, with a sigh.

"Come, little one, you must tell me what has caused your disappointment."

"Well, if I must, I must. I was going to ask you for two hundred and fifty dollars—just think of it! and I suppose you have paid four times that sum for this beautiful star."

"Oh! is that all? Why, you shall have it, and twice as much more if you need it."

"But you don't know what I am going to do with it."

"Nor do I wish to know. Do with it as you please."

Edith then told him that she had set her heart upon giving the orphans a Thanksgiving dinner, with plum-pudding and fruit. "The poor little things only receive the regulation-fare, and a change will delight their little hearts."

"Yes," said Mr. Wilde, "and destroy their little stomachs. But, Edith, seriously, you spend a great deal of time in that orphan asylum. I can understand your doing good, acting as secretary, and all that, but you actually do the work of a paid teacher. I am not finding fault; but I don't want you to grow into an ancient spinster, my dear." This was spoken —at least the latter part of it—in a bantering tone.

"My dear father, ever since the death of Mrs. Bailey I have continued to take a profound interest in the orphans; and you know I am a half-orphan myself. This lady, next to my mother, was the best woman I have ever known. She was so gentle, so patient, so kind to the children, even to the erring and wayward, that she often appeared to me like an incarnate saint."

"Ah! she was the mother of the young man who was sent to State-prison over ten years ago. He ought to be free by this time, poor fellow! I believe in my heart that he never committed that forgery. He was the victim of some vile conspiracy."

"I have no doubt of it, father. His mother told me the story over and over again; she informed me upon every point of his character. He was frank, fearless, and open as the day. No, no; the son of such a mother never committed an act of forgery."

"Here, little one, is your check for two hundred and fifty dollars, and here is your diamond star. Let us change the subject. Suppose you read aloud for me for half an hour, before we retire for the night."

Edith had just taken the book when the servant handed Mr. Wilde the card of "John Grady, Editor and Proprietor of the *Weekly Reformer*."

"Show the gentleman into the library. Edith, you need not leave. It is some applicant for money, and I can dispose of him in a short time; and then we can go on with our reading. What are you waiting for?" said Mr. Wilde, turning to the colored waiter.

"There are two of them, sir."

"Show them both in. Edith, keep your seat. I shall soon get rid of them. I want to hear you read; for, for some reason, the poetry is always better when you read aloud."

George Bailey and John Grady walked into Mr. Wilde's library. Owing to the kindly care of Grady, Bailey had completely recovered from the fever consequent upon his privations and sufferings during his protracted and vain attempts to obtain employment without the necessary "city reference." All traces of his recent struggle had disappeared. He was now attired in a decent suit of black, which showed to advantage the pallor of his complexion. In dress, in bearing, in manner he had the air of a quiet, dignified gentleman. Bailey's face wore the indescribable expression of a man who had suffered a great wrong. The chief ingredient of this expression was sadness; and yet, with this sadness, there was a subdued fierceness in his eye and a set determination in his lips, which indicated an immutable purpose that nothing but death could destroy. His face was difficult to read, because his purposes and his passions were under complete control.

"Be seated, gentlemen," said Mr. Wilde. "Mr. Grady, what can I do for you this evening? To what do I owe the honor of this visit?"

"Mr. Wilde," replied Grady, "allow me to introduce to you my friend, Mr. George Bailey."

At the mention of Bailey's name both father and daughter gave a slight start of astonishment, but Mr. Wilde recovered himself in a moment and shook the returned convict cordially by the hand. "Edith, this is Mr. Bailey, of whom we were just speaking; Mr. Bailey, this is my daughter, Miss Wilde."

Edith also extended her hand cordially to the returned

convict, and said she was glad to see him well. There was a shade of disappointment in her face as she sought in vain for some resemblance to his mother, whom she had so truly loved and so sadly mourned. But in the dark, pale countenance, strongly marked, and in the iron-gray hair—gray not with age, but with thought and suffering—she failed to trace a single feature of the fair and fragile lady whom she had known and cared for as the matron of the orphan asylum.

"Mr. Wilde," said Bailey, resuming his chair, "I have called to thank you and your daughter for the great kindness which you showed to my poor mother after my—my—conviction. Only for the cruelty of my jailers, I should have learned long ago how well you had provided for her; and this knowledge would have spared me many a sad hour in my—solitary confinement."

"We deserve no thanks, Mr. Bailey," said Mr. Wilde, "for we did but our duty by a good woman, undeservedly punished. Even had you been guilty, which we did not believe, we should have treated your mother as we did. However, if there is credit for the act, my daughter is entitled to it: I am not. You remember I was a witness—a most unwilling one—against you, for I always believed you the victim of a conspiracy—"

"Thank you, Mr. Wilde, for those words," interrupted Bailey.

"And in telling your sad fate at the dinner-table, I aroused the sympathy of my little daughter, who never rested until, with the aid of some of our influential friends and relatives, she had your mother installed in a good position, which placed her beyond the reach of want Miss Wilde learned to love your mother very dearly for her own sake."

All the subdued fierceness forsook Bailey's eyes, and an expression of exquisite gratitude and tenderness shone in its stead, as he looked the thanks to the beautiful girl, that he could not utter. The firm expression fell away from the lips that trembled with emotion.

"Mr. Bailey," said Edith, with the view of saving him from embarrassment, "it is a most singular coincidence that my father and I were talking of your mother at the very moment of your arrival at the door. As my father has just told you, I was your mother's very dear friend. I was with her at the time of her death; and she left her effects, papers, etc., in my charge for you whenever you could be found. She charged me to give you her blessing, and to warn you not to forget your God in your misery. She died with your name on her lips."

In spite of all Bailey's efforts the tears welled up in his eyes, and he was obliged to turn his head in order to hide them.

Miss Wilde, perceiving Bailey's emotion, and not wishing to witness the tears of a strong man, hastily arose and said,

"I shall go to my room and bring you the small writing-desk containing the papers, pictures, and trinkets which Mrs. Bailey left in my charge. The large trunk containing her other effects can be sent to your home."

On the way up to her room Edith soliloquized as follows: "Mrs. Bailey was right in loving such a son. At the very mention of his mother's name all that strange, subdued fierceness left his eyes, and they became as soft and tender as a woman's. The idea of a man of that stamp becoming a poor, paltry forger! The Van Hesses, father and daughter, were both idiots; the one blinded by a narrow bigotry, and the other by a selfish worldliness." Edith was as clear-headed as her father, and possessed all his keen insight into human character.

She handed Bailey the writing-desk, which he received with the simple words, "Thank you." His eyes, however, spoke volumes, which Edith failed not to read perfectly.

Honest John Grady had sat a silent spectator, until a general silence afforded him the opportunity for which he had been patiently waiting.

"Mr. Wilde," said Grady, "my friend here can find no employment for want of a city reference: nobody will employ a returned convict. Can't you, Mr. Wilde, do something to give him a start?"

"Hush, hush, Mr. Grady!" interrupted Bailey; "I would not for the world desecrate this hour by begging employment. Indeed, sir, I did not come here to embarrass you by asking work; I came simply for news of my poor mother, and to thank her benefactors."

"But Mr. Grady is right," interposed Edith; "Mr. Bailey must not be permitted to starve. He was wrongfully convicted, father, as you well know. He has suffered unjustly for ten years; and now, for his mother's sake, I ask you, father, as a favor to me, to procure him employment of some sort."

"Edith, my dear, I am afraid that you do not understand business. The only way in which I could find employment for Mr. Bailey is to employ him in our banking-house—and I have partners. Mr. Bailey" (turning from Edith to that gentleman), "you perceive my difficulty?"

"Indeed, Mr. Wilde, I do perceive your difficulty; and I regret exceedingly that my good, kind friend mentioned the matter. It really pains me."

"Mr. Bailey and Mr. Wilde," said Edith, looking with mock severity from one to the other, "I give you fair warning that this is my affair and—Mr. Grady's. I made a promise to Mrs. Bailey on her dying bed—no matter what. Now, father, I do insist that you explain the matter to your junior partners, and give Mr. Bailey a position. I will be bail for his honesty." The last sentence was spoken with a smile which would have charmed the worst misanthrope that ever breathed. Its effect on poor Bailey may be imagined.

"Miss Wilde," said Bailey, "I do protest. I would rather die than have the appearance of seeking employment in this manner."

"Well, well," said Mr. Wilde, "my daughter is right, as she usually is—always is—on every moral question. Mr. Bailey, you were an innocent man, unjustly convicted and punished, partly and unwittingly on my evidence. As I was unwillingly an instrument in the miscarriage of justice, I shall be a willing instrument in aiding your restoration to your former position. Come to the bank to-morrow morning, and I shall start you, at first in a humble place, from which you must work up by means of your own talents."

"I assure you, sir," said Bailey, "that I had not the most remote idea, when I came here, of asking for employment; but I thank you and Miss Wilde from the bottom of my heart."

"All right, Bailey," interrupted Grady; "Miss Wilde and I have done the business; that is, I blew the bellows and she played the music."

"One word before we leave," said Bailey: "Mr. Wilde —Miss Wilde, do you thoroughly believe in my innocence? Has either of you the shadow of a doubt?"

"Mr. Bailey," said Edith, hastily, "you ought not to ask such a question. Do you think that I would recommend or my father employ you, if we had the shadow of a suspicion? Was not your mother my most intimate friend?"

"I beg pardon for the question," said Bailey, "but, oh, Miss Wilde, you cannot realize what it has been to live for eleven years under the black cloud of a great crime; and I assure you that I am far more grateful for your implicit belief in my innocence than I would have been had your father by a stroke of his pen made me a millionnaire. I cannot express my gratitude in words."

Bailey and Grady left, with the understanding that the former was to enter on his new employment the next morning.

"Upon my soul!—pardon me, Bailey, for swearing—she is a trump! If I were a young man, and as good-looking as you, I would forfeit heaven—God forgive me!—to possess such a thorough-bred woman as that for a wife. She reminds me of an Arabian courser — beautifully formed, and with an eye as tender as it is full of fire."

"Hush, Grady, hush!" and George Bailey was silent almost all the way to Williamsburgh. He soliloquized inwardly, "My mother died in *her* arms! *She* obtained employment for her! *She* always believed in my innocence! *She* induced her father to give me work! Oh, my guardian angel! How coarse that expression of Grady's—my wife! —any man's wife! She is too good to be the wife of an archangel! How bright the stars look to-night! How beautiful the whole heavens appear! It seems to me as if I were born again."

And he *was* born again; for the spirit of love had entered his heart; a love which had its origin in profound respect for what was surpassingly good; a love which neither time nor distance could ever change. Blessed are the few into whose hearts this divine love enters!

CHAPTER XI.

"Nor all that heralds rake from coffined clay,
Nor florid prose, nor honeyed lies of rhyme,
Can blazon evil deeds, nor consecrate a crime."—BYRON.

DURING George Bailey's imprisonment and subsequent struggles, Myron Finch had grown to be one of the great merchant-princes of New York. He was a member of the leading clubs, a director in several corporations, and a cunning speculator in stocks and real estate. He was the owner of a beautiful steam-yacht, in which he gave magnificent entertainments to his friends, who were the political controllers of legislatures and conventions, or the gigantic financial operators on the Stock Exchange. Finch was one of the "Ring," whose approving nod was worth a fortune, or whose adverse frown was ruin to an enemy. He kept fine horses; he lived luxuriously; he fared sumptuously every day; and enjoyed with a rare relish all the good things of this life. He had long ago made himself the real head of the firm of Van Hess & Co., and had very quietly but decisively elbowed his father-in-law into an inferior place, with the remark, "My dear sir, at your time of life this work is too much for you." And Mr. Jacob Van Hess, in no little awe of this resolute son-in-law, had very tamely submitted to take a back seat in his own counting-house. The truth of the matter is, Mr. Van Hess had become very much afraid of Mr. Myron Finch. The old gentleman loved his daughter even more than his business; and he had discovered, within six months after her marriage, that she was wedded to a cold, cunning, unscrupulous scoundrel. No sooner had he been made a

partner, no sooner had the honey-moon been over, than
Myron Finch flung aside the mask of religion and temperance, with which he had won the confidence of Mr. Van
Hess, and gave loose rein to the infidelity and to the baser
passions of his evil nature. For the sake of Grace, Mr.
Jacob Van Hess smothered his anger, and endured the
domination of a man whom he despised and loathed.
Both father and daughter knew him to be simply a polite
and smiling fiend, without love, without gratitude, without
a single virtue. His master-passion was his intense desire
for money; because money alone could purchase the gross
sensual pleasures in which his frigid soul seemed to take
delight. He was the incarnation of selfishness.

Time has been very gentle with Mr. Myron Finch. During the eleven years that have passed away since we first
introduced him to the reader he has altered but little in
appearance. He has become inclined to corpulency, and
the pale hair has been slightly worn away from his temples. A puffiness, too, has appeared about his nether eye-
lid, indicative of intemperance and disease.

But if the husband has remained comparatively un-
changed, great indeed, and pitiful to behold, is the change
in the poor wife, the once petted and spoiled darling of
fortune. Mrs. Myron Finch has worn for years the timid,
frightened expression always found in the faces of weak
women who are constantly afraid of brutal husbands.
Whatever little spirit she had originally possessed has
been completely crushed out of her by stern, cool, system-
atic ill-treatment and unmitigated cruelty. For a long
time she had foolishly endeavored to hide her misery from
her father, and her father had dreaded to speak to her concerning her unhappiness. The same fear of the world (her
world of fashion) that had caused her to desert George Bailey in his time of trouble and disgrace, had caused her to
submit in silence to the inhumanity of Finch. She had
borne the villain three children, and for their sakes, as well
as for the sake of her own worldly pride, she had suffered
wrongs enough to have driven a stronger woman to suicide
or murder. Finch had completely subdued her. Thin,

dark, sickly, with dark lines around her eyes, she looked care-worn, faded, and prematurely old.

In all her misery the poor woman had nursed in her heart the image of the strong, frank, fearless youth who had loved her with the love of a true and loyal nature. In one of his drunken, angry fits, while abusing and beating her, Finch had boasted that he was the man who had sent her lover to State-prison. From that day forward she had felt that George Bailey was an innocent man, and the victim of a foul conspiracy. When she contrasted the two men her remorse was unbounded, and her old love revived with a strength that she did not even try to subdue.

A few days after the events recorded in the last chapter Mr. and Mrs. Myron Finch were sitting alone in the dining-room, each reading a morning newspaper. Breakfast was finished, and the children had gone to the nursery. Suddenly the husband dropped his paper, and, turning to his wife with a savage scowl on his brows, said,

"See here; your old lover, George Bailey, d—n him! has just turned up in the city. Quin saw him yesterday in the banking-house of Warrenton, Wilde & Co. Do you hear me, d—n you? What are you dreaming about, you idiot?—about your old sweetheart, eh? Remember, you must never see or speak to him. Don't fancy that I am jealous of such a thing as you. But this man may call to see you, or to inquire about your father, or his mother, or something of the sort. You must never see him; for the day that you do I shall separate from you and obtain a divorce."

To this tirade Grace made no reply: she seemed scared, and trembled from head to foot; and her aspect was that of a frightened bird when newly captured.

"I declare," continued the ruffian, "that the woman is trembling all over!" and changing his position so as to face his wife, he commenced to taunt her.

"So you married me to cover the disgrace of an engagement to a convict, did you? You married me because I was a pious young man, and went to church twice every Sunday, didn't you? And I married you because I loved

your old father's money-bags, eh? Wasn't it a fair exchange, my precious?"

Finch had often gone farther than this in his speech before now, and had even repeatedly struck her in his drunk-
en state; but never in his sober senses had he ventured to
taunt his wife in this vile way; for no one could ever ac-
cuse him of being a fool, except in so far as all knaves are
fools. There were feelings surging in the heart of Mrs.
Finch, aroused by the allusions to her first love, which her
husband did not comprehend, and which, had he known,
would have curbed the license of his speech. He failed to
see that he was fast driving his wife to desperation. A
hectic flush overspread her thin cheek, and a semblance of
the old brilliancy shone in her eyes, imparting for a moment a portion of the former beauty for which she had
been remarkable.

"Woman, I say, do you hear me?"

But Grace's mind was far away, and for a minute or two
she seemed to have lost or forgotten her fear of the tyrant.
Finch moved his chair close to her and shook his clinched
fist in her face, as he said,

"Mrs. Finch, have you lost your speech?—are you mad?
If you don't pay more attention to what I say I'll choke
the life out of you!"

Still Grace neither seemed to hear nor heed him. She
sat like one dazed, or perhaps like one who was slowly
making up his mind, and cared no more for her husband's
violence at this moment than for the howling of the idle
wind. Transported with rage at her continued silence, the
brute seized her by the throat with one hand, and smote
her repeatedly on the face with the other.

Myron Finch went too far this morning. He could not
see the effect of Bailey's return on a mind that had brood-
ed about him ever since she had discovered his innocence.
With a dignity which Finch had never before witnessed,
Grace simply said,

"Hands off, coward!" and seized a pair of large scis-
sors which lay near her, and holding the point out before
his face, said, "If ever you touch me again I shall kill you

on the spot! I hate you, I despise you, I scorn you! Separate—obtain your divorce, you contemptible wife-beater!"

Myron Finch, at this exhibition of spirit on the part of
his wife, turned deadly pale. He was thoroughly cowed.
It was now his turn to fear the woman whom he had so
long despised and bullied. He was first amazed, then awed,
and finally frightened. Had a dead woman arisen from
the grave and threatened him, he could not have been more
astonished. But, if cowardly, Finch was cunning; and no
man knew better than he how to adapt his conduct to the
circumstances of the hour.

"Grace, you exasperated me beyond endurance. Forgive me; in my passion I scarcely knew what I did. I
was jealous of your old lover."

"No, sir; you were not jealous, and you need not lie
about it. You cannot deceive me, Mr. Finch. I hate you;
and you had better go, or I may be tempted to stab to the
heart the father of my children. Go, go, go! you cowardly villain! I have borne your cruelty for eleven years; I
shall bear it no longer. Leave me! leave me, or I shall not
be responsible for my acts!"

Myron Finch retired, with the expression of a baffled
fiend marked on every line of his pale, flabby face.

For hours after her husband had left, Grace sat in the
rocking-chair, with her head thrown back and her eyes
closed. The only signs to indicate that she was not asleep
were frequent tremblings of the lips, twitchings of the eyelids, and deeply marked lines between the brows. The red
marks of Finch's brutal blows were plainly visible on her
cheeks. At length she arose and commenced walking backward and forward, as men frequently do when agitated with
unhappy thoughts—and, clasping her hands in a sort of
speechless agony, she murmured, in a tone of indescribable
grief and remorse,

"And for that brute I abandoned to his fate the truest,
bravest heart that woman ever won! Even had George
Bailey been guilty of the crime of which he was convicted,
a life in State-prison with him would have been infinitely
preferable to a life in a palace with such a fiend as Finch.

Oh! oh! oh! my punishment is greater than I can bear!
But I deserve it all—I deserve it all!"

Tears came to the relief of the suffering woman. Moaning and weeping, she continued her monotonous walk, ever murmuring, "Oh! oh! oh! I deserve it all—I deserve it all! But I must find him—I must find him." Then she cast herself heavily down in the chair, and, covering her face with both her hands, she said, "But how shall I ever face him? I would give worlds to look at him once more; but I dare not—I dare not! However, I must see him and ask his pardon. I have always loved him. I might have forgotten him, if that brutal fiend Finch had ever treated me with common decency. But now my husband and I are as far apart as the poles!" Again Grace arose, and strode back and forth like an angry man. An unwonted fire gleamed in her eyes, and her brow was knit with an energy born of her new resolution. "I shall see my father and tell him all—my good, kind father, who has borne with Finch these weary years for my sake."

Such was her eagerness to carry out her determination that she rushed up to her room, hastily dressed herself for the street, and in less than fifteen minutes was in an omnibus on her way down to her father's office.

Happily Finch was not in the counting-house when Grace arrived, or there might have been a scene, for the lady's soul was on fire, and had reached that condition in which regard for her world of fashionable society would have had no weight with her whatever. Finch's blows were still tingling in her face, and the very memory of them maddened her—at least she fancied so. But perhaps, after all, memories of George Bailey spurred her on more than she was aware of; or, at any rate, she was now moved by a combination of motives.

When father and daughter were seated alone in the private inner office, the former said,

"Well, Grace, my dear, this visit at noonday is something very unusual;" and the old gentleman looked uneasily at the door, in fear that Finch might enter and find them together.

"You need not glance so uneasily at the door. Let him enter—let him hear all I have to say! Father, I am going home to you with my children to-night. I shall not sleep another night under Finch's roof. I could not wait until evening—my impatience would have killed me. See these marks on my face: the fiend struck me this morning with his hand: he struck me moral blows that were far worse. He said that I only married him to hide the disgrace of my engagement with a convicted forger, and that he married me for my father's money-bags!"

"Grace! Grace!" groaned the father, "I have suspected this for years, and the thought of it has been killing me by inches. Oh, Grace, you cannot imagine what I have borne from this man for your sake!"

"I know it, father—I know it only too well. He has bullied and abused you; taken the business out of your hands and driven you into a corner; and for my sake you have endured it all. Know, then, that from the first month of our marriage he has ill-used me. I tried to hide it from you and the world through a false pride; but to-day, in his sober senses, he transcended his previous brutality. Know, too, dear father, that in one of his drunken fits he confessed and boasted that George Bailey was an innocent man, and had been sent to State-prison by his instrumentality."

"What! what! My God! my God! This is the worst blow of all! What! boasted that he was instrumental in sending an innocent man to State-prison for ten years? Oh no, no! this was only the idle, lying boast of a wicked man."

"Father, Bailey was innocent, and I must ask his forgiveness."

Jacob Van Hess's head fell forward on his chest, and either he did not hear or heed what Grace had said. The old man seemed lost in deep thought, and his face wore an expression of profound dismay.

"I had a note this morning," he said, "from George Bailey."

"You had?—what about?" eagerly interrupted Grace.

"Here it is," replied Mr. Van Hess, pulling the note out of his pocket; "read for yourself."

At sight of the bold, characteristic handwriting, which she knew so well, Grace's face and neck turned the color of scarlet. This was what she read :

"Warrenton, Wilde & Co.,
"New York, December 12th, 18—.

"JACOB VAN HESS, ESQ., *Sir*, — Having recovered the effects of my late mother, and failing to find among her papers the receipt for the fifteen hundred dollars which she paid you on account of the forged check that liquidated my debt to Mr. William Wilde, I take the liberty of asking you, as a matter of simple justice, to forward me a receipt, or to accord me the privilege of an explanation. You can readily understand my anxiety concerning this receipt.

"Truly yours, etc.,   GEORGE BAILEY."

"Did you give his mother a receipt at the time?" asked Grace.

"Very likely I did. But you know how careless women usually are in matters of this kind."

"My dear father, please write as I dictate. Do it for me; because you can furnish me the opportunity to beg Mr. Bailey's pardon."

Mr. Van Hess seized a pen and wrote George Bailey an invitation to call at his residence that evening.

Father and daughter then discussed their plans for the future. Grace and the children were to leave Finch forever, and make their home with Mr. Van Hess. Mr. Van Hess was to dissolve the partnership and retire from business. When this matter had been finally determined upon, both felt happier than they had felt for many years.

CHAPTER XII.

"A man of sense may love like a madman but never like a fool."
LA ROCHEFOUCAULD.

To the sad, solitary George Bailey, Edith Wilde seemed something more than human. To say that he thought of her day and night would but faintly convey an idea of his feelings toward her. It was more than love; it was worship. He rarely reflected on her loveliness, but always on her goodness. During the past eleven years he had seen and experienced so much ingratitude, wickedness, and cruelty, that he had been reduced almost to a state of atheism, and had begun to have a firm belief in human depravity. Nothing but his superior education and sound common-sense had prevented his falling into the haunts of thieves and burglars, and becoming, at the invitation of Williams, their organizer and captain. In Bailey's character there was a substratum of high honor and pure morality which came to him by inheritance, and had been developed by that best of all teachers, a wise, educated mother. But in the intervention of God in human affairs he had lost all faith; for he had seen the innocent unjustly punished and the wicked "flourishing like a green bay-tree." Into the darkness of his soul at this time the charity and goodness of Edith Wilde shed brilliant rays of light, which slowly and gradually dispelled the dark and gloomy scepticism that was surely corroding his better nature. Through Edith's eyes he fancied that he saw his mother's soul. In his thoughts Edith's image was always coupled with that of the Saviour. His first thought every morning, his last thought every night, was a prayer to God for her happiness. And this was the first prayer which Bailey had uttered since the day of his unjust conviction. The simple act of thinking about a good woman brought him back to a knowledge of his Creator. The face, the form, the eyes, the smile, the grace, and the very tone of Edith's voice were all indelibly impressed upon his memory. The pent-up passion, the exquisite tenderness of his nature went forth toward her with an irresistible energy, like the strong, steady, silent flow of a mighty river.

In the banking-house, Bailey, in his humble situation, soon won the approbation of his employers. He was quiet and industrious, always willing and ready to perform any work which might be assigned him; eager to assist his fellow-clerks when behind-hand, and anxious to do their work and his own whenever any of the younger men wished a holiday. He was the first in the office in the morning, the last to leave

in the evening.   None of his fellow-clerks knew his history;
but they all liked the cold, grave, sad man who was never
seen to smile.   His day's work over, he sought his quiet
room in Grady's house, and spent the evening in reading
and studying, and thinking of Edith Wilde.   His only
pleasure he took on Sunday.   As regularly as the Sunday
came, he dressed himself in a sober suit of black, and, no
matter what was the condition of the weather, went to the
Episcopal church which Mr. Wilde and Edith attended.
Had her church been a Mohammedan mosque, Bailey would
have gone to it in preference to any other, because it contained the one being in all the universe whom he adored.
He was placed in the gallery by the sexton, in such a position that he could see her without being seen himself.   He
looked forward all the week to Sunday, counting the hours
until he could see her again.   The Episcopal service appeared to him sublimely beautiful, because, in some mysterious way, she seemed to him the very incarnation of the
litany and of the teaching of Christ.   As he listened to the
fine bass voice of the rector, uttering the grand thoughts of
" The General Supplication "—" From all blindness of heart,
from pride, vainglory, and hypocrisy; from envy, hatred
and malice, and all uncharitableness, *Good Lord deliver us*"—
and caught her silver tone in the response (for, like all who
have suffered long from solitary confinement, his sight and
hearing were preternaturally acute), a new heaven and a new
earth were revealed to him; and because she was good, he
determined with all his might to be good likewise.   When
the minister came to the words, " That it may please Thee
to forgive our enemies, persecutors, and slanderers, and to
turn their hearts," Bailey could not and did not respond,
" We beseech Thee to hear us, Good Lord."   He had brood-
ed over his revenge so long and so steadily that it had become a part of his nature.   To punish Finch was the great
aim of his existence.   He could be a Christian for Edith's
sake in all things but this.   By a sort of perverse logic he
had reasoned himself into the belief that it was his duty to
assist in carrying out the vengeance of Heaven against his
moral assassin.   His human love was leading him toward

his God; and a time came when he would freely have given half the remaining years of his life to kneel by Edith Wilde's side and repeat with her those beautiful prayers of the Church. His vindictive passion was ever tugging at his newly-awakened spiritual aspirations, and dragging him down into a quagmire of wicked thoughts and hopes. The spirits of good and evil were fiercely contending in Bailey's heart.

This was the state of George Bailey's mind when he received the reply from Mr. Jacob Van Hess, making an appointment for an interview that evening. Bailey, in the prosecution of his plans for revenge on Finch, was greatly disappointed at not finding the receipt for the fifteen hundred dollars; and after mature deliberation he had resolved to obtain it, for he knew well its value in the future. He was aware that he was asking no favor; he was only asking for his right. Besides, he had never entertained bitter feelings toward Mr. Van Hess; nay, on the contrary, he had remembered him with gratitude for the favors he had conferred up to the period of his conviction. He had truly reasoned, If a learned judge and twelve jurymen had been deceived by the conspiracy, why not Mr. Van Hess and his daughter? In his heart he could not blame them.

As he slowly and meditatively walked toward the house in which he had wooed and won the love of the beautiful heiress eleven years before, what a contrast he presented to the frank, open, joyous youth who, in the exhilaration of his spirits, had seemed to spurn the very earth on that raw March day! He now wore the sad, reticent look of the prison. His expression of face was such that no man could now expect his confidence. "Ah," he muttered, with a look of pain, "this is the house; I surely ought to know it."

When admitted into the parlor, and while waiting a few minutes for his host, Bailey cast his eyes around the rooms and glanced at the well-remembered pictures and statuary. Everything appeared precisely as they were eleven years ago. He felt by contrast a terrible change in himself. He had not much time for reflection, for Mr. Jacob Van Hess entered the parlor at this moment, and approached Bailey as if for the purpose of shaking his hand; but the manner of the latter was so frigid and formal, as he arose from his chair and bowed, that the old gentleman paused in the middle of the room, greatly embarrassed, and hardly knew what to say. But Bailey came to his relief by saying, in a tone coldly polite,

"Mr. Van Hess, you will please pardon my writing to you for the receipt; but as it was indispensable to me, and mine by right, I took the great liberty of addressing you a note."

"No, no; it—it was not a liberty at all. I—I—am glad to give you the receipt," said Mr. Van Hess, still more embarrassed, for he had not anticipated Bailey's frigid politeness.

"Thank you, Mr. Van Hess. I knew that you would not refuse to do an act of justice."

The old gentleman having handed Bailey the receipt, and having in some measure regained his composure, went up to Bailey, and, extending his hand, said,

"Forgive me, George; I unwittingly did you a great wrong. I have suspected it for a long time, but never knew it for certain until my daughter told me this morning."

"I have nothing to forgive," replied Bailey, coldly; "you acted as you thought justly at the time. I have never blamed you."

"Say, at least, Mr. Bailey," pleaded the old man, "that you forgive me, even if you have nothing to forgive, for it will be a great relief to my conscience. Oh, Mr. Bailey, I made a fearful mistake, an irreparable blunder, worse than a crime!"

"If you desire me to repeat the words, I can easily do so: if I have anything to forgive, I freely forgive you." His manner and his words were icy, and cut Mr. Van Hess to the quick. It was unintentional on Bailey's part. The memory of that scene in the counting-house, when the forged check and the receipt for it were brought home to him, was vividly portrayed in his mind, never to be effaced, and the sight of Mr. Van Hess pained him.

George had arisen to take his leave, when the old gentleman said, "Mr. Bailey, please be seated; there is another who wishes to be forgiven;" and before Bailey had time to make any reply Mr. Van Hess had left the parlor. In a few minutes a lady entered the room, lividly pale, thin and worn, whom Bailey at the first glance failed to recognize. After a closer inspection he recognized the once beautiful Grace, the idol of his youthful affections. His bow to her was, if possible, more frigid than the one he had given her father. The whole interview was so painful to him that he now regretted having sought for the receipt. Of course, had he anticipated meeting Grace Finch, he would no more have entered that house than he would have entered the crater of Mount Etna when in full blast.

"George Bailey, can you forgive me?"

But this was too much for Bailey to bear. Here was the woman before him who had forsaken him in his time of trouble and disgrace, and had married the very man who had wrought him such misery.

"Who calls me George Bailey?—is it the wife of Myron Finch?"

"Oh, Mr. Bailey, forgive me—forgive me! Do not leave the house until you have spoken the precious words!"

"Madam, I don't understand you. With you I have no quarrel. I have nothing to forgive."

Grace, with all a woman's quickness of perception, clearly saw that Bailey cared no more for her than he did for one of the servants in her father's kitchen. She saw his anxiety to leave the house, and it must be confessed that his utter indifference pained her exceedingly. Had he only found fault with her, had he but upbraided her for her desertion, she would have had some hope; now she had none. She cast herself, pale as death, on a sofa, and murmured, "Lost, lost—forever lost!"

"Madam," said Bailey, "my presence is painful to you, and I wish you good-evening." He had now reached the door, and in another moment he would have gone, perhaps never to be seen by her again. Grace sprung from the sofa, placed her hand on the knob of the door, and closing it, said,

"Mr. Bailey, I must speak to you. You *must* forgive me —you *must!* Sit down, please—sit down."

"Who is it that speaks to me in this imperative manner?" said Bailey, half angry at the detention.

"I do—Grace Van Hess, whom you once loved!"

"Grace Van Hess," replied Bailey, in a deep, grave tone, "is dead; or was transformed, if report be true, into Mrs. Myron Finch. I have not had the honor of any previous acquaintance with Mrs. Myron Finch. This is the first time I have had the honor of seeing that estimable lady. I knew her husband once: I helped him to obtain a good situation; I was his very good friend; in fact, I was the instrument by which he gained his first start in life, and I believe his present wife, too, unless I have been greatly misinformed. Doubtless, for all my kindness to Mr. Myron Finch his loving wife is duly thankful." The hard, cold, flinty irony of these words smote Grace to the heart as if with cold steel.

"George Bailey, you are changed too," retorted Grace; "you are not the frank, brave, generous George Bailey whom I once knew and loved."

"There, madam, you speak most truly. The George Bailey whom you knew eleven years ago, and fancied that you loved — vainly fancied that you loved — is dead! He died, Mrs. Finch, in a solitary cell in State-prison; and, *mirabile dictu*, phœnix-like, out of his ashes arose the man you see before you. Ah! verily, madam, the frank, trustful youth whom you knew once died a very miserable death, killed by the— But why talk? Why waste words?"

"Mr. Bailey, I was young, inexperienced, and cowardly. I was surrounded by fashionable society; and I was, alas! proud, and unable to face the disgrace of being engaged to a convict. They convinced me of your guilt."

"Well, well, have I complained? You abandoned me, and I ceased to think of you. I have never blamed you. I have nothing to forgive; if I have, I forgive you. This interview, madam, had better end."

"Mr. Bailey," Grace persisted, "I have had the best possible proof of your innocence."

"Proofs are not necessary to those whose good opinion

I regard," replied Bailey, haughtily, doubtless thinking at that moment of Edith Wilde.

"I did not know of the terrible plot that consigned you to prison for ten years until after my—"

"Marriage," interposed Bailey.

"Mr. Finch," continued Grace, "told, in his drunken—"

"That will do, Mrs. Finch," interrupted Bailey. "It is better that I should hear nothing of Myron Finch from you; for some day I have a reckoning to make with that gentleman, and his wife ought not to be a voluntary witness against him." There was a bitterness and a severity in Bailey's tone which all his self-command could not subdue. If the sight of the father had pained him, the sight of the daughter was simply intolerable.

When George reached the street he seemed to breathe more freely. He commenced to talk to himself, for he had not yet overcome his prison habit. "So, this is the woman whom I once loved—this poor, weak, ill-used creature, with all the marks of Finch on her physical, mental, and moral nature! She might have been built up into an excellent woman; but this fiend, Finch, has evidently dragged her down to nearly his own low level. Evidently she hates her husband; and—and—I could strike the villain here! But no—away, away, base thought! 'Get thee behind me, Satan!' What would Edith think? What would my mother think? Nay, nay, I would rather forego all revenge than forfeit the good opinion of my guardian angel, who succored my mother in her time of destitution, and who procured me honorable employment when every avenue for honest work was barred against me. Bless her, O my God! bless her, and guard her for ever and ever!—Amen."

After Bailey's departure, Grace threw herself back in the chair and covered her face with both her hands, murmuring, with a tone of despair, "He loves me not! he despises me; and I deserve it all. My ruin was greater than George Bailey's. Mine is life long; his was for ten years." The poor woman rocked her body to and fro, and seemed a prey to remorse and despondency.

*   *   *   *   *   *   *

Edith Wilde remembered the son of her late very dear friend, and frequently asked her father how he succeeded in business. Two or three times she had met him leaving the church, and each time she had rewarded him with a cordial smile, and once she had shaken hands with him at the church-door. Bailey felt the touch of her fingers thrill through his body for a week.

One day, about six months after the admission of Bailey to a position in the banking-house, he was surprised by an invitation from Mr. Wilde to dine with him and his daughter.

"I may as well tell you," said Mr. Wilde, "that my object is to talk business with you. The nature of this business is partly private, and therefore I prefer to discuss it at my residence." But Bailey never gave the business a thought: his mind was entirely engrossed with the banker's daughter; and to meet her in this way was a happiness that he had never dreamed of; for a thought of courting or wedding his "guardian angel," as he chose to call her in his lonely self-communings, had never once entered his mind. She was too far above him, too good, too noble, ever to be his wife. He loved her hopelessly, and felt that he could never love any one but her. Realizing his position, he had firmly resolved to keep so close a watch and ward over his looks, his words, and his acts, that neither father nor daughter could ever by any possibility suspect his feelings. In his present frame of mind Bailey felt that any revelation of his passion would be the very depth of ingratitude; and the most he ever hoped for was that when on his death-bed he might take her hand in his, and tell her how truly, how purely, and how devotedly he had loved since the first hour he saw her.

Bailey took more than usual care in dressing for the dinner at the banker's house. He had not been so particular about his linen or his necktie since the time when he went to visit Grace Van Hess. As he stood before the glass a strange, sad smile lit up his grave face; for he recognized the return of the old vanity which prompted him to appear as neat as possible in the presence of the woman whom he desired to please. As a matter of course, he had informed his friend John Grady of the invitation; and that redoubtable champion of reform and temperance, always sanguine and hopeful, augured great good fortune to Bailey, and failed not to warn him to do his utmost to win the heart of "the best woman on the face of God's earth," as he chose to designate Edith Wilde.

The dinner was a very pleasant affair. Three highly educated persons, with many tastes in common, had no difficulty in finding subject-matter for conversation. In the presence of his two friends all Bailey's reserve and reticence disappeared, and the frank, joyous spirit for which he had been formerly remarkable returned with all its powers of fascination. His knowledge, wide and thorough, his habit of deep meditation, and his extraordinary memory, cultivated, as the reader may remember, in his prison cell, imparted to Bailey's conversation a charm and a raciness which held father and daughter almost spellbound. He presented himself to them in a new light; nor had either of them the least idea that there was so much in the mind of the man whom they had hitherto seen so grave and so sad. Bailey appeared at home on all subjects: theology, law, medicine, history, and politics were handled by him with almost equal brilliancy. At one point in the conversation he trod on dangerous ground.

"I do not believe," said he, "that man by himself, man standing alone, can be a religious being. He must worship with some woman—mother, sister, wife, or friend—or not at all. That Church will prosper most which has the greatest influence over the minds of women."

"How do you account for that, Mr. Bailey?" inquired Edith.

"I do not know that I can correctly account for it," replied Bailey. "It may be that there is in the beautiful but delicate organization of woman a higher emotion — the religious emotion—almost wanting in many men; and where it exists in some men in a high degree, it will be found, on investigation, that the religious faculty has been developed by some wise woman."

8

"Your mother," said Edith, "was a wise, religious woman; and, therefore, Mr. Bailey, by your own argument, or according to your own theory, you ought to be a very religious man."

"I might have been, but for my great misfortune," said Bailey, with a sigh like a sob.

He had seen his danger; he had seen that, if pushed, he might have stated that Miss Wilde's goodness had drawn him nearer his God.

Mr. Wilde turned the conversation to business.

"Mr. Bailey," said he, "my son Walter is managing a branch house in San Francisco, and I fear the work is too much for him. His health is not good, and from the tone of his last letter (reading between the lines, as I usually do) I fear he is growing worse. It is the desire of the house to wind up our business in California; and, after due deliberation, at my suggestion we have concluded to send you out to assist Walter, nominally, but really to do the whole work. I had two reasons, Mr. Bailey—one entirely selfish, the other founded on the principle of justice —for selecting you for this responsible post. I desired to place my son Walter in the hands of an honest, sensible man; I desired also to give this man an opportunity to recover the position which he lost more than eleven years ago, partly by my evidence."

"Mr. Wilde, your kindness overpowers me; I have no words to express my gratitude for this great trust. I assure you, sir, that your complete confidence in my integrity is the greatest boon that could be conferred upon me. I do not like to make professions; but you may rest assured that if my poor life is necessary to save your son's, he and you are perfectly welcome to it."

Dinner had been finished for some time, and Edith had taken up some worsted-work to employ her nimble fingers. Over this work she was gravely scanning, with those large, wide-open, weird eyes of hers, Bailey's sad face, and, with the intuitive perception of her sex, she clearly saw that the young man meant every word he said—that his life was freely at Walter's service.

During the week before the steamer sailed for Panama, and while the preparations for the voyage were being made, Bailey spent two or three delightful evenings with Mr. Wilde and Edith. The former had directions for his son; the latter had little presents for her brother; and these furnished the opportunities for Bailey to see and converse with the woman whom he idolized. Had it not been that he was doing father and daughter a great service—at least, so they esteemed it—Bailey would have been overwhelmed with grief at the bare thought of going so far away from Edith.

The evening before the ship sailed, Bailey called for the present for Walter which Edith had just finished with her own hands. They stood for a moment under the hall lamp. "Mr. Bailey," said she, "I want you to take great care of our Walter, for I am not only his sister but his little grandmother. We had no mother; and as I was the elder, I helped him with his studies, and the love between us was something more than that of brother and sister. But I need not ask you; I know you will." At these words their eyes met point-blank, and Edith read his heart like an open book. A great joy swept through her, for she knew that she was loved as not one woman in a million is ever loved. She pressed his hand and bade him good-bye.

The next day George Bailey was sailing away toward the Southern Cross.

Chapter XIII.

"One sin doth another provoke."—Shakspeare.

Timothy Quin, "wine-merchant" and ward politician, was now a thick-set, bull-necked, red-faced man about forty years of age. He had "risen" in the world since the time when he was the humble, obsequious porter of Van Hess & Co. Ignorant, cunning, and sycophantic when it served his purpose, totally without principle, and born without a conscience, he was ever ready "to turn an honest penny."

Whether that "honest penny" came to his pocket in the form of a bribe to carry a primary election, or by selling a horse (after innumerable lies) for fifty per centum above its value, or by retailing inflammatory and poisonous compounds misnamed rum, gin, and brandy, mattered very little to him ; for the great aim of his life was to "rise" in the world; and he had sense enough to see that money was power, and covered a multitude of sins.   He had half a dozen " wine-merchant's " stores on the corners of half a dozen streets where five-story tenement-houses most abounded.   He kept his horse and light wagon, drove once a day to his different stores, then through the Park, and sometimes to the races. He was ready to bet his money on anything, from an elec-tion to a rat fight; and as he was shrewd, he always man-aged to double the "honest penny."   Timothy was no longer obliged to duck his head by grasping the forelock of his hair, as had been his habit when serving in the ca-pacity of porter.   The fact is, Quin had grown to be a great man and a power in the " party."   He now dressed in shiny black broadcloth, wore a gold watch with an immense gold chain, and adorned himself with the most gorgeous of neck-ties.   It is true, his manners were not quite as polished as his patent-leather boots, and his finger-nails were not quite as clean as his linen.   When among gentlemen—and he did sometimes see gentlemen—it was amusing to listen to his commendable attempts to speak English like an Ameri-can.   The result was a sniffle through his nose, or a sepul-chral tone drawn down from some obscure region at the base of his brain.   In his efforts to disguise his origin and his brogue, he played the mischief with vowels and handled the consonants without gloves.   Nevertheless, among his own countrymen he was a patriot, and a true son of the Emerald Isle; he was a thorough Fenian, and knew all about Robert Emmett, whose portrait hung upon the walls of his bar-rooms, and could talk treason at a safe distance, and defy the British Lion when the brute was over three thousand miles away.

Timothy Quin was a type of the class that tried to rule New York.   Vulgar, impudent, greedy, the great metropolitan city was to him and his class what Rome was to the Goths of Alaric—a place in which to secure rich spoils. To the man who in his boyhood and youth was compelled to doff his cap to every petty officer and magistrate, to be on intimate terms with an alderman, or to shake the hand of a police-justice, was an honor that, twenty years before, he had never dreamed of attaining. If his gin, rum, and brandy, so-called, made widows and orphans, what was that to him? The wail of the widow or the cry of the orphan never cost Timothy Quin a thought, or caused him to lose one hour of sweet repose. Timothy's wife was even coarser and more vulgar than himself; for she had not received, like him, the "culture" which came from association with the sporting gentlemen of the race-course and the pool-room.

Since George Bailey's return to the city Quin had pondered deeply over his former connection with Mr. Myron Finch, and had slowly made up his mind to use certain transactions, that took place more than eleven years ago, in such a way as to enable him "to turn an honest penny." True, at the time honest Timothy had received many a thousand "honest pennies" from his intimate friend Finch; but what of that? Myron Finch was reputed to be a millionnaire; he lived in princely style; he was a great merchant; he had oceans of money. Did not he, Quin, give Finch his first start in life? Was he not instrumental in aiding the poor entry-clerk to become a partner in the firm? Did he not make this clerk the son-in-law of Jacob Van Hess? What were a paltry thousand dollars compared with Finch's millions? In those days honest Tim was modest, and his aspirations had never soared above a small grocery and liquor store. But since he had grown into a "wine-merchant," and the owner of six stores, into a ward politician, with all the word implies, and into a sporting gentleman of means, he had come to the conclusion that Mr. Myron Finch had treated him very shabbily, and had not given him his proper share of the spoils. Bailey was employed in a great banking-house, and doubtless was supported by influential friends. Finch knew it, and, likely,

feared the returned convict. Timothy Quin took in the
situation at a glance, and resolved "to turn an honest
penny" by *squeezing* his friend of other days.

His mind absorbed with great thoughts of gain, Timothy
shouldered his way through the most crowded streets below
the City Hall, just as he had done through life, obsequious
to the strong, and overbearing with the weak, until he reached the counting-house of Van Hess & Finch. He nodded,
half shyly, half impudently, to his old master, winked and
smiled familiarly at some of the clerks, and grinned in a
jocular way at some of his old companions, the porters and
carmen. Tim was a born politician. With early education
and culture he would have made a capital member of a cor-
rupt Congress or a mercenary Legislature. As a lobbyist
he would have been worth his weight in gold. A rich cor-
poration, in want of a charter with which to fleece the people, would have found him the most affable and approacha-
ble of men.

As Quin approached the desk at which Finch was writing, the latter threw down his eyes and pretended not to
have seen his unwelcome visitor.

"Misther Finch, I want a wor-rd wid ye, if ye plase,"
were the words with which Quin addressed the great merchant. There was a menace in their grating tone, and
there was an undercurrent of anger in the unadulterated
brogue, which he did not care to disguise. Myron Finch
grew a shade paler, for he divined the purpose of Quin's
visit. Finch now recollected, to his dismay, that since the
day he had paid Quin the last instalment of the thousand
dollars, he had systematically failed to recognize him, when
by chance they had encountered each other in the Park or
on the race-course. Timothy had felt cut at this. You
might cheat him at cards, you might strike him in a moment of anger, and he could forgive and forget; but hurt
his vanity by treating him with contempt or indifference,
and he would resent the injury, if it took him half a life-
time to do it.

"Misther Finch, I want a wor-rd wid ye, if ye plase!"
Quin repeated, in a much louder and angrier tone of voice.

"In a minute, Timothy; I am very busy. In a minute or two I shall see you in the inner office."

"Very well, sur; I kin wait."

Timothy took a seat, crossed his legs, and commenced to spell out the words in a newspaper, for he thought it the gentlemanly sort of thing to be found reading the news from Europe and the state of the stock-market. "Very well, sur," Timothy muttered to himself; "I'll charge ye, me boy, just wan hundthred dollars for every blessed minute ye keep me waitin'. Five minutes, five hundthred; tin minutes, tin hundthred! Just take yer toime, me brave boy; this is the best pay I iver got. Fifteen minutes sence ye tould me to wait a minute, and that's fifteen hundthred dollars. A hundthred dollars a minute! I wondther if ould Asthor or ould Sthewart kin mek money as fast as this?"

While Timothy was making "honest pennies" by the hundred thousand, Finch was thinking with all his might how he would meet and manage his old confederate. He was well aware that black-mail, once commenced, never ended but with the utter ruin of the person who submitted to it. Finch was not wanting in intellectual ability nor in quickness of perception. He knew the object of Quin's visit just as well as though he had announced it on his first entrance. Indeed, since the return and employment of Bailey he had rather anticipated annoyance from the ex-porter. Finch could not handle the "wine-merchant" now as he had handled the ignorant workman of eleven years ago. "What shall I do?" he muttered. "Ah, I have it! I'll promise; I'll put him off; I'll gain time; and if the worst come to the worst, why—why—I can pay to have him disposed of. I'll have no rat like this nibbling my hands and feet by half inches!"

"Well, Misther Finch, ye've kep me waitin' fifteen minutes very much to me profit, I can assure ye. I've been sayin' me prayers, Misther Finch, and me good angels have promised me fifteen hundthred dollars—a hundthred dollars a minute—for me patience and me piety. Ha! ha! ha! —ha! ha! Misther Finch, wud ye be afther tellin' me fwhat

I'm laughin' at?" The tone and manner of this speech were indescribably insolent, and yet Finch, with imperturbable coolness, replied,

"Why, Timothy, you appear in excellent spirits to-day. What good fortune has befallen you?"

"Och, thin, Misther Finch, to be plain wid ye, I've found me fortune at last; and I mane to have it, do ye hear? I mane to have it."

Quin was working himself into a state of anger, because he really feared Finch's subtlety, which was vastly more dangerous than his own.

"I don't understand you, Quin."

"You don't, eh? You may tell that to the marines! Ye don't know that George Bailey is back in New Yar-rk, and in the employ of Warrenton, Wilde & Co.? Ye don't know that, Misther Finch?"

"Well, what of that?" replied Finch.

"Fwhat of that? Everything of *that!* See here; you med yer millions, an' I got a palthry wan thousand dollars in dhriblets. You are a rich marchint, married to a rich wife, the only daughter ov an ould man as rich as Crasus, an' you've got all this by my manes. Come, Misther Finch, we ought to have gone halves; and, be jabers, it isn't too late yit!"

"Again I repeat, I don't understand you," replied Finch, with cool gravity.

"You don't, eh?" replied Quin, with an ugly frown on his beetle brow—"you don't, eh? Thin I'll soon tache ye. You are worth your millions—"

"Nonsense, Quin! my fortune is grossly exaggerated, and my expenses are heavy; I have lived up to my income. To-day, clear of all debts, I'm worth not much over one hundred thousand dollars."

"Very good, thin," said Quin. "Though I don't believe wan wor-rd of fwhat ye say, I'll take ye at yer own valeation. Ye say ye are worth a hundthred thousand dollars, or a little over it; let us say a hundthred and tin thousand. My tarms is these: give me fifty-wan thousand five hundthred—the fifteen hundthred for keepin' me waitin'

fifteen minutes—an' the wor-rd atwane us is *mum.* Now
do ye know fwhat I mane?"

The tone, language, and bearing of Quin were coarse and
aggressive beyond all powers of description. Every look,
every gesture, every wink, and every smile was an insult;
and yet Myron Finch was able to keep his temper, and to
gain time for reflection.

"Them's my tarms, Misther Finch; do ye hear? Them's
my tarms."

"Your terms are very modest, Mr. Quin—very modest
indeed!"

"I want none o' yer chaff! Them's my tarms; and if
ye don't consint to them, I'll carry me goods to another
market—to wan George Bailey; and that manes State-prison for somebody—eh, Misther Finch, doesn't it?"

Quin, knowing that he was violating the original compact with Finch, and aware that he was doing a dishonorable thing—dishonorable even among thieves—had deliberately worked himself up into a fit of anger, in order to bully his smooth, cunning confederate of former times. Finch
gave Quin a deadly look, as he replied,

"And what does it mean for you? It seems to me that
we were both in the same boat."

"It manes nauthin' at all at all for me, me brave boy;
for I have larned a thrick or two since I was a porther.
I was sint on an errand, an' I was not supposed to know
that there was anythin' wrong. The law can't lay a finger on me, and I don't care that for it!" said Quin, vicious-
ly snapping his fingers; "but you, you can be sint to State-
prison for life! Who forged the check, eh, Misther Finch?
Who spint hours an' hours in this very office imitatin' Bailey's handwrite, and copyin' ould Van Hess's signature?
You know that the evidence of Misther Wilde and the ex-
pirts nearly saved him, for they had their doubts; and that
nauthin' convicted him but the *motive,* and the *receipt* which
you put in his coat-pocket jist in the nick o' time. Come,
Misther Finch, I've thought it all out. Down wid yer fifty-
wan thousand five hundthred dollars, or I'll go straight off
to Bailey and tell him all!"

Timothy Quin would have trembled in every joint had he been able, at this moment, to read the heart of Myron Finch. While Quin, with bad manners and worse temper, was driving the hardest sort of bargain, Finch was simply pondering and taxing his fertile brain for some plan whereby he might destroy this enemy who had suddenly arisen to torment him. Finch thought: "Could he kill him in that office and bury his body in the cellar? or cut it up, put it in a barrel, and consign it to Galveston? Could he poison him? Could he hire some one to slay him at midnight? Whatever he intended to do must be done quickly: no living soul knew the crime committed against Bailey but themselves. If he poisoned Quin, or stabbed him to the heart, or put a bullet through his brain, suspicion would never fall on him, Finch; for what *motive* could he have had for murdering an Irish rum-seller? But he must have time to think; he must not act hastily. One thing he was certainly resolved never to do—he would never give Quin a single dollar." Finch was a man of clear and accurate perceptions, with plenty of brains, but without heart or conscience. Cowardly, cruel, ungrateful, and supremely selfish, he was nevertheless a man of no ordinary intellectual ability. He was resolved to poison Quin, or pay for his assassination, rather than give one dollar in the way of hush-money or black-mail. These fearful thoughts were taking shape in the mind of Finch, while that paragon of a "wine-merchant" was trying "to turn an honest penny" by acting the part of an insolent, angry bully. To maintain appearances and to lull suspicion, Finch commenced to haggle about the price.

"Your terms are very high," said Finch, in a low, quiet tone. "Could you not take a less sum than half my fortune? Consider your way of life and mine. Twenty thousand dollars would be as much to you as eighty thousand to me. Suppose I should offer you twenty thousand, would you give me a paper in your own handwriting confessing that you were equally guilty with me, and that on the trial of George Bailey you perjured yourself? In that case each would be in the other's power."

"No, no; I'll be —— if I do! Give you a paper? Why, wid that paper you'd sind me to jail or hang me in less than no time. Misther Finch, I know ye too well for that!"

"I shall give you a paper in my handwriting similar to the one that you will give me. We shall then mutually checkmate each other. What do you say to this?"

"I'll give no paper, I'll write no writin'," replied Quin, who was more afraid of a piece of writing than he was of a pistol at fifteen paces' distance. He had just learned enough in his business, in politics, and in betting, to beware of signing his name to a piece of paper.

"Well, I see we cannot agree," said Finch, "and my being here so long with you alone will be noticed. Can you not meet me at some hotel, where we can talk this matter over more at our leisure? Besides, I must see about raising a large sum of money, and it takes a little time to do it."

"See here, Misther Finch; I don't want to be hard on ye: say thirty thousand, an' it's a bargain."

"No; I cannot possibly part with more than twenty thousand."

"Split the difference," said Quin; "make it twenty-five, and we'll be the best of frinds."

"I cannot go one dollar higher," said Finch, disguising his hatred and disgust as best he could. "Are you willing to take this, and then swear, in the presence of two witnesses, that that amount is in full for all demands?"

Satisfied that this sum was four times as much as he expected, Quin gave his assent, and promised to meet Mr. Finch at the A—— House on the evening of the third day from the present. As Timothy Quin retired from the counting-house he chuckled at his success; and Myron Finch strode up and down that inner office for half an hour, thinking with all his might how he could get rid of Timothy Quin. Ah, Timothy! if a little bird of the air could carry you the thoughts of Mr. Finch, instead of chuckling you would hurry home, bar your doors, kneel down and say your prayers—those prayers which you have never uttered since you were a little boy at your mother's knee!

CHAPTER XIV.

"The bread of deceit is sweet, but it afterwards turneth to gravel in the mouth."—PROVERBS.

On the day appointed for the meeting with Quin at the hotel agreed upon, Myron Finch, the wealthy and well-dressed merchant, might have been seen slowly wending his way through Broad and Wall Streets to Broadway. He was thinking so profoundly that he failed to notice several of his acquaintances until accosted; and, as soon as the ordinary salutations were exchanged, he resumed the same attitude of deep meditation. We are at liberty to state his reflections. "This coarse, vulgar fellow would suck me like an orange," thought Finch, "until nothing is left but the rind. The cancelled check was secured and destroyed. There was no witness but Quin. Why not deny the whole thing, and defy this leech? Had Quin any other testimony? He must have, or he never would have been so impudent and arrogant in his demands. What could that testimony be? Had he, the cunning rascal, an accomplice?"

Finch was a man who slowly and carefully concocted his plots. No military engineer ever built a fort more skilfully to withstand the assaults of the enemy than he his schemes to prevent detection; but, as in the best armor there are joints, and as in the strongest fortification there are weak points, so in the plans of Myron Finch there were acts of oversight which even his caution did not guard against. He had staked all to make a fortune which he keenly relished; and now to have it torn from him piece-meal by this ignorant fellow, Quin, was worse than death. His crimes against Scroggs, the pastor's niece, and against Bailey, were not committed through any hatred or malice, but simply to advance his selfish interests. He respected his school-master, whom he had injured; he loved, after his cold fashion, the girl whom he had ruined; and he admired

Bailey, whom he had destroyed! But the destruction of each was necessary to his happiness, and so he destroyed them without scruple or remorse. Had his own mother been an impediment, he would have removed her too, and his conscience would never have given him an instant's pain. He never hated or bore malice until after he had wrought evil on his victims. His feeling against Quin was a combination of fear, hatred, and disgust. "It is strange," he thought, "if I cannot manage this ignoramus. To-day I shall play with him, watch him, pump him, and see what he knows; and if he has nothing against me but his single word, I shall have him arrested as a black-mailer." These reflections brought Finch to the steps of the hotel, where Quin was waiting to see him.

"We shall meet in a private room," said Finch, in a cold, distant tone.

"Very well, sur; I'm your 'umble sarvint to command," replied Quin, in a tone of mock humility which was very galling to Finch.

We shall leave these two worthies in their private room to discuss their monetary affairs, while we turn to another and better character of our story—honest and kind-hearted John Grady. It so happened that Grady had that morning been commissioned by his wife to carry an invitation to her niece, Miss Jenny Edwards, the head-stewardess of the hotel, to make them a visit next Sunday, and to remain with them all night, as her own room, recently occupied by George Bailey, had been vacated. John Grady had no difficulty in finding his niece-in-law, for he was well known in the hotel on account of his visits once or twice a month to see her. As the uncle entered Miss Edwards's room he greeted her most cordially, seized both her hands, and kissed her most affectionately on the forehead.

"And how's my little niece to-day, and how is every bone in her body?" said Grady, holding her small, delicate hand in his great strong grasp. "Your aunt requested me to call and ask you to come over on Sunday, and stay all night. Bailey sailed for San Francisco last Saturday, to be gone about three or four months."

"Your little niece is all right, Uncle John. But hush! There's *somebody* in the private room at the end of the hall."

"What difference does it make who is in the private room?" replied Grady. "There are fifty private rooms in this house, and there may be fifty private parties in them; but what do we care about them?"

"Hush, uncle! *He* is in there (pointing to the room) with a coarse, rough-looking Irishman—I beg pardon—in one of the small private dining-rooms. As you came, I was considering whether my sense of honor would permit me to discover what they are doing."

"*He?* Do you mean that precious rascal, Finch?"

"Yes; I mean Myron Finch."

"Is it a sense of honor you are talking about with such a villain as he?" And honest John stretched out his "carnal weapon," as he was pleased to term his right arm, as if longing to try its weight on the villain aforesaid.

"I saw him pass, but he did not see me. Indeed, I am so much changed that I doubt if he would recognize me if he met me face to face." This was uttered by the young woman in a tone of deep sadness.

"Jenny, my dear, is there any way in which we could overhear what he is talking about? for I have good and sufficient reasons for desiring to know."

"Yes: there is a door connecting the room in which they now are with a smaller room. If the door is unlocked, as it usually is, we can open it about an inch without being observed, and overhear every word that is said."

"Jenny, you are a jewel! Just bring me to that room, and I'll pray for you all the rest of my life!"

Jenny Edwards was a young woman of about thirty years of age, pale, thin, and angular, with a strong jaw and firm lips. Her eye was quick and her movements prompt; but over her whole face there were indelible marks of much suffering. There was, too, the confident air of one who, through anguish of spirit, had acquired a self-poise and a self-reliance that nothing could shake. But for these signs of past tribulation, which had left a certain hardness on her countenance, she would have been a handsome woman. In her younger day she must have been very beautiful.

"Beautiful, my dear!" continued Grady. "We can see them and hear every word the precious pair of rascals may utter."

"It is growing dark, and the room is not well lighted," said Jenny; "so there is little chance of our being discovered."

John Grady and Jenny Edwards stood at the door connecting the two rooms, his head above and hers below, with eye and ear at the little opening about an inch wide, and overheard as follows:

Finch. "Suppose I deny the forgery, what proof have you? The check I destroyed long ago."

Quin. "Go an, Misther Finch: jist show me yer whole hand of car-rds at wanst." (It may be remarked that Quin's figures were of the gambling and betting order.)

Finch. "Suppose now—only suppose, remember—that I were to deny everything, and have you arrested as a blackmailer; wouldn't that be a nice turning of the tables? I only, mind you, use this for argument's sake. But which would be accepted in a court of justice, your unsupported word or mine?"

Quin. "Go an, Misther Finch. Play yer hand out. I'll play mine by-and-by."

Finch. "Come, Quin, you must be reasonable; you must lower your demand: if you don't, I shall leave you this instant and denounce you as a black-mailer. Come, what is the lowest figure that you will accept?"

John Grady could see the two men from his place of observation. It was cold, clear, heartless intellect against cunning brute force. Quin was evidently afraid of Finch, and eyed him as though he were a rattlesnake.

Quin. "Not a cint less than the tarms I've already mintioned."

Finch. "Then—I—shall not—give you—one—cent. So, do your worst!"

Quin. "Eh, Misther Finch, that's your game, is it? You have played yer last car-r-d. It's my turn now." So saying, he put his hand in his pocket and pulled out a large greasy memorandum-book. Shaking the book in Finch's face, and then opening it with a rapid, impulsive movement, he exhibited several curious pieces of red blotting-paper, with ordinary writing-paper, which had been torn and crumpled, pasted over it, and so matched that the writing was quite legible.

Quin. "See here, Misther Finch; do you know that? an' that? an' that?" showing piece after piece, and each piece containing the words, "William Wilde," "fifteen hundred dollars," "November 20th, 18—" and "Jacob Van Hess & Co.," written and rewritten. One of the papers contained a fac-simile of the check, complete in all its parts, which had been the means of sending George Bailey to State-prison. The body of the check was an excellent imitation of Bailey's handwriting; the signature was an equally exact imitation of that of Jacob Van Hess. Quin produced over a dozen of these papers, which were simply the attempts of Finch, many times repeated, to imitate the writing of Jacob Van Hess and George Bailey. "What do ye think of these, Misther Myron Finch? Whin ye came down to the office afther dark to practise, and whin ye wor thinkin' an' schamin', I was watchin' ye. I knowed there wor siven divils in yer heart, an' I kep' me oye on ye. Bright as ye are, ye wor foolish enough to tear up yer practisin' papers an' throw the pieces into the waste-basket. Afther ye left, Misther Myron Finch, I picked these pieces out, an' sorted them, an' fitted them together, an' pasted them on the red blottin'-paper, an' here they are. How do ye like them? That's my hand ov car-r-ds, an' it bates yours all hollow, Misther Finch. I howld the five-fingers, an' the ace, ay, an' the *knave* too, Misther Finch. Maybe ye niver played 'forty-foives,' Misther Finch; but if ye knew that ilegant game, ye would know that I howld the winnin' car-r-ds, an,' be ——, I'll play them! So ye won't give me a cint?—an' so ye'll hand me over to the police as a black-mailer, Misther Myron Finch, marchint-prince—will ye, eh?"

The vulgar insolence of this vulgar brute would have driven a weaker or a better man than Myron Finch to desperation. The reiteration of "Misther Finch," with the low, vicious malice of a wretch whose instincts were cruel and savage, was in itself an insult of the grossest kind, and sufficient to arouse the wrath of a man of the most saintly disposition. But Myron Finch was no ordinary character. An exhibition of anger, or a blow struck in vindication of his manhood, even had he possessed the physical courage to strike it, would have been utter ruin. He realized his danger, and paid little attention to the abuse. While Quin was pouring out vials of spite, Finch was making up his mind to murder him. In pursuance of his plan, he let his head fall on his breast with an air of extreme despondency, as if he had given up the fight and confessed himself vanquished. "Ruined, ruined, ruined!" Finch exclaimed, in a low, broken tone. "Lost, lost, lost! The game has been played" (using Quin's favorite figure) "and I am thoroughly beaten. I am lost—ruined!"

Quin eyed him suspiciously, but the acting of Finch was so perfect that he was completely deceived and thrown off his guard.

Finch. "Make your own terms, Quin; you can take every cent I have in the world. I confess myself in your power."

Quin. "Now see here, Misther Finch; ye med me angry wid yer talk about black-mail an' all that sort o' thing. But if ye'll only be rasonable, I won't be hard on ye. The day that you give me the twinty-five thousand dollars, I'll burn these papers, every wan of them."

Finch. "I give up the fight! I'll do anything to escape State-prison. Oh, I'm burning with thirst—I feel sick—I am upset! This, this has driven me nearly crazy! Come to the store to-morrow, and I shall give you a certified check for twenty-five thousand dollars; and—and you will surely burn all the papers—those you have at home as well as those you hold in your hand?"

Quin. "I have them all here, every wan of them. I swear to you, Misther Finch, that they are all here," tapping the pocket-book as he replaced it in his pocket.

Finch. "Let us have a drink. This unpleasant interview

9

has parched my throat, and I am horribly thirsty." Finch rung the bell, and ordered a bottle of the best brandy and some cigars.

Quin was elated with his success; he rubbed his large red hands with glee; his eyes fairly danced at the certainty of receiving on the morrow the large sum of twenty-five thousand dollars; and physically and mentally he was in a fit condition to imbibe good brandy at another's expense. Finch, on the contrary, appeared despondent and half crazy, anxious for strong drink to drown his misery.

Quin. "Cheer up, Misther Finch! What is twenty-five thousand dollars to you? The papers will be desthroyed, an' you'll still be a very rich man. Let us dhrink to our future frindship."

Timothy, in his present state of exhilaration, drank glass after glass of strong brandy, while Finch took little more than a spoonful. The latter held his glass, after he had taken a sip or two, below the table, and quietly spilled the liquor on the floor—a proceeding which the former could not by any possibility have suspected. The idea of wasting first-rate imported hotel brandy in this way appeared to honest Tim simply preposterous. Myron Finch pretended to be half drunk. His spirits rose. He shook hands with Quin across the table, laughed and joked, and sung snatches of songs. He called for a bottle of old Burgundy, the most treacherous of wines, which on top of brandy was intoxication of the most stupid kind. He poured out the red wine, and as Quin drank he smacked his coarse lips, and pronounced it "foine!" Finch sent the waiter for some coffee and the bill; and pulling out the money with which to pay the reckoning, purposely allowed several gold pieces to roll on the floor. But Quin, now almost stupidly drunk, essaying to stoop to pick up the money, fell from his chair and rolled to the floor; and before he had time to recover himself, Finch poured the contents of a small vial, already uncorked, into his wine. As soon as Timothy had regained his seat, Finch said, "Come, Quin, one more glass before the coffee arrives." Both villains staggered to their feet, the one pretending to

be and the other really drunk, clinked glasses, and swallowed the wine. The waiter handed in the coffee, was paid the
reckoning, and received a large fee, with which he disappeared. For a minute or two Finch and Quin sipped their
coffee and smoked their cigars in silence. Finally Finch
closed his eyes, threw his head back on the chair, and remarked that he was dreadfully sleepy. Quin began to
nod. Every minute or so his companion would open his
eyes, rub them, and then cast a rapid glance at the drunken
sot before him. At last Quin fell into a deep sleep; for,
what with the brandy and cigars, and what with the forty
drops of laudanum which Finch had slyly dropped into the
liquor, a cannon fired at his ear would scarcely have aroused
Quin from the drunken stupor that now oppressed him.
He breathed stertorously, like one in a fit of apoplexy;
and, owing to the position of his head, the usual red of his
face had changed to a purple, and his heavy snoring could
be distinctly heard by the keen and deeply interested lis-
teners in the next room. But, singular to relate, the more
soundly Quin slept the more wakeful Finch became; he
became not only wakeful but alert and cautious. He rose
from his seat, looked at the door by which the waiter had
retired, nay, examined the very hall outside, but never once
thought of looking at the door leading into the small bedroom, taking it for granted that that door was securely
locked; and then on tiptoe, with the sly and stealthy step
of a cat, he softly approached Quin, paused for a moment,
and, observing no change in the position or breathing of
the insensible sot, deliberately put his hand in the breast-
pocket of Quin's coat and abstracted therefrom the memorandum-book containing the fatal "practice" papers—the
imitations of George Bailey's handwriting. "Ha! Timothy, you beast, snore away!" he whispered; "these proofs
will be destroyed before I sleep to-night." He restored
the memorandum-book to Quin's pocket, and, taking out
his own pocket-book in which to put them, paused for a
moment, and said to himself, "I had better burn them.
Dead men and burnt papers tell no tales!" He arose to
walk over to the fire to execute his purpose, and had ac-

complished about two-thirds of the distance, when he found
the wrist of his right hand, which held the fatal papers,
grasped with a grip of iron, and heard the words hissed
into his ear in a low, terrible whisper,

"Utter one syllable, and I hand you over to the police!"

Before Finch could recover from the shock of amazement and fright caused by the suddenness of the assault,
John Grady had snatched the papers out of Finch's hand
and quietly crammed them into his own trousers' pocket.

"Speak one word and you are lost! I have a witness
here whom you have good reason to know. Come here,
Jenny; take a look at the cowardly scoundrel, forger, and
robber, whom you once thought an angel of light and
power."

The entrance of this woman almost paralyzed Finch.
Had her ghost arisen from the grave he could not have
been more astounded. He stared at her with wide-open
eyes, and seemed, in the daze caused by her presence, to
have forgotten his danger, and the object for which he had
committed robbery from the person of Quin. Finch staggered to a chair, and murmured, "Jenny Edwards! Jenny
Edwards! Jenny Edwards!"

"Yes," she replied, "Jenny Edwards, whose happiness
you ruthlessly destroyed—whom you first betrayed and then
abandoned. You supposed I had sunk from one slum to
another, until finally I had found a nameless grave in Pot-
ter's Field. But no, Myron Finch! I might be deceived by
a great love, but never by a baser passion. I arose out of
my misery, asked my God to forgive me, and here I am,
with the power to punish you; and revenge is sweet! Oh,
what a base villain you are! With a fair exterior and good
powers of mind, you used your talents to ruin all who approached you. You drove the poor school-master, Scroggs,
from his position; you killed my good uncle in Vermont,
who had been a father to you; you ruined and cruelly sent
to State-prison George Bailey, who had been your benefactor; and me you heartlessly cast off in a great city to rot
and die! Money has been the god of your idolatry—money
for your own sensual gratification. For this you flung me

aside and married a poor weak creature, whom you never even respected—a weak creature who had not the strength or the courage to save her noble lover, as she might have done by showing her idiot of a father that George Bailey could no more commit a crime than you could perform an act of virtue. And so you grew rich and prosperous, Myron Finch—lived in a grand house and drove your carriage; you kept your steam-yacht and your fast horses; and, beast that you are, you were false to the wife who brought you fortune and position. Oh, I have watched you! oh, I know you! Often and often, Myron Finch, when I was struggling out of my misery; when I feared that remorse and despair would drive me insane; when I was starving with hunger, and shivering with cold, and fighting down temptation—for I was young, and considered beautiful in those days—and saw you, with all your crimes, rich and prosperous, I was tempted to doubt the justice of God, and in despair to commit suicide. I had one satisfaction, Myron Finch—your rich wife brought you neither comfort nor happiness. Oh, I watched you, and was delighted to find that you mutually hated each other!"

John Grady listened to this outpouring of wrath and indignation in silence; Finch, in abject fear and trembling. If the truth must be told, Jenny's passion for this wicked man was not wholly dead. At times she would have killed him with her own hands, and again the memory of her year of happiness in her New England home with her young and handsome lover would come back like the memory of a sweet dream, but a sweet dream obscured by heavy black clouds. In her lonely musings she had built castles in the air, and in one of these airy, unsubstantial edifices she had placed Myron Finch, reformed by her means. Had Myron Finch been free from his present wife, and possessed of all the wealth of the world, Jenny Edwards would not have married him, to be taken by her and treated as a husband. She would have had the ceremony performed, and would have left him the next minute. This was her feeling when her practical mind reflected by daylight; her midnight musings and fancies were only vagaries of the imagination,

which could never be vitalized by action. It was not her
intention now to send him to State-prison for life. There
could be no reform there: and it must be confessed that
Jenny Edwards's great aim in life was to reform Myron
Finch, and make him right the wrong he had done her.
How she was to accomplish this aim she did not know, but
she had a vague idea that God would interpose to show her
the way; for Jenny had a pure, simple faith in the religious
teachings of her early youth. When she had finished her
"lecture" to Finch, and almost exhausted herself by the
force and vehemence of her language, she turned quietly to
her uncle, and said,

"Wake that man, if you can; the drug may kill him,
and then we shall have a case of murder on our hands.
We ought to let the carrion rot, and his partner swing for
it; but, after all, he is one of God's creatures, with an immortal soul, I suppose—if such as he and Finch have souls
—to be saved. Ring for a waiter, and ask him to bring
you some strong coffee, which is the best antidote for poi-
soning by laudanum. Rub him, shake him, and pour the
coffee down his throat." Then turning to Finch, who, in
a kind of stupor, was watching the efforts of Grady to restore Quin to consciousness, Jenny pointed imperiously to
the door, and said, "Go! Begone! The very sight of you
sickens my soul!"

Finch went out as he was ordered, muttering, almost unconsciously, "Jenny Edwards! Jenny Edwards come back
to torture me!"

The vigorous efforts of Grady soon roused Quin to a
partial state of wakefulness and sobriety; and having ascertained the number of one of his many stores, the worthy
"wine-merchant" was hustled into a cab and sent to his
home.—John Grady carried the good news to his wife.

CHAPTER XV.

"Look here upon this picture, and on this."—SHAKSPEARE.
"We can easily learn to be vicious without a master."—SENECA.
"A good man and an angel! these between,
How thin the barrier!"—YOUNG.

FINCH walked up Broadway toward his home—if home it might be called, from which his wife had fled with her three children—like a man in a dream, trying to recall all the incidents of the evening. The cool air and the prevailing quiet refreshed his mind and body, and very soon his clear intellect grasped the catastrophe in its true light. Had there been but one witness, he would have brazened it out and denied everything. But, in addition to Grady, whom he remembered as an old enemy after Bailey's conviction, here was this woman, who had such good cause to hate him, suddenly arisen, as it were, from the dead to strike the fatal blow. He perceived that all his money could not save him from conviction, nor buy up either of these two formidable enemies. Before he reached Union Square he had arrived at the conclusion that the city of New York was no longer a safe place of residence for him. He must abscond; he must fly to some country with which the United States had no extradition treaty; but he must not fly a poor man. He had committed too many dangerous crimes to obtain wealth, and a portion of this wealth he must carry into some foreign land. To wander about again seeking employment, to endure the rebuffs of merchants, such as he himself had administered to his own clerks, and to feel the stings of poverty as he had felt them eleven or twelve years ago, were simply intolerable—he might as well go to State-prison at once. It was evident that Jenny Edwards, for some reason which he could not comprehend, did not desire his immediate arrest, and that

John Grady was controlled by her wishes. But how long would this state of feeling last? They might have him arrested at any moment. As he pondered these matters, he came to the conclusion that Grady, having obtained possession of the proofs of his forgery, and having seen the act of robbery, would use his power over him to extort money. He saw, too, that Grady was a totally different order of man from Quin. Before he reached his house, his mind was made up to convert all his stocks and bonds into ready money, and, with about one hundred thousand dollars, retire to South America, and live like a gentleman on the interest. His real estate and business he would sacrifice, as a matter of necessity.

He opened a safe in his bedroom, and took out all his papers. With lead-pencil he carefully computed the value of his railroad bonds and stocks, and his coal and mining stocks. He took out all his jewellery. He went to the front-room in the second story, and with a skeleton-key opened his wife's private boxes and drawers and ransacked them all. Mrs. Finch, having fled the house in a hurry, had not yet called for her private property, and, unfortunately for her, her valuable jewellery, worth many thousands of dollars, was left behind. This her husband seized, and wrenched the precious stones out of their settings. The diamonds, the rubies, the emeralds, he placed in a little casket, and the gold he cast into the sink in the bath-room. "This," he said, grimly, "will pay me to some extent for the houses and lands, which are not portable property."

After securing his property, he stole quietly out of the house, entered an omnibus, and took a room in a second-class hotel. He feared to remain in his own house, and he did not intend to enter again his own office. He left his three children behind him without one pang of remorse, or the slightest feeling of regret. He slept soundly that night, because he was convinced of his security, and had no doubts of his escape. Finch was the personification of selfishness. It is doubtful if he ever realized his sins against his own soul, or his crimes against his fellow-men. Such men as he may feel, and in fact do feel, acute fear, but remorse and repentance are to them unknown emotions. Cold-blooded as fishes, they seem as devoid of affection as of moral emotion.

The next morning Finch disposed of all his bonds and stocks, and converted them into cash. This, with the precious stones stolen from his wife, and his own jewellery, made him worth about one hundred and twenty thousand dollars. Before twelve o'clock Myron Finch was quietly waiting at the depot in Jersey City for the one o'clock train to Philadelphia. At four o'clock he was lost, in an obscure lodging near the shipping, in a large city. Toward evening he went out and bought two common trunks, such as sailors take on long voyages, and two or three suits of plain, unfashionable clothing : he went to a barber, and had his hair cropped short and his face clean shaven : he went to a drug store and purchased some black hair-dye; and to a cigar store and purchased some tobacco. He re-entered his room, colored his face with tobacco-water, and dyed his hair, his eyebrows, and his eyelashes. His disguise was now so thorough that it is more than probable that even Jenny Edwards would have failed to recognize him.

One thing was very remarkable about this man Finch— he rarely smiled, and he was never known to laugh. Even in his sensual pleasures he was grave and sedate, and he always bore the exterior of a decorous gentleman. As he finished the work of disguising himself, and saw, as he critically scanned himself in the glass, how complete it was, not even the shadow of a smile passed over his face. He simply said, " I think this will do." A villain with more heart and a little sense of humor would have uttered at least a low laugh of satisfaction at the perfection of the change. Finch did not even hate anything except he first feared it ; and when the fear was gone so was his hatred. Yesterday he feared Quin; to-day he never once thought of him. This morning, while disposing of his property for cash, he feared and hated Grady ; to-night, all danger being past, he had no ill-feeling toward him. The only time he had ever hated Bailey was when he returned from State-prison, and there was danger that he might wreak vengeance for the wrong that had been inflicted upon him. All Finch's plans

were for the future.   His money would enable him to gratify
all his gross appetites ; and, provided he could do so, it mattered little to him whether he lived in Vermont, New York,
Europe, or South America—at least so he fancied.   "Gold,"
he repeated to himself, "is ease, pleasure, self-indulgence in
every land and clime, from Labrador to Japan."

Thoroughly disguised, and dressed in the garb of a commercial agent, Finch found a brig bound for Valparaiso, in
which he took a small state-room as cabin passenger, under
the name of Alexander Brown.   He would have preferred
a larger and more commodious vessel than the *William
Penn* (for that was the name of the brig), but feared to remain any longer so near the scene of his crimes.

While Myron Finch is on his way toward Cape Horn, we
shall follow the fortunes of the hero of our story.

When George Bailey had reached San Francisco, he found
Walter Wilde's health much worse than he had expected
from the tone of the letters which the young man had sent
to his father and sister.   About one year ago he had graduated head of his class in Columbia College—a feat which
almost cost him his life.   His frame, never very strong at
the best, had been worn down by excess of study ; and
though his father had sent him to California more for the
purpose of improving his health by a sea-voyage and change
of climate than for the sake of the business—for any one of
his clerks could have attended to that—it was really a great
mistake to send him so far away from friends and kindred.
Besides, the winding up of the financial affairs of the branch
bank required skill, patience, and experience — qualities in
which the young student was very deficient.   Walter Wilde
was worried and lonely ; and when Bailey came to take his
place he found him homesick, and suffering from a cough
of long standing.   Walter was exceedingly relieved when
Bailey assumed the charge of closing up the business.   Every day, after a hard day's work, Bailey had a carriage at
the door, and almost compelled the youth, who was very
fond of reading, to lay aside his books and come out for a
long drive outside the city limits.   At first young Walter,
with the indolence of ill-health and much reading, almost

resented the importunity of his friend; but in a short time these rides, by the force of habit, and on account of the exhilaration of spirits which the bracing air of the country aroused, became exceedingly pleasant. Bailey sought the advice of the ablest physician in San Francisco, and had Wilde carefully and minutely examined. The medical diagnosis was favorable: "No organic disease; delicacy of constitution, and irritation of the bronchial tubes; nourishing diet, plenty of sleep, fresh air and moderate exercise, and a tonic of quinine and iron." Walter Wilde laughed at the examination, half in fun and half in anger. He had a sort of respectful dread of his grave, earnest nurse and man of business; but having the fine blood of the Wildes in his veins, and all their generous impulses, and seeing Bailey day after day drive him out, or, if the day was unfit for a drive, read aloud for his amusement, or talk to him by the hour, he soon came to entertain not only a profound respect but a deep affection for his untiring friend. Bailey would remind him of his meals and his medicine, and would be inexorable until the orders of the physician were conformed to.

One unpleasant afternoon the two young men were sitting in their own parlor of the hotel; and Bailey was reading aloud, in a deep, sonorous tone, "The Prisoner of Chillon" with a tremulous pathos in his voice more pitiful than tears; and his friend was watching the lights and shadows flit over the reader's face with a peculiar look, as if trying to read his character. At the close of a stanza Bailey raised his eyes and encountered the inquiring gaze of Wilde.

"George, old boy, you're the best fellow alive! Where on earth did you learn to be so gentle and so patient? I was looking at you and wondering as you read."

"Nonsense, Walter! I am neither gentle nor patient; but, on the contrary, I am hot-tempered and impulsive."

"Then why have you been so patient and gentle with such an ill-conditioned fellow as I? Why, when you first came here I almost disliked you as a prig, and scarcely treated you with decent respect."

"I have done nothing," replied Bailey, "but my duty. Your father sent me to take the trouble of business off your

shoulders, and to help restore you to health; and—and—
your sister requested me to—to be a brother to you, or
something of the sort."

"Say, Bailey, do you know my sister?"

The young man asked this question after a long pause,
and it caused Bailey to blush a dark red.

"Ye-e-s; I had the honor of seeing her a few times.
The first time was when I went to her to thank her for her
great goodness to my poor mother, and when she begged
your father, for that mother's sake, to give me employment.
During the week before the steamer sailed I saw her almost
every day."

"Got you employment, did she? Oh, I remember, now:
your mother was the old lady, the doctor's widow, for
whom Edith procured a situation, and in whom she took
such great interest. Oh, I remember it all very well. So
you are the son of that old lady, Edith's friend? And
where the deuce were you all this time?—sowing your
wild-oats, or off on a whaling voyage?"

"I was neither sowing wild-oats nor sailing on the sea;
I was doing the State some service," replied Bailey, with
grim irony. "Some day I shall tell you the honorable employment that the State assigned me."

"But Edith," pursued the young man, meditatively, "does
not usually take to strangers; in fact she is rather shy and
reticent, except with those whom she likes. So she made
the governor give you a place in the bank? Bravo! that's
like her: once she takes a good thing into her wise little
head, she never ceases until it is accomplished."

"My mother died in her arms: she was my mother's
dearest and best friend. Can you wonder that she took an
interest in the son?"

Bailey jerked out these sentences, partly by way of apology for Edith's interest in him, a stranger.

"I do not wonder in the least. Why, George, that girl
had a whole regiment of old men and women whom she took
care of. Don't be offended. I do not mean to class your
mother among them. I simply wish to show you that she is
the kindest, the bravest, the purest, the best little woman on

the face of the earth! Ah, if you only knew her as I do,
you would worship her! What a wise little creature she
has always been! She is two years older than I. From
the time that my mother died she has been a mother, a
more than mother, to me; always helping me in my studies, always providing for me, always taking care of me.
She was so little, and so wise, I nicknamed her 'grandma.'
She seemed, too, to know everything. She used to help me
with my Latin and my mathematics; and—would you believe it?—after I became a 'soph,' she took private lessons
from an old Scotch professor on the sly, so that she might
have the pleasure of assisting me, her stupid grandson. I
don't believe that I could have graduated at all, much less
with honor, had it not been for Edith. Now, old fellow,
don't be offended at what I said a moment ago; for I
am sure your mother must have been a lady—I mean,
a real born and bred lady, not one of your *parvenu* vulgar ladies—or my sister never would have made her a
friend."

George, instead of being offended, could have listened all
night to Edith's *brother* (though scarcely to any other man,
except her father) pronouncing eulogies on the woman
whom he has idolized from the first moment that they
met. Bailey continued to speak of his mother, but for the
purpose of hiding his confusion when Edith Wilde's name
was mentioned.

"Yes, Walter, my mother was, as you say, a real lady in
every sense of the word—polished, refined, good, and charitable—and she suffered unmerited punishment. Oh! oh!
had she only lived to see me this day in my present position, and to know who put me in the way of well-doing!
But perhaps her good spirit watches over me and knows
all. I trust it is so."

"But what most astonishes me," said Walter, "is your
gentleness and patience with a cross-grained, irritable fellow
like me. I noticed your anger the other day when, crossing the bridge on foot, the hackman almost ran over me;
and I observed the way in which you caught the horse's
head, and hurled horse, man, and hack from the arch of the

bridge back to the street. Whew! what a giant's strength! What wouldn't I give to have your muscle!"

"For ten years that muscle was admirably developed by hard work on a wholesome but spare diet," Bailey replied, in a tone of dry irony.

"So long? What the deuce put such a severe course of training into your head? Were you practising as a professional gymnast?"

"No, not a gymnast, but a—a— Did you know a merchant in New York named Myron Finch? He was the man who put me in the service of the State."

"I knew him but slightly. If I remember correctly, he was a light-colored man, with light eyes, light hair, and light all over—almost like an Albino."

"Yes," continued Bailey, "that is the man; light without, but black within; and particularly black about the heart and white about the liver. That man put me on my course of physical and mental training."

At the thought of Finch, Bailey's eye and brow became dark and fierce. His constant struggle against the desire for vengeance was difficult and trying; and nothing prevented his seeking out the villain and punishing him with his own hands but his absorbing love of Edith Wilde. In spite of all his good resolutions, the old, deadly, vindictive feeling would arise in his heart and shake his whole frame with its intensity.

Walter Wilde, unconscious of the storm he had raised in the heart of his friend, rattled away without reserve concerning Edith, his father, and himself. For Bailey he now entertained feelings of esteem and affection; for the young man was not slow to perceive the solid intellect and sound sense, as well as the Titanic strength, which had aroused his admiration; and Bailey loved Edith's brother. He would have loved Edith's cat, or dog, or bird, or glove—anything, in fact, that belonged to Edith.

Finally, the business was wound up, and the two friends took their passage in the good ship *Sebastian Cabot*, bound for New York. Bailey had informed Warrenton, Wilde & Co. of the success of his financial operations, and Walter had written to his sister a long fraternal letter, eulogizing his friend, and speaking in the most glowing terms of the pleasures of a long sea-voyage around the Horn.

Chapter XVI.

"Yet is there one more cursèd than they all,
— That canker-worm, that monster, Jealousie."

SPENSER.

MORE than five months have rolled away since the clipper ship *Sebastian Cabot* passed through the Golden Gate and sailed toward the Southern Cross, and not a word has been heard of her. It has been generally supposed that she foundered in one of those terrific gales which frequently occur south of Cape Horn. As day after day and month after month passed without tidings of the ship, long overdue, Mr. William Wilde and his daughter became extremely uneasy, and this uneasiness gradually grew into a chilling fear. Every afternoon, as her father came home, Edith mutely searched his eyes for news; but the only reply of Mr. Wilde was a sad-shake of the head, more eloquent than any language that he could have employed. Sometimes they sat down to their cheerless dinner without exchanging a single word; and at other times Edith would simply say, "No tidings yet, father?" and he would reply, in a dreary monotone, "None, my child, none!"

Once Edith asked him if the insurance companies had given up the ship as lost, and he was obliged to say that they had. Mr. Wilde disliked to talk on the subject; and when forced to reply to the questions asked him, did so in monosyllables, and then relapsed into a brooding silence. As an experienced merchant and banker, he well knew that ships traversed beaten tracks on the ocean almost as travellers do between great cities on the land. Were she still afloat, some ship in passing would have seen and spoken her. Mr. Wilde, therefore, had less reason to hope than Edith; he believed in his heart that the *Sebastian Cabot*

had foundered, and that all hands were lost. To him this
was a bitter blow; for he had fondly hoped that his own
name, through Walter, would be preserved in the great
banking-house of which he was the principal manager.
Nor was this ambition inconsistent with his parental love,
which was deep and strong; indeed, the one feeling seemed to intensify the other. He had toiled all his life for
money; not for its own sake, but for the pleasure and excitement he found in making it; and when once made, no
man could be more willing to expend it, or more liberal in
his charities. What he valued most, next to his own and
his children's honor, was the good name of the house of
Warrenton, Wilde & Co. Had his only son lived to take
his place, had he seen him an able merchant and banker, he
would have been pleased to say to his Creator, "Now let
thy servant depart in peace." The instinct of living again
in our children, common to strong natures, predominated in
the mind of Mr. Wilde.

One afternoon he came home looking so pale, weary, and
care-worn, that Edith, very much alarmed, exclaimed,

"Father, father! what ails you? You are sick! You
have bad news—I know you have: I see it in your face—
I see it in your eye. Tell me at once. Anything is better
than suspense."

"My darling—" But Mr. Wilde could say no more.
He covered his face with his hands and groaned in agony.

"Father! dear, dear father!" and she put her arms
around his neck and kissed him on the forehead. "Father, dear, I know the worst: the ship is surely lost, and
my brother and my — brother is drowned!" The blank
was meant for Bailey, but even in that hour of woe she had
sufficient self-restraint to refrain from mentioning his name.
The look of agony in her eye and over her face was something appalling; and yet in that awful moment, when her
misery was more than twice as great as her father's, her
first thought was to comfort the old man.

In broken accents and in disjointed sentences Mr. Wilde
informed Edith that a ship had arrived that morning the
captain of which reported that off Cape Horn he saw por-

tions of a wrecked vessel, and part of the bow containing the letters *Sebas— Ca—*. "There is no longer the least doubt," he said. "Oh, my poor Walter! Oh, my son, my son! Would that I had died instead of you!" The gray-haired man wept like a child.

Edith uttered not a word, shed not a tear: she turned the color of marble, but did not swoon. She kept quietly smoothing her father's white hair and brow, and gently trying to comfort him. As she mechanically stroked his hair or his hands, her weird, wide-open gray eyes gazed into the fire with a far-off look. The supreme suffering of her soul could only be seen in the introverted expression of the eyes and in the compression of the lips. At length, when Mr. Wilde appeared somewhat composed, Edith said,

"Father, I would like to retire to my room. May I leave you for this evening only? To-morrow I shall be able to resume my usual duties, and be henceforth to you, if I can, a comfort and a consolation."

"Certainly, Edith; go and rest. You will need it more than I. God bless you, my darling!" and they kissed each other a sad good-night.

As soon as Edith reached her room, she threw herself upon her knees and prayed long and fervently. She asked God to give her fortitude and courage to do her daily duty under the burden of her two-fold affliction. She arose from her knees, cold, desolate, and tearless. She had known for months—ever since his departure for California—how tenderly, truly, devotedly, and passionately she loved George Bailey. She loved him with a singleness and strength such as strong women feel once and forever. She had never felt the slightest semblance of love for any one of the many suitors who had sought her hand. But for him, the son of the noble lady who had died in her arms—for him, the persecuted, the brave, the noble, the true, the heroic and the gentle—she allowed the great fountain of her love to flow forth in unmeasured currents. When she gave him her heart she gave it without stint or reservation; she gave it with all the generosity of a noble nature. As he was the first man who had ever aroused in her the tender emotion, her imagination clothed him with all the attributes of a demigod. A fearful thing is this first and only love of a strong woman. If Edith Wilde lived after such a bereavement, she would live as much a widow as though the marriage ceremony had been performed between her and George Bailey. She felt herself his through all the countless ages of eternity; and to her it would have appeared a dreadful sin ever to think of any other man in the relation of lover or husband. Pale and motionless as a marble statue, Edith sat gazing into the slowly-dying embers of the fire, and thought of the dear young brother, whom she had trained to everything pure and honorable, and of her lover, with whom she had never exchanged a single endearing epithet. It was a pitiful sight to see this good, strong woman thus stricken down by so fearful a blow.

The fire in the grate died out; the room grew cold, but Edith heeded it not. For hours she remained in the same fixed attitude, more like a corpse than a living person. At last a slight noise seemed to startle her, and, as if conscious for the first time of her terrible bereavement, she wrung her small hands in agony, and then threw her arms upward with a gesture of intolerable pain. Then she arose and paced the room backward and forward, as if seeking relief in motion; and clinching her hands, compressing her lips, and occasionally closing her eyes, she seemed as if nerving herself against the overthrow of reason. She had no likeness of Bailey except the ineffaceable one graven on her heart; she had not even a line of his handwriting; no visible thing of his had she: she would have given her whole fortune for a small lock of his iron-gray hair. She blamed herself for thinking so much about her lover and so little about her brother. She endeavored to drive Bailey out of her mind, and retain Walter there; but in vain; for the greater grief seemed to swallow up the less; and her thoughts, in spite of herself, would again and again recur to the man whom she loved beyond everything on earth.

Again she sought consolation in prayer, and forced herself to dwell on the darling brother whom she had lost forever; but with every effort, the two dear forms came before her imagination intermingled, and sinking down, down into the hungry ocean intertwined in each other's arms. Again she arose from her knees and paced the room as before. Not a tear came to her relief. At length, from sheer exhaustion, she threw herself on the bed and lay like one in a trance. But "Sleep, the twin brother of Death," weighed not upon her eyelids. She could never tell afterward how she had passed that first night of supreme misery. Nature, gentle and kindly, helps the miserable more than they can realize, by blunting the edge of agony which, if prolonged, would destroy life or overthrow reason. While reclining on the bed, a sort of stupor took possession of her faculties; and in this condition the storm, the shipwreck and the death of Walter and Bailey passed before her like the phantasmagoria of a fearful dream.

The pale rays of the rising sun, the harbingers of a new day, struggled through the blinds and curtains of her chamber, and still Edith lay with her eyes wide open, staring at the ceiling with a stony look. In another hour the crimson light filled the room, and extinguished the artificial light which had burnt steadily through the long hours of the night. Edith arose wearily, like one who rises for the first time from a bed of sickness, and staggered to the wash-stand, and bathed her hands and face in cold water, inwardly resolving that she would bear her cross and comfort her feeble father. She had now the appearance of one who had suddenly grown old. She was determined that no human being should ever know of her love for Bailey: that secret she would carry with her to the grave. At eight o'clock she went down to breakfast, and silently kissed her father. Neither spoke; neither could eat a morsel; each feared to mention the subject uppermost in the minds of both. Here we shall leave them to bear their misery as best they can, and ask the gentle reader to accompany us to another father and daughter, whose acquaintance he has already made.

The beautiful mansion in which George Bailey had paid his addresses to Grace Van Hess had long ago been abandoned. Father and daughter, with her three children, oc-

cupied a humble house in one of the poorer quarters of the
city. Jacob Van Hess is now a very old man, broken and
sickly, a prey to remorse, and struggling to keep his commercial credit above water. The discovery of Myron Finch's
character, so soon after wedding Grace and becoming a partner in the firm; the fear that his son-in-law had for years
inspired; the wholesale squandering of the money of the
firm without the power to prevent it; the evil treatment
which he knew that his darling Grace had received from
her brute of a husband through the entire period of her
married life; the strong suspicion, recently established into
a terrible truth, that Finch had cheated Bailey out of wife
and position, and had used him (Van Hess) to carry out his
villanies; his recent absconding with nearly all the remaining resources of the firm—all these had made Jacob Van
Hess prematurely feeble and timid, had crushed his spirit
within him, and destroyed that energy and enterprise which
had made him so successful a merchant. For the first time
in twelve years Grace and her father feel comparatively happy. The absolute terror which Finch had inspired is lifted
from their hearts, but the debasing effects remain and will
remain forever. Terror is the most morally destructive of
all the emotions, and seems to have a paralyzing influence
both on the body and the mind. The old man is a coward
now, and dreads poverty and the poor-house. The daughter, who, under the kindly treatment of a strong man like
Bailey, might have grown into a strong woman, is now
mean-spirited, selfish, and unreasonable. Finch had the
fatal power of dragging all with whom he came in contact
down to his own very low level. Ah! if Jenny Edwards
only knew it, it was much better for her to have been cast
off and forgotten, than to have been wedded, like Grace
Van Hess, to this moral monster.

Through her father Grace had learned of Bailey's promotion and voyage to San Francisco, and had kept herself ap-
prised of all his movements, from the time of the unsatis-
factory interview when he called for the receipt, up to the
day of his departure. In some unaccountable way she had
learned, in addition, that Edith Wilde, whom she had some-

times met in society, had been very kind to Bailey's mother; had procured Bailey himself employment; that he had gone regularly every Sunday to Miss Wilde's church; and that he had been very handsomely treated by Mr. Wilde. She had actually discovered Bailey's lodgings and habits of life. The love which she had quietly nursed for eleven years, like a slow fire smothered with much fuel, had burst out into a strong, fierce flame on the day that her brutal husband struck her; and the cold, hard manner of George Bailey, on the occasion of their one interview, combined with her own feminine suspicion or instinct, had convinced her that his heart had been given to another woman, and that woman she believed to be Edith Wilde. She was now unreasonably and savagely jealous. This jealousy had spurred her on to ascertain all George Bailey's movements, and had given her a penetration and a determination of purpose hitherto foreign to her character. She had been delighted to hear of Myron Finch's absconding; not that she feared him, or could ever again fear him, but because she was rid of an obstacle that stood between her and the man she loved. Even if her husband should return, he could be arrested and imprisoned; and she had resolved, at any rate, to obtain a divorce. Finch's selfish brutality, as before stated, had had its effect on Grace's character. She saw no wrong in loving Bailey, or in hating Edith Wilde. She dreamed dreams and saw visions; and in the blindness of her passion she built airy habitations, in which she placed herself as the wife of the man whom she had abandoned to his fate. She would say to herself, in her solitary musings, "Who knows but his old love will reappear? If he saw me often enough, his passion would revive. But for this Edith Wilde—" Then a dark scowl would overspread her face. She had been starved and stinted so long during her life with Finch, that her heart fairly ached for such love as she knew Bailey was capable of feeling. She would have freely risked her immortal soul to bask one hour in the sunshine of the love which she had deliberately cast away twelve years ago.

The same day, and at about the same hour that Mr. Wilde

had communicated to Edith the loss of the ship *Sebastian Cabot*, Mr. Van Hess was reading the *Evening Post*, and Grace was reading a light novel, translated from the French. The old gentleman started and exclaimed,

"Eh! what is this? George Bailey and Walter Wilde among the list of passengers!"

"What do you mean, father?" said Grace, in a startled tone. "What passengers? What ship are you talking about?"

"The ship *Sebastian Cabot*, which foundered at sea and all hands lost, including George Bailey and Walter Wilde. Here is a full account in the *Evening Post*." Mr. Van Hess, however, did not read the article aloud, as he had intended; for, happening to turn his head, he saw that Grace had fainted. He rung for assistance; and by a liberal use of cold water and considerable hand-chafing she was quickly restored to consciousness. When strong enough to speak, and when the servant had left the room, she said,

"Father, it was unkind of you to be so abrupt. You startled me dreadfully, and you know that my nerves are not strong. Show me that paper."

Grace read the fatal article with compressed lips, and a face the color of the dead. When she had finished she said, "I won't believe it! There are small boats, and rafts, and all that sort of thing. Men are picked up at sea. I won't believe that George Bailey is drowned—I won't!"

"Very true, Grace, my dear; they may have been picked up and they may not; more likely not. I am glad I asked and received his forgiveness; for he was a good lad, and would have made you an excellent husband instead of that —Finch."

"Yes," said Grace; "and whom am I to thank that my husband was Finch?—Keep quiet, father, keep quiet! Bailey, I repeat, is not drowned."

"My dear, I did all for the best."

"Yes, yes; I know you did. Good-night, father, I am tired;" and Grace Finch walked out of the room for the purpose of escaping the garrulity of the feeble old man, for whom she had little respect.

She, too, sat and pondered; and she, too, strode back and forth like a man; and she, too, threw herself on her bed and groaned; but there was this difference between Edith Wilde and her—Grace never once prayed, and never once thought of anything but her own selfish sorrow. At breakfast next morning word came to her father that she had a headache and could not leave her room. During the afternoon she dressed and went out. She wandered here and there without aim or purpose. She bought an evening paper and scanned it carefully for news of the lost ship, but in vain. She thought that perhaps the Wildes might have some information; but what excuse could she make for calling at such a time? Could she invent something? No, she could think of nothing which was reasonable. At last a thought struck her—the receipt. Bailey was in Wilde's employ. Mrs. Bailey had lost the receipt—that is, if she ever received one. She need say nothing of Bailey's having received a receipt sometime before his departure for California. She now hurried home in time to meet her father at dinner.

"Father, don't you think that Mr. Wilde should have Mr. Bailey's receipt—that is, the receipt which you gave him before he went to San Francisco?"

"No, I think not. That would be a rather strange proceeding," said Mr. Van Hess.

"But," said Grace, "the whole proceeding was very strange. Mr. Bailey owed Mr. Wilde the money which the forged check paid to Mr. Wilde. Mrs. Bailey paid this debt with honest money, and left no receipt for her son. He was so anxious about it, doubtless for the purpose of showing it to Mr. Wilde, that he wrote to you about it. Now, it is more than likely that this receipt was lost when the ship went down. Don't you think it would be an act of generosity to hand Mr. Wilde a receipt this evening, and to tell him your fearful mistake?"

"Well, Grace," replied the old gentleman, "it is not very business-like to give a second receipt in this way; but, as you remark, it would be only just to tell Mr. Wilde that I believe now that we sent an innocent man to State-prison."

Whether it was business or sentiment mattered little to

Grace Finch, as long as she accomplished her purpose. She was anxious for news, and she was morbidly curious to see if Edith Wilde suffered very much in consequence of her twofold loss. The passion of love in low minds is a ready condoner of crime, and a logical justifier of every sin committed in its own behalf. Her causeless hatred of Edith was a sin, but Mrs. Finch saw it not; her love for Bailey was a crime against her womanhood, but she never realized it.

The giving of the receipt and the conversation about the old forgery naturally led to the very thing which Grace had desired — namely, a private interview with Edith. These two women presented a singular contrast as they sat facing each other on the sofa. Thought, study, and high moral principle had chiselled the features of Edith Wilde into a beauty and a purity surpassing the best models of Grecian art: strength, and firmness, and intellectual power shone in the steady glance of her clear gray eye; and over and above all was that expression of goodness which had won the heart of Bailey at their first interview. Self-indulgence and abject fear had left their impress so distinctly on the former girlish beauty of Grace Finch, that one was unconsciously reminded of a beautiful peach on which the damp of a cellar has left the stain of mildew.

"You must excuse us, Miss Wilde," said Grace, "but we could not rest until Mr. Wilde had the assurance that Mr. Bailey had been a grossly-wronged man. We have had the proof of it, and desired to communicate this proof to all his friends. Now that, perhaps, he is no more "—and at this point Grace searched Edith's face keenly, but saw no sign of emotion—" now that he is no more, we wished those who trusted him to know that he was deserving of their confidence and esteem."

Edith Wilde looked at Grace Finch with a frigid, distant, stony expression of face. At first she had been simply amazed that one calling herself a lady should intrude upon a mere acquaintance at such a time. Her amazement changed to contempt, and this contempt gradually grew into a feeling of dislike. She thought to herself, "So this is the woman who was engaged to George Bailey; and per-

haps she loves him still." Like all who love deeply and
truly, she fancied that it would be impossible for any woman to be long in Bailey's society without loving him. As
these thoughts went through the mind of Edith, she had
not lost one syllable of what Mrs. Finch had said.

"Madam," said Edith, in cold, measured accents, "Mr.
Grady has told us all; but his statement of the gross
wrong, of the horrible crime committed against Mr. Bailey,
was not necessary. My father believed him innocent, and
I had the pleasure of knowing his mother very intimately.
Had I not known his excellent mother, and through her of
her son's purity and integrity, I would never have urged my
father to employ him in an important position."

"You were intimate, then, with his mother?"

"Very," replied Edith; "she was my dearest friend."

It required all Mrs. Grace Finch's self-control to keep
down the "green-eyed monster."

"I—I—came to give the proofs of Mr. Bailey's innocence; or—or, I mean my father came for that purpose;
but—I—I see it is not necessary. Pardon me, but the suddenness of the news rather upset me. You—ah—you may
have heard that George Bailey and I were—ha! ha!" (the
slight laugh was hysterical), "were engaged once, and that
it—it was broken off about the time of the forged check."
This little speech, broken with suppressed emotion, left its
sting in the heart of Edith, as Grace intended; but anxious now to change the line of conversation, she continued,
"Miss Wilde, has your father received any additional news?
Has he any hope?"

"No, Mrs. Finch; no news, and but little hope," replied
Edith, in a frigid tone.

The two women sat silent, not knowing what to say to
each other; and though they had been accustomed all their
lives to mingle in the best society, and to feel perfectly at
ease, each felt embarrassed, for each became conscious that
the other loved the same man. They read each other's
hearts like open books. Men, under similar circumstances,
could never have made the discovery of rivalship. Let two
women, even of the ignorant class, talk five minutes togeth-

er about the man beloved by both, and by some subtle free-masonry each will know the other's feelings just as thoroughly as though they had proclaimed their love from the house-top.

While silently facing each other on the sofa, Edith wondered that the weak, coarse woman who had abandoned Bailey and married his rival, could have the audacity to talk to her in such a way; and Grace thought it very strange if George Bailey could think anything of this pale-faced, queer-looking girl, who was only a sort of intellectual blue-stocking. Mrs. Myron Finch had great faith in her own faded charms — that is, after they had undergone a slight burnishing. She believed in small hands, small feet, small mouth, small head, and small waist; in fact, small-ness constituted seven-eighths of what she considered beauty, and the other eighth was made up of length without breadth or thickness—length of neck, of limb, of hair, with here and there a dash of red to relieve the general dead level of insipidity. As Edith Wilde had none of these qualifications, but had, on the contrary, a good-sized head, containing at least forty-eight ounces of firm brain, and a high, broad forehead, below which beamed a pair of large gray eyes, and below these again a nose indicative of strength, and a mouth formed to say something more than "prunes and prisms," Mrs. Finch began to feel a sort of contempt for the personal appearance of her rival, and to think that, after all, she had not much to fear from her powers of fascination. It had never once entered the mind of Mrs. Finch that a man could possibly love a woman for anything but mere physical beauty. And yet the small, faded, burnished charms of Grace Finch were to the characteristic, intellectual beauty of Edith Wilde, what the female show-figure in a milliner's window is to the finished Greek statue from the hand of Praxiteles.

Thus the two women sat for a few minutes unconscious of the lapse of time, for each was busy with her own thoughts. At length Mrs. Finch arose, and again apologizing for her unseasonable visit, and requesting Miss Wilde to send her word in case she received any tidings of her brother and Mr.

Bailey, took her departure, leaning on the arm of her aged father.

If ever a feeling of dislike, not to give it a harsher name, had found a home in the heart of the good and gentle Edith Wilde, it found it that evening for the coarse, selfish, and feeble Mrs. Myron Finch.

Chapter XVII.

"——— upon the watery plain
The wrecks are all thy deed; nor doth remain
A shadow of man's ravage save his own,
When, for a moment, like a drop of rain,
He sinks into thy depths with bubbling groan,
Without a grave, unknelled, uncoffined, and unknown."
BYRON.

"Water, water everywhere,
Nor any drop to drink."—COLERIDGE.

THE good ship *Sebastian Cabot* was borne along toward the equator by a fair north-west wind over an ocean as smooth as an Italian lake. When crossing the "line" the wind died away, and baffling calms prevailed for more than a week. Finally, a fresh breeze arose in the west, and the stout ship, under a full press of canvas, bore away to the south of Cape Horn; and here she was struck by a southeast gale, accompanied by a snow-storm so blinding that the man at the wheel could scarcely see the length of the quarter-deck. As the gale increased and grew into a raging tempest, the officers and sailors suffered intensely from the cold; and, to add to their misery, the ropes, spars, and rigging were covered with a thick coating of ice. Many of the men had become badly frost-bitten. The foretop-sail had been torn in fragments from the yards; and the ship was plunging before the wind under bare poles. Huge seas were shipped, and washed the deck from stem to stern; and the strong ship shivered and shook like a thing of life in the grasp of her relentless enemy. The bulwarks were swept away, and all the small boats, save one, smashed to pieces. The carpenter reported a leak; and all hands, at the imminent risk of being swept overboard, were ordered to the pumps. To ease the ship, now laboring heavily in the trough of the sea, the captain commanded the fore and main masts to be cut away. Day and night, after the tempest had died down, officers and men, with Bailey, Wilde, and the other passengers included, took turns in pumping out the water, which was fast gaining on them in spite of all their efforts. The carpenter had made several vain attempts, by means of canvas, to stop the leak. As the ship was in ballast, the sand choked the pumps, and the sailors were ready to give up in despair. The ship *Sebastian Cabot* was slowly but surely sinking. It was finally agreed that one portion of the crew and passengers should construct a raft, and the other portion take to the only remaining small boat. Including Bailey, Wilde, and four other passengers, there were twenty-nine souls on board, who were distributed as follows: the captain, the third mate, the four passengers, the carpenter, and six sailors were assigned to the boat; and the first and second officers, Bailey, Wilde, and the remainder of the crew to the raft. They took with them navigating instruments, and as much water and provisions as they could with safety carry. By observation they found themselves about eight hundred miles south-west of Chili. The boat and the raft had each a mast and a small sail; and four men in turn were kept at the oars. For two days, owing to the almost dead calm that succeeded the late storm, they kept together within speaking distance; but on the third night, a breeze having sprung up, the boat sailed away, and was never afterward heard of. Being overloaded at the start, she was evidently swamped in one of the minor gales that followed the first calm. The sufferings of the men on the raft were simply intolerable. Wearied, with rowing and want of sleep, and constantly in danger of being washed away by the seas that swept over them, death seemed to most of them a happy release. As they moved slowly toward the north-east the weather became very warm, especially at noon, and a raging thirst was added to their other miseries. During the seventh night the second mate had either fallen or thrown himself into the sea; for in the morning he was missing, and no one knew how or when he had disappeared. The first mate found it extremely difficult to maintain discipline among the sailors, the majority of whom were Spaniards and Portuguese. On the fourth day they had abandoned rowing, and now depended solely upon their small sail, which did not seem to carry them forward more than five or six miles a day. In fact, they were at the mercy of the winds; and unless they were picked up by some ship which had been driven out of her course like themselves, their chance of being saved was exceedingly slight. The sailors demanded a larger allowance of water, which the first officer refused; and this refusal would have caused a mutiny but for the presence of mind of Bailey, who drew out his revolver, and, standing in front of the men, said he would shoot the first man who disobeyed the orders which were given for the good of all. Bailey, Wilde, the mate, and the steward kept together at one end of the raft, in charge of the provisions, which were dealt out fairly and equitably to all; and the sullen sailors remained at the other end, waiting for the opportunity to seize and devour the whole stock.

Bailey's great aim was to preserve the life of Walter Wilde, whose constitution, at the best, was none of the strongest. He placed Walter near himself, compelled him to sleep with his head pillowed on his shoulder, gave him slyly more than half his allowance of bread-and-water, and forced him, during the scorching calms, to wash his body several times a day with the salt-water, warning him at the same time against allowing a single drop to pass his lips. Bailey washed his own body repeatedly, and allowed his inner clothing to remain wet, knowing that through the pores he would receive considerable water from which the salt would be eliminated and remain on his skin in crystals. He made young Wilde take his allowance of water in teaspoonfuls; and it was while he slept that Bailey poured the greater portion of his own allowance into Walter's cup.

Bailey's great fear was that his friend would succumb and die. How then, if he survived himself, could he face Edith, if the brother whom he had promised to preserve at the risk of his own life were dead? Walter clung to George like a child to its mother, and was treated with all the self-denying devotion which a mother would exhibit under similar circumstances. It was in this day of sore trial and suffering that Bailey's great qualities came to the surface. He was no stranger to privation; for he had spent sixty days in a dark cell in midwinter on bread-and-water. For ten years he had worked in a stone-quarry and slept on a hard cot, had eaten the coarsest fare, and worn the thinnest clothing. His enemies had taught him patience and fortitude, and his great physical strength and superior power of mind had made him a natural ruler of men. These qualities caused him to live where ninety-nine out of every hundred would have died, and enabled him quietly to support the power of the mate and quell the dangerous attempt at mutiny.

One after another the sailors died, raving maniacs, or, in the madness caused by trying to quench their thirst with salt-water, jumped wildly into the sea and were drowned. The carpenter had already died, and the first-mate was extremely low from exhaustion. The water was consumed; and the only sustenance left was a little bread, badly injured, and unfit for human food. Bailey became the very life of the party; he managed to rig up some fishing-tackle with which he caught one or two fish; by patiently waiting and watching, he shot with his pistol a sea-bird, and, as the raft could not be steered, he was obliged to swim for it. This fresh food he divided equally among the survivors. One morning the mate and two more of the sailors were missing. Owing to a slight swell of the ocean, it was supposed that in their weak condition they had rolled off the raft and been drowned. But four sailors, with Bailey and Wilde, remained of all who had sought to save their lives on their frail vessel. Day after day they eagerly scanned the horizon in search of a passing ship, but no sail ever gladdened their sight; and as the first rays of daylight dawned, every eye was turned in all directions, and the look of bitter disappointment in every face was pitiful to behold.

Walter Wilde was rapidly sinking, and his mind at intervals began to wander. The young man's condition filled Bailey with a nameless terror; for he was, on Edith's account, determined to save his life at the expense of his own. He was resolved not to survive him. A new horror was added to his other miseries. He found the four surviving sailors in frequent whispered consultations, and he clearly saw the wolfish glare of famine in their eyes. As young Wilde was evidently dying, Bailey read their thoughts, and became convinced that they wished to kill him in order to drink his blood and eat his flesh! While Walter dozed Bailey fished; and this day, while stealthily watching the sailors, he was more than usually successful. Notwithstanding the evident conspiracy to murder his friend, he made the customary equal division, resolved to give them no cause for an attack.

As the dusk of evening drew on, Bailey, who could see pretty well in the dark (another qualification for which he was indebted to his prison life), perceived the demon of blood-thirstiness gleaming in their eyes, and he trembled from head to foot with a fear which almost paralyzed him. He dared not apprise Walter of his danger. He placed him behind him, with his own body between him and the vampires who sought his blood. He held his pistol ready cocked to shoot the first man who moved toward their part of the raft, and endeavored with all his might to keep awake and to beat off the drowsiness which oppressed him.

George Bailey had suffered enough in his dark, solitary cell; he had felt the pangs of hunger before in the streets of his native city; but all his sufferings combined did not equal the horrible misery of his mind at this moment. His soul revolted and his heart sickened at the bare contemplation of the deed which the four starving demons meditated.

About eight o'clock in the evening the strongest of the sailors commenced to creep very slowly toward Bailey and his friend; but Bailey was on the watch, and having seen

the man run a large knife up his sleeve—at least he concluded it was a knife—was thoroughly prepared to meet
him, and waited until he had approached within three feet
of him.   He then exclaimed, "Back to your part of the
raft, or I'll shoot you on the spot!" and the baffled vam-
pire slunk to his place with a low howl of rage.   Bailey
then arose, and drawing a rope across the raft, said, "The
first man who crosses this line I shall kill!"   He retired to
his place beside Walter, who asked him what was the matter; but Bailey gave his friend an evasive answer.

All night long George Bailey kept himself awake by a
superhuman effort of the will.   Walter slept, leaning his
head on Bailey's shoulder—slept fitfully, uneasily, and tossed and tumbled in a state of half delirium.   Bailey held
his pistol in his right hand while the fingers of his left ran
through the dark locks of the brother of his darling Edith;
and he felt a strange pleasure, amidst all the horror of his
position, in being in such close contact with one who so
closely resembled his beautiful idol.   At one time during
this night—this horrible night—when Bailey felt his eyelids becoming heavy, the desperate thought entered his
mind of quietly slipping with his young friend into the
ocean, and of gently ending their miseries in each other's
arms!   Should he become so weak as to be unable to defend Walter, he well knew the dreadful death which was
in store for them both.   The very terror which his position
inspired seemed to give Bailey something more than mortal
endurance.

Daylight at last dawned, and Bailey commenced fishing,
the line in one hand and the pistol in the other, and his eye
never for a moment turned away from the four blood-hounds
lounging not four yards off.   He caught a single fish, after
two hours' toil.   He fired his pistol into a piece of dried
canvas, and with little pieces of wood chipped from the raft
he made a small fire and cooked it.   He gave Walter two-
thirds and ate the other third himself.   He would not
divide any longer with the assassins, for he clearly perceived that it was now a life-and-death struggle between
them.

The sailor who had tried to make the assault on Walter the evening before, and whom Bailey had driven back at the point of his pistol, now arose, and in broken English demanded that they should all cast lots; for it was better that one should be killed than that all should die of hunger and thirst. Bailey quietly told him that he would permit no cannibalism while he had a single bullet left in his pistol.

As evening was coming on again, all Bailey's terror returned. While it was yet daylight he asked Walter if he was sure he could keep awake, and watch for one hour while he slept. Walter thought that he could. "Remember," said Bailey, "if you feel yourself becoming drowsy, wake me instantly: don't hesitate one moment."

Bailey had slept for fully two hours, while Walter was keeping watch. It was now nearly dark, and, as the latter was looking indolently at the four men on the after-part of the raft, he saw one of them seize a knife, and begin to creep slowly and stealthily toward them. Walter pinched Bailey on the arm to awake him. In one instant—quicker than we can express it—George Bailey and the assassin were on their feet, the one with his pistol, the other with his knife. The assassin made a plunge forward to strike the fatal blow; but, ere he had accomplished half the distance, Bailey's pistol-bullet went clear through his brain, and the wretch lay dead at his feet. Bailey hurled the corpse into the sea, for fear his three comrades might devour his flesh. He warned them that on the slightest movement toward the dividing-line he would fire and kill them in succession. "Now, dear Walter, you may sleep in peace; I can watch for twenty-four hours if necessary."

Another day dawned. One of the sailors stood bolt-upright, scanned the horizon, and seeing no ship in sight, bounded far from the raft and sunk into the ocean. He feared the very fate that he had intended for Walter. Another sailor died about noon; and the last of them rolled into the ocean, being so weak that he could not help himself. Bailey rushed to save him, but too late.

They were all alone on the great deep. If death now came, it would be, at least, a decent death, since the fear of cannibalism was gone. The weather was exceedingly fine, and as they drifted'toward the north the atmosphere became cooler. The hungry ocean, like a huge monster, lay everywhere around them, ready to devour them; with no food to eat nor water to drink, covered with sores, and worn to mere skeletons, the two survivors almost envied the lot of those whom the greedy ocean had already swallowed up. Another day came, and not a sail in sight. Bailey had to exert every faculty of mind and will to make the effort to fish, but he caught nothing.

As day changed to night, and as there was a light swell, which caused the raft to roll, Bailey was afraid to sleep, for fear either or both might fall off and be drowned. He caused Walter to rest with his arm around the mast; and he so arranged his own body and limbs on the opposite side, and so held Walter's hand, that it would have been almost impossible for either to roll into the sea without awakening the other. The sleep of both was light and fitful, and each had annoying dreams of eating human flesh and drinking human blood. To their utter astonishment and delight, they were awaked from their uneasy slumbers by feeling large drops of rain falling on their faces. Blessed rain! It perfectly poured in torrents. The young men opened their mouths, took off their outer clothing, now white with salt, and allowed their under-clothing to be completely saturated with fresh-water. They filled the tin cups and the cask, and they washed their tattered garments with the soft rain. Refreshed and invigorated, Bailey commenced to fish; and as fortune, like misfortune, never comes alone, he caught a larger fish than any that had hitherto rewarded his labors. This, with the fresh-water in abundance, furnished the best meal which they had eaten in several weeks. That afternoon, evening, and night, the two young men slept a deep, heavy, refreshing sleep. Toward morning, as their sleep became lighter, each dreamed of delicious repasts, iced wines, and cooling fountains. But the little strength remaining was fast giving out; and each knew that unless picked up in a day or two they must inevitably die of starvation. Bailey fished all day but caught nothing; he fired his pistol at a sea-bird and missed it; and both, making their supper on a draught of rain-water, lay down in each other's arms, for the sea was now smooth again, and tried to forget their sufferings in sleep.

"George, old boy, I cannot last much longer. I am very weak, and I suffer from dreadful pains in my stomach. I wish we could die together, for I don't like to leave you here all alone."

"Walter, my brave fellow, do try to keep up for another day. I know by the appearance of the gulls that we are approaching land, and we must be nearing the track of passing vessels."

"Only for leaving you alone, I would pray for death as relief from my sufferings;" and the young man fell off into another light, uneasy slumber. In a few minutes he awoke and clung closer to Bailey, as if to derive hope, relief, and life from the contact.

"George, if I die and you survive, will you tell Edith something? Will you tell her that I said that if I had been a woman I would have loved you with my whole heart and soul? But you will not—you—will—not—you-u—" and again Walter fell into another light doze. In a minute or two he was partially awake again and said,

"My dear George, you—have—been—the noblest—the bravest of friends—you have—been a—hero—hero—gave me your—bread and—water—tried—to save me—at the risk—of—your own—life." He slept once more.

"George, George! my good George! I have just been with Edith—and—and I told her how you—loved her, and how, for her sake — you starved yourself to — keep me—alive."

Walter's head reclined on George's bosom. Bailey supported him with one arm, and pressed his cold, thin fingers in grateful reply to all that he had said.

"Walter, Walter, hush! Don't talk. Sleep. Make up your mind to live. I have a presentiment that we will be picked up to-morrow. It will soon be daylight. Ha!—

See! See!—There's a light!—a ship's light, right in our track! Thank God!—Thank God! But, heavens! if she should pass us without seeing us! See, Walter! There's the light, about five miles astern of us!"

The sight revived Walter, who raised himself on his elbow, and gazed long and steadily on the approaching light. At first the vessel could be seen like a dim dark cloud moving along the sea; but, as day gradually dawned, the sails became whiter, and the outlines of a large brig were clearly defined. What if, in the uncertain light and at that early hour, the lookout should fail to see them! The very thought was horrible, and seemed to inspire Bailey with new strength. He took off his shirt, attached it to an oar, and lashed the improvised flag-staff to the mast of the raft. He tied Walter's handkerchief and his own to another oar, and kept waving it to and fro, to attract, if possible, some wary sailor on board of the brig. But no one seemed to see them. The vessel was now nearly in a line with them, and about three miles to the westward. The agony of Bailey was fearful; he waved the oar in vain. He knew that the raft itself could not be seen from the brig; but surely, surely they must see the mast, sail, and white shirt flying from the top of the oar. Almost frantic with despair, Bailey climbed the frail mast and waved the oar with superhuman energy. In breathless expectation he fancied that he perceived a movement of the men on board: he imagined that he saw a slight change in the course of the brig: then he became sure of it, and let the oar fall from his hand, exclaiming, "Hurrah! Walter, we are saved!" and glided down to the raft in a swoon.

Poor Walter crawled over to his preserver—the indomitable, the iron-willed—and poured a little of the rain-water down his throat, and sprinkled some over his face; he chafed his hands, and rubbed his temples, and prayed to God to spare the life of his noble friend. Bailey's condition seemed to rouse the feeble Walter to new life and energy.

In the mean time a boat arrived from the brig, containing the second mate and four sailors; and as the officer stepped on board and glanced at the two skeletons, his first question was,

"Is he dead? No! Hand me that flask of brandy."

He poured a spoonful down his throat, which in a short time brought Bailey back to his senses. The kind-hearted seaman also administered some to Walter, and the stimulant greatly revived him. The two men were tenderly helped into the small boat and gently lifted on board of the brig; for sailors, though often rude and rough, have kindly hearts. With their hollow, sunken eyes, high cheek-bones, matted hair, and unshaven faces; with their clothes in tatters, and with their bodies covered with salt-water boils, the two young men presented to the captain and crew a most pitiable spectacle. As they were gently lifted on board the *William Penn*, a passenger with jet-black hair and eyebrows, and clean-shaven, sallow face, cast upon the two sufferers a glance as devoid of sympathy as if the two men had been two logs of wood.

CHAPTER XVIII.

"It is the nature of the human disposition to hate him whom you have injured."—TACITUS.

THE captain and crew of the *William Penn*, with that generous hospitality which characterizes their profession, did all in their power to nurse the young men into health and strength. Bailey's condition was far worse than Wilde's; for he had eaten less food and taken less rest, and had suffered, besides, from constant anxiety, particularly during the time when the four half-crazy sailors had sought to kill Walter for food and drink. George Bailey lay for several days in his berth almost unable to move, and had to be fed like an infant on the lightest kind of food—a biscuit broken in hot water and flavored with a little sugar. Providentially his stomach could retain nothing stronger or heavier, or the sailors would have literally killed him with kindness. He was perfectly rational, but thoroughly exhausted;

and, from his previous study of medicine, knew that he was
in danger of gastric fever, which, in his present condition,
must inevitably destroy his life.   Each day, however, he
gained a little, and the severe pains began to subside; but
still he was hardly able to move his hands or speak above a
whisper.

Walter's recovery was rapid, thanks to the excellent care
he had received on the raft, and it was now his turn to
nurse his preserver—a labor of love which was performed
with a gentleness and patience truly womanly.   He constantly sat beside Bailey's bed in the little state-room which
the mate had given up for his use, and coaxed him to eat
his food and drink a little rum diluted with water.   Sometimes Walter read aloud, in a low, rich tone, which strangely harmonized with the splash of the sea against the sides of
the brig, old tales of shipwrecks and disasters at sea, or the
"Life of Captain Cook," or the voyages of Vasco de Gama
or Magellan; or sometimes he read several chapters out
of the Bible; for, if we except the lower order of "yellow
covered" literature, there was nothing else on board to read.
For hours Bailey would shut his eyes and lie awake, drinking in the mellow tones of Walter's voice; and when Walter, thinking him asleep, would cease reading, close the
book, and arise to prepare his food or medicine, Bailey would
open his large sunken eyes, and gaze tenderly and fondly on
his young friend—for was he not Edith's brother? and had
he not saved his life on the raft?

"How are you to-day, old fellow—stronger, eh?" Walter
would ask.

"I am slowly·gaining, thanks to your watchful care and
patient nursing.   The danger of fever is past, for my food
rests easily on my stomach and no longer causes pain."
Bailey spoke very slowly and with some effort.

"There, now, that will do," said Walter; "go to sleep
and don't talk any more."

"Walter, does it tire you to read aloud?"

"No, not at all; for you know that I read in such a low
monotone it cannot hurt me in the least.   I could read
aloud all day."

"Well, my friend, if it does not tire you, and if you have nothing better to do," said Bailey, "it soothes me very much to listen to your voice."

So Walter read these lugubrious accounts of sufferings similar to their own, which, after their recent misery, had a strange charm for both of them. Bailey lay and listened and thought. He heard the voice, but caught no idea from the book, because his mind was thinking of his beautiful Edith (beautiful to him, if not to others), of her intellect and her goodness; and her brother's reading enabled him to realize the more readily that he had obeyed her wishes in risking his life to save that brother from a horrible death. He thought it would be a pleasant thing to die now, and let the grateful Walter tell her how he had kept his promise. Perhaps she would then shed a tear for his memory and his fate, and this solitary tear would amply compensate him for all his sufferings. Poor George! Had you known how at this very moment Edith Wilde grieved far more for you than she did for that beloved brother, and that her grief was even too great to find relief in tears, perhaps this knowledge would have created such an intoxication of delight as would have superinduced that very fever which you dreaded a few days ago.

"Walter, will you please let me hold your hand? I think I can sleep better in that way. Thank you!"

The swash of the sea, the low, rich voice of the reader, the touch of *her* brother's hand, soothed his soul to such a sweet repose as he had never felt before. He was relieved of all pain, and this caused him to feel a certain luxury in mere existence. Walter Wilde's attendance was inconceivably pleasant to George Bailey. He compared his present position with the fate which had almost overtaken him in New York—of dying in the streets like a houseless, ownerless dog, and thought himself in paradise.

George Bailey grew stronger day by day, and at the end of the second week since the rescue he was able to appear on the deck, leaning on the arm of Walter. The sunshine and bracing sea air, and, above all, the perfect content of mind, rapidly hastened his recovery.

The passenger with the very black hair and eyebrows and the swarthy complexion took good care to shun the company of the two friends, as they paced up and down the deck for exercise; and well he might, for that passenger, as the reader will remember, was no other than Myron Finch, the forger, fleeing from justice and the vengeance of the man whom he had so foully wronged, under the *alias* of Alexander Brown. When Finch had cast a look of utter indifference at the two human skeletons whom the crew had saved, he failed to recognize either of them, and whether they lived or died was a matter of no consequence to him. He had heard the younger man address the elder, sometimes as George and sometimes as Bailey; and it is doubtful, but for hearing the names, if he could have recognized in the attenuated face and figure of the grave, middle-aged man before him the once gay, gallant, and light-hearted George Bailey. He made the discovery, too, that the younger man was the only son of William Wilde, of the banking-house of Warrenton, Wilde & Co.

While Bailey and Wilde were pacing the deck, Finch was standing before his little glass in his state-room, carefully scanning his own face to see if his disguise were complete; for at the sight of Bailey all his fear and hatred were revived. Satisfied that he could not be recognized, he muttered to himself, "We shall reach Valparaiso in a few days, and I can avoid them. I can be ill, and keep my state-room. Suppose he were to recognize me—what then? He has no proofs. Pshaw! I shall trust to the twelve years which have elapsed since then, and to my disguise." Notwithstanding this bracing up of his courage, he fairly trembled at the bare idea of being recognized by George Bailey.

Finch was too self-indulgent to feign sickness and to be put on a spare diet; and so he appeared at the dinner-table in the cabin as usual, on the first day that Bailey was able to dine with the captain and officers. George was seized with a strange feeling of loathing for this Alexander Brown —something like the feeling one has for a noxious reptile. He could not avoid thinking that he had seen those pale eyes before, so out of harmony with the ebon hair and eyebrows, and the uneasy, furtive glance seemed familiar to him; but where or under what circumstances he had seen him, he could not form the most remote idea. Perhaps, had he not known that Myron Finch was a prosperous merchant, living in grand style in New York, his suspicions might have been aroused; for, in brooding over the crime committed by this heartless rascal, Bailey had his every feature, nay, the very color of every feature, photographed on his memory.

In the course of conversation at the table Walter Wilde remarked, in the easy tone of a man accustomed to the usages of the best society,

"I suppose, Mr. Brown, you have been a great traveller by sea and land?"

"Yes," replied Brown (we shall call him for the present by his *alias*), "I have crossed the Atlantic ten times; I have been several times to Calcutta and Melbourne, and I am now on my way to some of the cities on the west coast of South America, on the business of our firm."

"You are not an American, then?" asked Walter.

"Oh, bless you, no! I have not that privilege, for I am a native of London. Our house has its head-quarters there, but we have correspondents in every part of the globe. I am only their humble agent."

Although this was spoken by Brown with the easy, careless drawl of an Englishman, not overdone, there was something in the tone which caused Bailey to start—a movement that was not lost on Mr. Brown. There was nothing in the simple question asked by Walter that would lead the confidential agent of a great English house to enter into minute particulars about his business, had he not had an object in letting them know who and what he was. He was too explicit by half, and a keener observer than any person sitting at the table would have been able to detect "the lie circumstantial." In vain Bailey racked his brain to recall when he had before seen those colorless eyes and heard that peculiar voice. It must have been some Englishman who had had business relations with Van Hess & Co. when he was their head-clerk.

In order to change the subject, Brown asked Walter, for he never directed his conversation to Bailey,

"How long were you exposed on that raft?"

"For nearly seven weeks," replied Walter; "and had it not been for my friend here, I would have died two or three weeks before we were rescued. Such patience, strength, and fortitude as Bailey showed I have never even read of."

"Nonsense, Walter! you showed as much pluck as any of us," interposed Bailey, who could not bear to hear himself praised. "Mr. Brown," he continued, "did you ever have any business relations with the house of Van Hess & Co. about twelve or thirteen years ago? It seems to me that I must have seen you before."

"Me?" faltered Brown, "me? Why, what on earth could I have to do with the firm of Van Hess, *Finch* & Co.? I—I—I believe that is the present name of the firm; is it not, Mr. Wilde?"

Brown had unconsciously betrayed himself by his hesitation and stammering, and by using the right name of the house. He had lost his usual presence of mind, when he found Bailey scrutinizing his features and trying to search out his identity beneath the dyed hair and discolored skin.

"Did you ever see or know Finch, the junior partner?" asked Bailey, in no friendly tone. "You have mentioned his name; did you know him?"

"Ye-e-s, ye-e-s," faltered Brown, trying with all his might to cover his fear; I—I met him in society, at the club, but never in business."

"Then," said Bailey, with a fearful frown knitting his brows, and an expression of concentrated rage on his face, "then you met the greatest liar, the greatest hypocrite, and the greatest rascal unhung! you met a forger; you met a man who stole another man's good name, who stole another man's position, who stole another man's betrothed, and then maltreated her. Oh! you met a man meaner and more villanous than the very devil of the Scriptures; and woe, woe, woe to that man or devil if he ever crosses my path!"

Words could give no adequate idea of the hatred, the

vindictive hatred, displayed in Bailey's low, deep, sonorous voice. Brown grew pale even below his tobacco-stained face, and his hands and knees shook with fear. A deadly terror filled his heart; for Bailey might yet detect him in spite of all. The truth was, that, without knowing him, Bailey *felt* his presence, and hence the outpouring of his wrath. Once or twice Bailey came within an ace of recognizing Finch, who was only saved by the imperfect light of the cabin.

"Why, old boy," asked Walter, "what's the matter? This is the first time I have seen you angry. You look as if that Finch had stolen all those things from you—as if you had been the victim."

"The matter, Walter? The matter? Oh ay! excuse me; but when I think of that consummate villain, I seem to forget everything—everything. Let us go on deck: the air of the cabin suffocates me!"

When alone, Bailey turned to Wilde and said, "Yes, Walter, I was the victim. Your father and sister know all about it. A perfectly innocent man, that devil Finch sent me to State-prison for ten years, after robbing me of my reputation, my position, and my betrothed! and the cruelties inflicted on me in that earthly hell would have killed me in a year but for the hope of vengeance. Oh! what were the sufferings on the raft compared to the agony of the shower-bath and solitary confinement in a dark cell on bread-and-water, with no companion for sixty days but the rats! It was an honorable death to die on the raft, doing one's duty and struggling for life in the light of day. Walter, you know now why I was able to bear up when others succumbed. Ah, my lad, I had a terrible training, as I told you one day, ironically, in San Francisco. I fell so very low, I sounded the very depth of misfortune. The face and voice of that man Brown remind me so much of Finch that, did I not know he was in New York, I would almost think it was he in disguise; but I know it is only a delusion, caused by the weakness of my nerves. Ah, Walter, mine has been a sad, sad story! The opening chapters were beautiful, but farther on it became a tragedy. Only

for your good sister my poor mother might have died from
want, and I might have starved in the streets of my native
city."

"My dear George"—and the tears were streaming down
Walter's eyes as he spoke—"my poor friend, your sufferings have been awful! God bless Edith for what she has
done for both you and your mother!"

Bailey's reply to this was an AMEN! uttered in a deep,
sincere, feeling tone.

Mr. Alexander Brown did not dare any longer to trust
to his disguise. The fierce denunciation of Finch at the
dinner-table made him really sick; and hence he crept into
what he termed his "hole," and remained there for the remainder of the voyage. In a few days the *William Penn*
entered the harbor of Valparaiso, and Bailey and Wilde retired to a hotel to recuperate. Walter had abundance of
money, which he had preserved in a belt around his waist;
and even if he had not, he could have drawn on his father
for any reasonable amount. Mr. Myron Finch, *alias* Alexander Brown, did not remain an hour in the city, but fled
as fast and as far from the man whom he feared as the limited means of conveyance in Chili would permit.

CHAPTER XIX.

"The night of sorrow now is turned to day."—SHAKSPEARE.

EDITH WILDE had resolutely resumed her social and domestic duties. The only difference observable in her bearing and conduct was a certain air of sad seriousness toward
her friends, and a quiet, thoughtful affection toward her father, whose every wish she seemed to anticipate. Toward
the little orphans she manifested a spirit of kindly care
which relieved orphanage of half its misfortune. While
her father was busy at the bank, she devoted hours to
teaching the children, consoling the afflicted, and nursing
the sick. There was a pleasure in the work, for it brought
her nearer, she fancied, to George Bailey and his mother.

The little ones loved her. Those who were cross and irritable with fever went asleep in her arms; and often, while lying in their little cots, recovering from measles or mumps, the children, at the sound of every step on the stair, would turn their eyes anxiously toward the door to see if Miss Wilde were coming; for they well knew that she never came empty-handed. Oranges, peaches, pears, grapes, and other fruits in their season, she invariably brought to them in her little basket. She stroked their hair, kissed them, and soothed in a hundred gentle ways the poor little motherless waifs.

Her great grief she resolutely locked within her heart; and she endeavored with all her might neither to pine nor mope, nor shorten her life, if she could help it. Work, wholesome work, she found to be the very best medicine, the great panacea for the aches of the heart and the brain; and of all places she preferred to work in the orphan asylum, because there she could best minister to innocent and suffering humanity.

Her interview with Mrs. Myron Finch had upset her nerves for a day or two; for even if George Bailey were dead, Edith did not wish to know that he was mourned for by such a woman. Mrs. Finch's passion was, in the eyes of Edith, besmeared with a moral slime which contaminated whatever it touched. Something akin to hatred—perhaps we had better term it a very strong dislike—arose in her heart toward this unprincipled and shameless woman. She dreaded to see her again; she feared even to hear from her. And yet Mrs. Myron Finch had not said or done much to evoke this feeling of aversion. In truth, Edith's feelings and motives were so mixed and indefinable that she herself would have found it extremely difficult to explain them. Good as she was, she was, after all, only a woman; and what woman can bear to know that another woman loves her lover?

Two months have passed away since the visit of Mrs. Finch, and not another word has been heard of the crew and passengers of the *Sebastian Cabot*. One day, at dinner, Edith observed an unusual expression of enjoyment on her father's face, and she wondered very much to see it, for ever since the news of the wreck he had been despondent, and took no interest in anything—not even in the bank. His present pleased expression could not have been caused by any afflux of money to his coffers; in fact, she was at a loss to know what had happened to give him so much pleasure. The old gentleman eyed her very slyly from time to time; and he, in turn, wondered why she did not ask him the reason he felt so happy this evening. It was a part of his little game to make her ask him, and he was somewhat annoyed at her delay in doing so. He had good news for her, and he desired to give it by degrees rather than abruptly, on account of her nerves. At length she said,

"Father, why do you look so happy to-day?" and then, as a sudden thought flashed through her mind, she said, "You have good news—I know you have—they are saved!" Edith turned the color of the dead; her heart for a moment or two ceased to beat, as a great hope rushed into her soul.

"Edith, my love, there is hope—just a little hope. But calm yourself. The news was very sudden, and I myself was almost killed with joy."

"Father, you may tell me all: you need not fear for me."

"He is alive," said Mr. Wilde—"rescued from a raft. He is on his way to New York, and he may be here at any moment!"

Edith Wilde well knew that her father referred to Walter. She was extremely anxious to hear about Bailey, but hesitated to ask the question. The old gentleman was so wrapped up in his only son, the inheritor of his name and his business, that he used the singular pronoun instead of the plural: he thought of Walter only, while Edith thought of both.

"Thank Heaven!" said Edith, no longer able to withstand her anxiety, "Walter is safe; but what became of his companion, Mr. Bailey? Was he, too, rescued?"

"To be sure he was," replied Mr. Wilde; "they were both together. But here is Walter's letter, written in Valparaiso ; read for yourself, and see what he says about your protégé. It seems that Bailey acted nobly, and that my son thinks him a perfect hero—a sort of Chevalier Bayard or Sir Philip Sidney."

With trembling fingers Edith read the letter.

"Hotel Bolivar, Valparaiso, October 19th, 18—.

"MY DEAR FATHER,—This note will startle you not a little, for doubtless you have long ago given me up as lost. I direct to the bank, because if it were to go to the house it might fall into Edith's hands and shock her delicate nerves. Your nerves are not easily moved, and you are always prepared for every contingency.

"I will reserve my story for a winter's evening around the library fire. Suffice to say that Mr. Bailey took such excellent care of me in San Francisco that, before I left, my bronchial trouble had almost disappeared. The voyage home had been prosperous and pleasant until we were overtaken by a most terrific gale south-west of Cape Horn. The ship foundered. One portion of the crew and officers took to the only remaining boat, while another portion, with Bailey and myself, took to a raft. For nearly seven weeks we suffered such misery as no pen could describe—cold, heat, hunger, thirst, cramps, boils—every torture that you can think of assailed us. All died or went mad, and jumped into the ocean, except Bailey and me. It would take a whole volume to tell you how Bailey preserved my life; how he starved himself and endured the horrible thirst in order to give me the greater portion of his bread-and-water ; and, in spite of all my protestations, he continued this to the very last. Then, when those nasty Portuguese sailors wanted to kill me for the purpose of—but I cannot horrify you by telling you the purpose—Bailey frightened off the four crazy men, and shot one of them dead, who had attempted to stab him. He soothed me, nursed me, and kept me alive. Only for George Bailey, my father would have no son, my sister no brother to-day. This man is a hero, if there ever was one ! and yet, with all his strength, skill, and courage, he is as gentle as a child, and as patient as a wom-

an.   He never gave out until the moment of rescue ; and
then, when he knew that my life was saved, he succumbed
to the utter weakness caused by privations which would
have killed nine hundred and ninety-nine out of every thousand men.   He is now to me something more than a brother—he is my preserver.   I send my best love, and he his
kind regards, to you and Edith.   You may expect to see
us almost as soon as this note.

" Your affectionate son,
" WALTER WILDE.

" P.S.   DEAR EDITH,—You never performed a better
action in all your life than that of inducing our father to
employ Mr. Bailey.   W. W."

Edith read the letter over twice and drank in every word
of it.   Many emotions stirred her heart—pride in the superior moral and physical qualities of the man whom she
loved, gratitude to God for the preservation of Bailey and
her brother, and, dominant over all, an ecstatic joy pervaded
her whole being at the mere certainty that both were living
and likely to be home in a few days.   There was a feeling
of exquisite pleasure, too, in the thought that she had not
been mistaken in her estimate of George Bailey's character,
and that her brother and father now knew him for what he
really was.

After the reading of the letter, Mr. Wilde and Edith sat
a few minutes in silence, as if for the purpose of fully realizing their happiness.   The silence was at last broken by
the former, who asked Edith, " How had she managed to
find out what manner of man Mr. Bailey was ?"

" I knew his mother.   Mrs. Bailey, next to my own
mother, was the best and noblest woman I had ever known.
She had constantly spoken of her son, and by this means I
came to know his character almost as well as if we had
been brought up together.   I believed him entirely innocent of the crime for which he suffered such cruel punishment, and I deeply sympathized with the stricken lady.
When her son came, not to ask employment but to express
his gratitude for the little kindness I had extended to his

mother, and when Mr. Grady asked you to give him work, I saw the justice of the request, and urged you, against your 'business principles,' to employ him; and this you did, like the good, kind father that you are; and have you not had your reward?"

"You are right, my dear, perfectly right. What a man this little woman would have made! In her, or rather his, hands the house of Warrenton, Wilde & Co. would have held its own."

"I never want to be a man. I prefer to be as it pleased God to make me. I despise those women who are perpetually exclaiming against their sex, and wishing that they were men."

"Why, Edith, my dear, I prefer to have you as you are —my comfort and my consolation — as you always have been since your mother's death."

"I have learned," said Edith, "two great lessons by my association with Mrs. Bailey. The first is, that to prevent crime we must begin with the very young; and the second is, that to lessen crime we must provide wholesome employment for returned convicts. Suppose those orphans had been left to the tender mercies of their surroundings, at least one-half of them would grow up criminals; and suppose all released convicts were refused employment because they could not be trusted, what are they to do? They must live: they will not starve, as poor George Bailey did; they will join the ranks of the criminal class, and prey upon that very society which refused them honest work. Take care of the orphans, the worse than orphans (that is, children with drunken, vicious parents); establish schools, reformatories — I mean real reformatories, and not prisons; take care of all released convicts, and trust them as far as they deserve; and the money saved in reducing the cost of prisons and almshouses would more than support all these institutions for the prevention of crime. Take the millions that it costs to support what is called 'justice,' from the judge down to the policeman, from the magnificent courthouse down to the dingy police cell, and expend but one-quarter of the amount on asylums, reformatories, and schools,

and see what a blessed change for the better there would
be! This 'eye for an eye and tooth for a tooth' doctrine
is exploded; and we are everywhere suffering from the
relics of Oriental barbarism.   There was once an Oriental
Preacher who came from God—who was the Son of God—
who taught something better, higher, holier: to 'do good
for evil;' to save the sinners; but though the name of this
great Teacher is often on the lips of professing Christians,
his acts they will not imitate, nor his example follow.   My
dear father, if I have anything to leave in my will, it will
be left to the young children who may be tempted to fall
into crime, and to a society for the employment of released
convicts."

    "My dear, you are talking like a statesman!   When and
where did you form these opinions?   Society could not
exist under such conditions as you contemplate."

    "I have been much alone," replied Edith, "and I have
studied out my theory, if I may so term it, from the start-
ing-point of the orphans whom I have under my care, and
from the miscarriage of 'justice' which deprived Mrs. Bailey of a son and sent her to her grave."

    At this point in the conversation the servant announced
Mr. John Grady, and the words were scarcely spoken when
into the library stalked the gentleman in question, accompanied by Washington Scroggs, M.D., and Miss Jenny Edwards.   Grady had heard the good news of the rescue from
Mr. Van Hess, and had run off to inform his two friends, the
doctor and Jenny, both of whom were well acquainted with
Bailey.   The warm-hearted and impulsive Grady could not
rest satisfied until he had the information from the "foun-
tain-head," as he termed it; and so he dragged Miss Edwards and the little quack off with him to Mr. Wilde's
house.

    "Mr. Wilde," said John Grady, "I am delighted to hear
the good news.   Miss Wilde, I am more than delighted to
hear the glad tidings.   Our friend, the brave Mr. Bailey,
and your son" (turning to Mr. Wilde) "are both saved,
glory be to God!"

    Grady had never asked if the report were true, for in a

single glance he had read it in the two faces before him;
and he was too much in the habit of believing what he
hoped, to have the least doubt at the present moment. It
would have been treason, in fact, to doubt; and had any
one had the presumption to doubt in his presence, it is
more than likely that he would have felt inclined to a liberal use of the "carnal weapon." Grady had forgotten to
introduce his two friends, who had been standing in his
wake all the time he was speaking, like two small boats at
the stern of some large steamer. But perceiving that Miss
Wilde and her father were both looking at the two strangers, he simply said,

"Oh, never mind—this is Dr. Washington Scroggs, and
this is my niece, Jenny Edwards. Now, tell me all about
the rescue. I am dying to hear all about my good friend
Bailey."

Mr. Wilde handed Grady his son's letter to read, and
during its perusal Edith requested Miss Edwards and Dr.
Scroggs to be seated. As for John Grady, in his present
state of mental excitement it would have been impossible
for him to remain quiet or seated. As he read, he ejaculated, "Yes, yes!"—"Just so! just so!"—"Truly a brave
lad!"—"Just like him!"—"Good, good!" (This was at
the place where Walter mentioned the shooting of the crazy
assassin.)

When he had finished the reading of the letter, to the
amazement of the father and the amusement of the daughter, John Grady walked over to the part of the room where
Edith sat and deliberately shook her hand, and uttered the
following words in a husky tone, choked with strong emotion,

"Miss Wilde, upon my honor I congratulate you!"

Edith, blushing, but at what it would have been difficult
to say, simply replied,

"I thank you, Mr. Grady."

Grady walked back to his friends and said, "Jenny, my
dear, read that!" and when she had finished, he handed it
to the little quack, saying, "Dr. Scroggs, you had the hon-
or of seeing and knowing my friend, George Bailey—read

that!" and when the little man had ended its perusal, he laid the letter on the library-table, walked over once more to Miss Wilde, and seizing and shaking her hand—he had thoroughly mastered this great American habit of hand-shaking—repeated his former remark in a louder and firmer tone, "Miss Wilde, upon my honor I congratulate you!" Then turning to his two friends, said, "Come, let us go. God be praised, George Bailey is alive!"

Chapter XX.

"O thou invisible spirit of wine, if thou hast no name to be known by, let us call thee—Devil!"—SHAKSPEARE.

"RESTLESS as a second Cain," Myron Finch wandered from city to city, seeking pleasure and finding none. Imperfectly acquainted with the Spanish language, and having no affinity with the Spanish-American people, he felt lonely, ill at ease, and completely discontented. His money did not bring him the enjoyments that he had anticipated; and he had not the resources of books and studies to fall back upon to kill the time which hung so heavily on his hands. He frequented the theatres and restaurants, and drank a great deal more hard liquor than was good for him. The habit of drinking grew on him apace; he drank at his meals, he drank at night, and to cure his headaches he drank in the morning before his breakfast—in fact, he seldom laid a sober head on a pillow. In his wanderings from place to place he carried his little brandy-bottle with him, and frequently "refreshed" himself with unwatered potations. He drank about a pint of brandy every day, and yet he was never seen intoxicated; for, unfortunately for himself, his head was as hard as his heart, and his drinks were pretty evenly distributed over the sixteen or seventeen hours of the day when he was not asleep. The inroads that this course of life made on his constitution could be seen in the flabbiness of his flesh and the puffiness below his eyes. In quest of excitement, he sought the gambling-houses; but in his dazed condition he was no match for the professional gamblers, whose business it was to fleece such men as Finch. He lost a great deal of money, and in his vain efforts to recover his losses he almost ruined himself. What with his hotel bills, his liquor bills, and his heavy losses at the gambling-houses, his money was fast taking wings. He had not a single real friend in the world; but this melancholy fact gave him no trouble. He desired the association of the fast men of New York, because they had always administered to his pleasures; they spoke the same language, and possessed the same low tastes; but as for these Spaniards, they were worse than the negroes of the South in his estimation. There came a time when an insatiable desire took possession of his mind to return to New York. He began to reflect that the Empire City was the only city in the world worth living in, and that he had been a great fool for ever leaving it. He said to himself, in the bitterness of his regret, that he might have braved the whole business of the forgery by making a proper use of his father-in-law and Jenny Edwards.

Myron Finch was a thoroughly miserable man. In addition to the destruction of his constitution by liquor, he had received a sound drubbing from a jealous Spanish-American, whose wife (Finch's washer-woman) he had grossly insulted. In the encounter the bridge of Finch's nose had been broken. He was now so changed in one short year that it is doubtful if even Jenny Edwards could have recognized him. For several weeks he had been confined to his room from the combined effects of the beating and the stimulants, and it required all the physician's skill to subdue the fever and to restore him to a partial state of health. Poverty, like an armed man, stared him in the face, and as he lay on his sick-bed, and found himself sinking lower and lower, and becoming daily poorer and poorer, the desire to return to New York grew into a sort of passion. What he intended to do there, or what was to become of him when he got there, never once entered his mind. In his present mental and physical condition, had he been offered all Peru, with the proviso that he must live in the country for the remainder of his life, he would have indignantly refused the bribe. When so far recovered that he could walk out into the streets and public squares of Lima, the utter loneliness of his situation among thousands of strangers, not one of whom knew him except the sharpers who had cheated and robbed him of his money, was forced home to his heart, stony as it was, with an energy thoroughly depressing. Aimless, sick in body, and suffering tortures from a diseased liver, Finch wandered from his lodgings to the public squares, and from the public squares back to his lodgings. His appetite for drink increased as his appetite for food decreased; and even he knew that a few months more of such a life must inevitably kill him.

In this wretched state of body and mind Finch never felt one pang of remorse for the ruin he had wrought. He thoroughly hated all whom he had wronged—Jenny Edwards, Washington Scroggs, George Bailey, and his own wife and harmless children. Nay, in this dark hour he could have found it in his heart to kill all his victims; and he could have felt an exquisite pleasure in their sufferings and death.

But he sorely missed the excitement of the stock-gambler of Wall Street; of the heavy commission-merchant, whose daily gains or losses amounted to thousands of dollars; of the large dealer in real estate, who doubled his capital every two or three years; and in all these callings Finch remembered to his cost that he had been an expert and a power. Though cold and selfish to the core (as the reader already knows), he sadly missed, too, the yachting parties and the horse racing, together with the general dissipation incident to life in a great city like New York. The craving to return almost crazed him; it haunted him day and night; he would dream that there were high, impassable mountains between him and this paradise of his hopes; and on the summits of these mountains he would fancy that he saw Jenny Edwards and his other victims standing with flaming swords to bar his passage. Out of one of these dreams, which were always superinduced by deep drinking, he would awake in a fright, with the cold perspiration streaming down his flabby face. By-and-by he began to fear that New York was as impossible to him as the moon. But reach New York he must, or die in the attempt. His finances were reduced to fifty dollars, but he still had his wardrobe and his jewellery, and these he could dispose of for about one-fourth of their value.

As soon as he was able to walk with some degree of endurance, he started on foot for Callao, the nearest port where he would be likely to find a vessel bound for the United States. He was afraid to expend a cent of the little money which remained; he lived on the meanest food and slept in the lowest hovels. But, unfortunately for him, no ship appeared. Day after day Finch waited and watched, starved himself to save his passage-money, and lived almost entirely on the single glass of bad brandy which had now become necessary to his existence. But in spite of everything, his money, his trinkets, and his wife's jewellery, which he had stolen, were all gone, and still no ship came to take him away from the accursed country. Had he been willing, he was unable to work. In fact, the once "merchant-prince" was obliged to beg his bit of bread and his glass of brandy in the public streets of Callao; and such was the vile nature of the man that he cursed in his heart alike those who gave and those who refused.

Finch became a fearful spectacle; his clothes became ragged and dirty, his face red and swollen, and his broken nose grew scorbutic and out of all shape. His delicate hands — delicate though dirty — trembled, and his weak limbs shook beneath the weight of his dropsical body. In this condition he daily begged alms at the hotels and gambling-houses; but he was not a smiling, he was a scowling beggar. He begged ungraciously; and he hated the whole race of man with a diabolic hatred. Notwithstanding all these things, the brain of Myron Finch remained uninjured; for the intellectual part of him had been originally of the best material. As he scanned his features in the looking-glasses of the hotels and restaurants in which he plied his vocation as public pauper, he saw how completely changed he was, and rejoiced in the fact, because he knew that if he ever reached New York, his most intimate companion would fail to recognize him. As he wandered along the streets and docks of the city, he reflected that a sea-voyage would improve his health, and that he had ability to carve out another fortune if he could only get back to New York.

At last a ship touched at Callao bound for the Empire City. Finch, who was never at a loss for resources, went boldly to the captain and told a dismal story of shipwreck, and of being picked up by a Spanish-American vessel. When rescued he had been on the point of dying of thirst and hunger; and he had lost everything but the ragged clothes which he then wore. He begged hard for a passage to the United States; told the captain that he would work as cook or waiter, and that he would perform any duty that might be assigned to him. The captain, though doubting the truth of his story, took compassion on him, and gave him permission to work his passage home.

CHAPTER XXI.

"O Love! thou sternly dost thy power maintain,
And wilt not bear a rival in thy reign;
Tyrants and thee all fellowship disdain."—DRYDEN.

GEORGE BAILEY had resumed his position in the banking-house of Warrenton, Wilde & Co.; and although his salary had been largely increased, and although he was now a tried, trusted, and respected clerk, the favorite of Mr. William Wilde, and his son's beloved friend, often invited to dine at their house, and always an honored guest, he still remained at his humble lodgings in the house of his first and firmest friend, John Grady. Bailey seemed to shun all society except that of the Wildes and the few friends whom he met at Grady's house. He had also resumed the habit of going every Sunday to the church which Edith Wilde attended. Sometimes, when leaving, Bailey and she exchanged bows or shook hands, and she always gave him the

sweetest of smiles. The touch of her slender fingers, as before stated, thrilled his frame for a week. To say that he
loved her would but faintly express his feelings; he worshipped her as the personification of goodness; and her
image was ever present to his mind as that of his "guardian angel." She was too good, too high, too holy, he thought,
for him ever to aspire to her hand in marriage. The thought
of ever telling her of his love was, in his estimation, the
very height of absurdity, and appeared, indeed, a kind of
sacrilege: as well make love to one of God's holy angels.

Bailey became a great reader. The Bible and Shakspeare
were his favorite authors. The book of Job he had read
twenty times through; and the plays of Hamlet, Othello,
and Richard the Second had a peculiar charm for him. All
the bad characters, all the villains, became simply so many
types of Myron Finch; all the sweet and lovely women became representatives of Edith Wilde, only they were not quite
up to his idea of the lovely Edith; she excelled them all.

While Bailey could talk well and intelligently on most
subjects in a mixed company—for his thoughts, like those
of men who have suffered much and meditated long in solitude, were very striking and sometimes profound—in Edith
Wilde's presence he found himself silent and embarrassed.
When Walter Wilde would commence at the dinner-table,
for the twentieth time, to tell their adventures on the raft,
and to narrate in glowing language the courage and self-
denial of Bailey, he, Bailey, would endeavor to silence him
or change the subject. To Edith the story was ever new
and always charming. In all sweet and womanly ways
Edith endeavored to make Bailey feel at ease and at home
in their house. But in spite of this, and in spite of her
knowledge of his heart and her own, a singular sort of
estrangement arose, or rather grew, imperceptibly between
them. She was afraid of transgressing the bounds of maid-
enly modesty, and he was in dread that she might discover
the nature of his feelings and be offended at his audacity.
He turned almost sick at the bare idea of the ex-convict,
who had spent ten years in prison, the companion of thieves
and burglars, aspiring to the hand of the rich banker's daugh-

ter—the peerless Edith. Had she been very poor, oh, how
he would love to toil for her! And Edith thoroughly comprehended his modesty, his delicacy, his patience, and his
self-denial; but she could make no advances while he held
his feelings in such complete subjection. His profound respect for her character only added fuel to her love.

Bailey's large salary was far more than enough for his
support; and while saving half of it, he managed to expend
the greater part of the other half on the household of John
Grady, whose *Weekly Reformer* was not in a very thriving
condition. His studies and his love kept his mind and his
heart in a healthy state; for there is no better moral pre-
servative than a pure and holy love. Be it for sister, or
mother, or for one nearer and dearer still, the wholesome
and refining influence of unselfish love is far above all hom-
ilies and sermons. Love is a grand poem. It beautifies and
enlarges to sublimity whatever it touches. True love is true
poetry, because it creates, and combines the real with the
unreal. Even the heart of the peasant who loves purely is
full of unutterable poetry; and, had he the power of expression, he could sing his feelings to the streams, the trees,
and the flowers like a Petrarch or a Burns. To the true,
pure lover the sky is bluer, the grass greener, the flowers
brighter, the brooks clearer, the song of birds sweeter, and
all earth grander and holier for this very love which perme-
ates and thrills every fibre of his being; and man himself,
the last and noblest creation of God, appears in a new light,
and wears an aspect of dignity hitherto unfelt and unseen.
Such a love was Bailey's. It even softened his heart toward Myron Finch, and caused him to turn aside for fear
of treading out the life of a poor worm.

One Sunday, Mr. Wilde at the church door asked George
Bailey home for an early dinner. Of course the invitation
was accepted; and naturally Edith and Bailey walked together a little in the rear of Mr. Wilde and Walter. Their
conversation was commonplace — about the weather, the
service, the sermon—and the lovers felt a certain constraint,
to each almost inexplicable.

About one hundred yards behind them, and on the oppo-

site side of the street, Bailey and Edith were closely and
carefully watched by a lady, who had not missed being at
her post of espionage, within half a street of the church entrance, since the first Sunday after the return of George
Bailey to New York. She had managed to elude observation, and she had invariably covered her face with a thick
veil. Authors are, of course, privileged to know everything,
even the private thoughts of their characters; and hence
we shall take the liberty of revealing the thoughts of Mrs.
Myron Finch, now a free woman, she having obtained her
divorce from her worthy husband. First, it may be stated
that the lady in question, ever since the day that she shook
off the yoke of her brutal helpmate—that is, since the day
he struck her—had grown active, unscrupulous, and selfish.
She had not been in close contact with Finch for ten or
twelve years without suffering from the contamination of
his very presence. There are some people who impart a
moral poison as readily as others do the germs of varioloid
or scarlet-fever; and Mr. Myron Finch was one of these.
He insensibly corrupted his companions, for he was morally rotten; and poor, weak, proud, foolish Grace Van Hess,
under the influence of Finch, degenerated into a cowardly,
selfish, passive creature, until her old love was revived, or
called into activity, by the culmination of her husband's
brutality. But perhaps it is better to reveal her character
in her thoughts:

"How I hate that white-faced creature! What right has
she to his love? Every Sunday I torture myself by watching them. Oh, I could poison her! He is mine: he was
engaged to me. Oh, my God! why, why did I not
stand by him? I could have unravelled that plot and sent
Finch to prison. How she smiles on him! I do hate her!
Oh, I would give my heart's best blood for that look of
love which he has just thrown away on that poor chit of a
thing! How I love him, love him, love him! For one
week of his love I would freely die! But she must not
have him, and she shall not. I will shoot him first, even if
I hang for it! No, no; I must put jealousy between them
—separate them. I must think, think, think!"

So Myron Finch has taught Grace how to think; and
see how wickedly strong her evil passion has made her.
She paused at the street in which Mr. Wilde lived, and never took her eyes off Bailey and Edith until they disappeared within the hall-door.

Among the visitors at the house of Mr. Wilde was an old
school-mate of Walter's, Henry Fawcett, who had just returned from a three years' residence in Europe. Like many
young Americans whose fathers have grown rich in trade,
he was ashamed of the business to which he was indebted
for his education, his station in society, and the means to indulge in foreign travel. Nay, further, he was ashamed of
the institutions which had destroyed the castes of the Old
World, and had enabled his father to rise from the station
he was born in—that of a peddler of vegetables—to be a
railroad manager and a heavy speculator on the Stock Exchange. Mr. Henry Fawcett aped the manners of the
youthful aristocracy of England, and thought it the fashionable thing to condemn universal suffrage, and to advocate the establishment of a limited monarchy modelled after
the plan of the "mauther" country, as he was pleased to
term Great Britain. This young man, with his recently acquired English drawl, was not deficient in brains, nor in a
certain "smartness" of repartee, which sometimes made his
conversation, if not instructive, at least amusing. He had
ability enough to cull out the defects in the American system, and to extol whatever he found superior in the European. He had sense enough, too, to perceive that Edith
Wilde would adorn any position in life, and that she would
inherit the fortune of a princess.

Henry Fawcett had become a frequent visitor at Mr.
Wilde's house; and it was soon observed that Edith was
the attraction. Whatever notions Walter had formed,
when hovering between life and death on the raft, of Bailey's love for his sister, they soon died out after his return
to New York; and as for Mr. William Wilde, he had never
dreamed for one moment of a marriage between his beloved
child and a penniless ex-convict, however high-minded his
conduct might prove him to be. Although not a syllable

had ever been uttered in regard to Mr. Fawcett's attentions to Edith, it was tacitly understood by both father and brother that he was a suitor for her hand. As for Edith herself, she never once imagined that Mr. Fawcett had any other motive in calling than the society of his former friend and school-fellow, Walter.

It had so happened recently, that every time Bailey had called at Mr. Wilde's house, he had found Fawcett there a welcome guest. The case, the elegance, the dash, the flippancy, the cynicism of this young man were a strong contrast in all respects to the bearing, the manners, and the general character of George Bailey. Fawcett termed Bailey a "cad"—a flash word which he had imported, like the cut of his trousers, from the "mauther" country—and this in the hearing of Edith, whose only reply was a frown and a look of extreme displeasure, which the young man remembered for a week. In fact, Bailey and Fawcett disliked each other intensely. Edith very quickly perceived that Henry Fawcett's presence inflicted great pain on her lover; and for this reason she avoided him, Fawcett, as much as good-breeding and the laws of hospitality would permit. If Mr. Fawcett should propose, she would send him about his business in short order; nor would the young man break his heart at a refusal. If Bailey would propose, her acceptance would end his jealousy and make him a happy man. It distressed her exceedingly to know that her lover suffered, and she did all in her power to show him that she sympathized with him.

On one occasion, when Bailey and Fawcett were present, the conversation turned upon the relative merits of American and European society, laws, and institutions; and Mr. Fawcett, as usual, favored everything belonging to the Old World.

"Society," said Mr. Fawcett, "in England is divided into castes, almost as unyielding and unchangeable as those of India, so that the son of a shoemaker cannot aspire to rise above his father's position in life, nor can he hope to associate with the son of a physician; nor can the son of a physician expect to meet on equal terms the son of a nobleman. This is as it ought to be everywhere."

"Then," replied Bailey, with some asperity of tone, "Washington, the greatest uninspired man the world has ever known, should have lived and died a country surveyor; and Lincoln, who will rank next to Washington, according to your theory of castes, should have remained a rail-splitter and a river boatman."

The word "boatman" had smitten hard on the ear of young Fawcett, for his father had commenced life boating vegetables from Staten Island to the city of New York; and if his own theory were good for anything, it would have doomed him to the society of common sailors all his life, instead of associating, as he did now, with Bailey and Wilde, who were born in the purple. Bailey's allusion to Mr. Lincoln was purely accidental, but Fawcett thought otherwise, and took it as a personal insult. He so far forgot himself as to say,

"I beg pawdon; but, aw, such-aw-remawks are moah *ap-wopo* at-aw-demoquatic wad meeting, among the-aw-vulgaw Irish and Germans."

The cool insolence of Fawcett, and the abominable drawl in which he spoke, aroused the wrath of Bailey, who replied,

"Mr. Fawcett, my remarks are true, if trite; and since I am not at a ward meeting, and since I am not a politician, seeking favors from Irish and German voters, allow me to say that your remarks were uncalled for and wholly irrelevant."

"In-deed! Mr. Bailey," said Fawcett, "in-deed I did not intend to have any discussion with *you*."

Whenever Fawcett became angry, he ceased his drawl, his *aws*, and his hesitation, and spoke in quick, curt American fashion, which was unmistakable, like the fine emphasis which he now threw on the word *you*.

"And why not with *me*, sir?" demanded Bailey, a slight flush overspreading his usually pale features.

"Well, sir, I would rather not discuss - aw - aw" (insolently returning to his drawl) "pubwick affairahs with *you*."

"I would like to know," asked Bailey, "why you do not desire to discuss public affairs with *me*?"

Mr. Wilde interposed, thinking it high time to put an end to the altercation. He simply said, "Gentlemen, we must all agree to differ; we have our fixed opinions on many subjects, but that is no reason why we should quarrel. Let us change the subject." And so the conversation turned to matters which caused Mr. Wilde to be the principal speaker.

Bailey and Fawcett disliked each other even more intensely than before, for each imagined that the other had covertly stabbed him in a tender place. The former was unduly sensitive about his conviction for forgery, and fancied that for that reason the latter had declined a discussion with *him.*

Edith was thoroughly distressed. She had learned to read every thought in the heart of Bailey by the expression of his face, and she failed not to perceive how deeply he was wounded. How she longed to console the sad, lonely man, and by womanly tenderness to make amends for the wrongs and sufferings of his youth and early manhood! Fawcett was a conceited bore, in her estimation, and she wished him a thousand miles away from her father's house.

Bailey almost vowed, on taking his leave, to refuse all invitations in future, and never again to enter the house; for during the entire afternoon and evening he had been very unhappy, and consumed by a jealousy which would drive him mad. He would continue to love Edith in the solitude of his chamber; and he would endeavor to see her every Sunday, and feast his eyes on her good and beautiful face. All thought or jealousy of Fawcett he would expel from his mind; he would fall back on the past, as a refuge from the present, and think only of his "guardian angel," who had succored his mother and himself in the darkest hour of his distress. In this frame of mind he reached his humble lodgings in the home of John Grady. But what was his astonishment to find a note for him, written in a hand which was curiously familiar, and which he could not recall. He looked for the signature, but name there was none. The note ran as follows:

"Mr. Geo. Bailey,—You are grossly deceived: you deceive yourself. Miss Wilde esteems you as a friend, nothing more. She loves Mr. Henry Fawcett. They are engaged, or soon will be. He is rich; you are poor. Don't be so foolish as to think Mr. Wilde would permit his daughter to marry *you*. Excuse an anonymous note, but necessity forces me to remain your unknown   Friend."

Bailey read this precious note over half a dozen times, and each time he came very near detecting the strangely familiar handwriting. Evidently it was partially disguised by slanting the letters toward the left, making it what is sometimes termed back-handed writing. He was too wise a man to pay attention to an anonymous letter; and in an ordinary case of business, or even in his usual state of mind, he would have cast it into the fire; but now, in his present agitated condition, it affected him exceedingly, because the tenor of the note bore directly on the nature and tendency of his own thoughts.

He refolded the note and put it in his pocket. For hours afterward he sat gazing into the fire, a thoroughly miserable man. He regretted that he had not died on the raft. He might then have sent Edith a message of love, just as he was leaving this world to meet his mother in a better. That night he dreamed that he and Edith Wilde were on board the raft, and that one of the hungry sailors who wanted to kill and eat her was—not the Portuguese, but Mr. Henry Fawcett!

Chapter XXII.

"The animal with long ears, after having drunk, gives a kick to the bucket."—*From the Italian.*

It was a delightful afternoon in the season of the Indian summer. The sky was a deep blue, streaked here and there with purple clouds, behind which could be seen many a delicate tint, to which no artist's brush could ever do full justice. The sun was slowly sinking toward the south-west, and there was a roseate tinge in his rays which cast a mellow beauty on all they touched.

On the afternoon in question a dirty, bloated, red-faced man, clad in a ragged, greasy suit of clothes, which had once been fashionable, might have been seen slowly walking up Third Avenue, in the city of New York, and carefully examining, with weak, watery eyes, the sign-boards of all the corner groggeries which he passed. His gait was uncertain and shambling, his knees seemed to tremble beneath his weight, and he walked like a man whose feet were very sore. As he raised his hand to shade his eyes from the rays of the sinking sun, it might have been noticed that that hand was comparatively white and delicately formed, and that it had never been accustomed to heavy manual labor. His hair was long and unkempt, of a dirty dry brown, and hung in straggling locks down his neck and cheeks. His face was covered with a beard of about two weeks' growth; and if he wore any linen it was completely hidden by a red "muffler," like those worn by sailors in severe weather. Altogether he was a most wretched-looking tramp. As he carefully scanned the sign-boards his lips moved as if uttering imprecations, and the expression of his hard, cruel face was not a pleasant thing to look at. He had painfully pursued his weary way up as far as Thirtieth Street, but had not been able to discover the name which he wanted. He had already been at a groggery near the East River, having ascertained the address from a directory, but his toilsome journey had been in vain, for the person of whom he was in quest had moved up town on the first of May last. The patience of the tramp was almost exhausted, as, after searching the sign-boards of all the "wine-merchants" once more, he muttered to himself, "It must be somewhere about here that the infernal scoundrel holds forth and retails his poisons. Let me see—Thirtieth Street, Fortieth Street, Fiftieth Street— How tired I am! Not a cent—not one red cent!" And here the poor wretch swore some oaths which it is better to suppress. "How tired and foot-sore I am! I am dying for a glass of brandy. I wonder if one of these cursed Irishmen would give me a

13

glass of whiskey? The last place I tried the brute of a barkeeper threatened to kick me out for disgracing his place, and called me thief and tramp."

"Say, Boss," addressing a young man with a clear, healthy face, who had evidently avoided his own poisonous compounds—"say, Boss, for God's sake give me a glass of liquor? I am weak, and dying for the want of a little stimulant."

The young man eyed him for a moment, and noted his hands, and clothes of fashionable cut, though greasy and in tatters. After a pause of a minute or two he replied,

"Well, I don't know: it seems to me that you have seen better days, old man. I suppose you would like 'a hair of the dog that bit you.' What 'ud you like?"

"Anything strong—the stronger the better," replied the tramp.

The young man handed him a decanter containing a liquid labelled "Jamaica Rum," which the tramp seized with an eager, trembling hand, and lifting a tumbler in the other hand, poured out a very large quantity for a single drink —so large, indeed, that the generous youth was forced to say, "See here, old man, haven't you taken a leetle more than's good for you?"

To this remark the tramp made no reply; but looking at the glass with a gleam in his watery eye as ardent as the liquor itself, he drank off the whole of it in a single gulp. Its fiery strength caused the tears to roll down his dirty, flabby cheeks, and made him smack his lips as if the poison had been the very elixir of life. It was a very painful sight to see this man vainly trying to hide with his fingers the double quantity of rum which he intended to take.

"Young man," said the tramp, "do you know a man in your line named Timothy Quin?"

"Do I know Tim Quin? Why, this is one of Quin's stores: he has half a dozen stores like this. But he is not now in the retail trade; he manifacters."

"Distils, you mean," said the tramp.

"I mane what I say—he manifacters."

"Manufactures what?"

"Manifacters everythin' drinkable, even that Jamakey that you've just drunk," replied the temperate youth.

"Do you never drink anything yourself?" asked the tramp, now comfortably seated on the head of a whiskey-cask, and expecting to be asked to take another drink.

"No, sir-e-e! Catch me drinkin' poisons! They are very good to sell—very profitable, do ye see—but very bad, as the doctors say, for digesching."

"Does Quin drink, himself?" inquired the tramp.

"Oh yes, of course," replied the young man; "but out of private bottles of genuwine liquor. He don't drink sich stuff as this."

"Is Quin very rich?" asked the tramp.

"Now see here, old man, you're mighty smart; you'd better clear out before our reg'lar customers begin to come."

"Boss," said the tramp, in a wheedling tone, "couldn't you give a poor fellow another dose of that poison—a poor fellow who would like to end his sufferings in a sea of good liquor?"

The young bartender, anxious to get rid of the disreputable tramp, took down the decanter and poured out a very large glass, and handing it to the tramp, said,

"Here, throw this down your throat and clear out: my customers will soon be here."

The tramp seized the glass, scanned it with one eye partially closed, with the air of a connoisseur, gloated for a moment over it, as if prolonging the pleasure by a little anticipation, and then swallowed it, as before, without water and in a single gulp. The tramp leaned his elbow on the bar, slowly laid the glass down without removing his dirty fingers from it, and with a half-drunken, cunning leer, said,

"Young man, you had better keep a civil tongue in your head, for I know your master well; he is a very old friend of mine; he was once my servant—do you hear? He was once my servant. And what are you? Nothing but a miserable Irish rumseller. If you don't hand me out another glass of that poison, I'll tell my friend Quin how you have characterized his noble business of distilling."

At first the young man was lost in amazement at the ingratitude, and then he grew angry at the insolence, of the filthy wretch whom he had condescended to notice. Placing his hand lightly on the bar, and vaulting over it with ease, he seized the tramp by the collar of his greasy coat, and administering to him several severe kicks, hurled him headlong into the street.

"There now, ye ungrateful cur, take that for yer impidence !"

Muttering horrid imprecations in a half-drunken undertone, the tramp picked himself up as best he could, and was endeavoring to make his escape through the crowd, which seemed to spring out of the sidewalk at the noise of the row, when a policeman came to his rescue, or that might have been the last of Myron Finch (for such was the tramp, as the reader has long ago seen); for the bartender had explained to the crowd the tramp's abuse of the Irish people, and this is something that the Irish do not readily condone or forgive.

The policeman had no excuse for arresting Finch; for, though half drunk as to his limbs, his head was as clear as a bell. Finch wandered on and on, examining the signs, by the aid of the gas-light, for the name of Timothy Quin, "wine-merchant." Finally, after walking about a mile north of the scene of his encounter with the temperate rumseller, he espied a man alighting from a wagon, whom he instantly recognized as his former confederate in crime. For fear he might lose sight of him in the darkness, in the house, or in the liquor-store, Finch ran with all the speed his trembling limbs would permit, and hailed Mr. Quin as he was entering the "store." Quin paused, looked carefully around, and seeing no one save the dirty, ragged wretch before him, he accosted him in no very pleasant tone of voice:

"Who are ye? an' what do ye want?"

"Don't you know me, Mr. Quin? Look closely at me: search my features—listen to my voice—surely you know me?"

Quin examined the tramp from head to foot; he glanced at his broken nose, his red, pimpled face, and his bloated body; he noticed his trembling hands; but in the dim light of the store-window he failed to recognize his old employer.

"Walk into the store," said Finch, "and see if you cannot recognize an unfortunate friend."

The two men walked up to the bar, and steadily gazed in each other's face; and still Quin was unable to trace in the face and form of the wreck before him the once dashing and wealthy Myron Finch.

"Mr. Quin," said Finch, "if you have no objection, I would like to steady my nerves with a glass of brandy, for I am weak and hungry."

Quin eyed the ragged tramp uneasily, and failed not to catch below the husky voice the tone and language of a man used to good society—at least, of a man who had received a good education. Had it not been for the change of voice caused by the inordinate use of strong drink, doubtless Finch would have been recognized in a moment. Quin noticed the hands of the tramp, and began to suspect a detective; for ever since the capture of the forgery-practice papers he has feared arrest as *particeps criminis*. Quin, even as porter, had proved himself observant and cunning; and his subsequent training, as the founder of rum-shops and the manager of political societies, had sharpened his wits and blunted his conscience. He had grown rich, and as his wealth increased his appetite to add to it became voracious. The more money he made the more he wanted; hence his attempt two years ago to extort, in the form of black-mail, a very large sum from Finch. While Timothy Quin was pondering over these matters, Myron Finch was waiting for his glass of brandy to steady his nerves.

"Mr. Quin," repeated Finch, "I greatly need a little liquor; for, as I said a moment ago, I am both weak and hungry."

Quin, starting out of a reverie, ordered Patrick, the man behind the bar, to produce his best brandy. From some hidden recess below the bar Patrick brought forth a bottle of genuine imported brandy, which was always kept in reserve for the "wine-merchant" and his particular friends.

Quin took little more than a thimbleful, while Finch nearly filled a large tumbler, which he drank off undiluted. Evidently Timothy Quin was resolved to bring this matter to
a close; so, with sundry oaths which we take the liberty of
suppressing, he demanded,

"Now that you have had your skinful of good liquor, I
want to know who ye are and what ye want?"

"Mr. Quin," said Finch, in a deprecatory tone, "there is
a back-room—can you not step in there and hear me out?
Will you please hear my story in private?"

"Now, see here; I don't know what right ye have to tell
me any story. I don't undherstan' what business ye can
have wid me. But we may as well ind it here an' now; so
step in here—we'll be alone."

Finch could have had no private interview with Quin had
it not been for the nameless fear of a detective, already alluded to. Quin was naturally a low-born tyrant, and thoroughly despised rags and poverty; hence, under ordinary
circumstances, the dirty tramp would have been hustled
head-foremost out of the "store." The worthy pair now
entered the little back-room, usually devoted to gambling on
a small scale—to "forty-fives" for drinks all round. Finch
carefully closed the door, and then took his seat in front of
Quin at the little round gaming-table which, with a few
wooden chairs, constituted the entire furniture of the room.
There were two or three very cheap pictures of prize-fight-
ers, in very cheap frames, ornamenting the whitewashed
walls. Something in the wary closing of the door, something in the stealthy step, albeit a little shaky, and something in the cunning expression of the pale, watery eyes,
recalled to Quin's mind a vague recollection of some one
whom he had known before; but still he failed to place
him—he could not possibly identify him.

Again the two men looked at each other long and steadily. Finally Finch raised his torn and battered felt hat,
revealing a brow as white as a lady's—a broad, high brow,
which seemed to have escaped the general ruin of the remainder of his body. The contrast between the upper and
lower portions of his head and face was startling.

"Mr. Quin," said Finch, after removing the old hat, and with a voice and manner quite histrionic, for Finch was nothing if not a first-class hypocrite, "Mr. Quin, the unfortunate man before you is—Myron Finch!"

Finch folded his arms and awaited the result. All Quin could utter, so complete was his amazement, was,

"My God! my God! Can I b'lieve me eyes? You Misther Finch? you—you?"

"Yes, you know me—you know me. I see it in your eyes that you recognize me."

"How, in the name of Heaven," said Quin, "have ye fallen so low? Ye must have taken away wid ye at laste a hundthred tousand dollars. Where has the money gone to?"

"It would be a long story," replied Finch, "and I am not in a fit condition to tell it to-night. Some other time I shall tell you all. Suffice it now that I felt very lonely among strangers, who spoke a strange language, and I took to drink and gambling. I was fleeced out of my money, abused and beaten, had my nose broken, as you may see, and I was left for dead at my hotel. When a man gambles, Mr. Quin, he cannot afford to drink; I drank relying upon my ability to bear it, but I was mistaken, and lost. The more I lost the more I drank, and the more I drank the more I lost. It did not take very long to exhaust my exchequer."

"Your what?" asked Quin.

"My money-bags. In fact, I found myself a beggar in Callao, and was obliged, after much solicitation, to work my passage to New York as assistant-steward on the ship. Now you have in outline my misadventures since I absconded two years ago. But it was not to speak of these matters that I called to see you: I have other business."

One by one Quin was able to recall the features of his old employer. Timothy was not a man of very nice moral perceptions, and he had never been over-scrupulous about his methods of making an honest penny; still, he was not actually cruel by nature, like Finch; nor was he deficient in kindly feeling, if it did not mar his material interests. He was really sorry for the miserable wreck before him. Per-

haps he remembered that it was the thousand dollars given
him by Finch for his aid in effecting the forgery which
gave him, Quin, his first start in life as a "wine-merchant;"
or perhaps he may have recollected that it was his attempt
to levy black-mail which was the beginning of Finch's misfortunes; or, being vain of his wealth and prosperity, his
vanity may have been gratified at patronizing his former
master. From whatever motive—and it may have been
from a combination of motives—Quin was influenced, he
resolved to aid—judiciously, of course—Mr. Myron Finch
to get on his legs again.

After gazing a long time at Finch in silence, Quin arose,
and opening the door, cried out,

"Patrick, ordher from the restherant beefsteak and onions for two; and bring in a bottle of 'Mum,' and a bottle
of the best brandy—the very best, mind ye." As he resumed his seat, he continued: "So the black divils of Spaniards were too smart for ye, an' got howld of all yer money,
did they?"

"I don't know about that," replied Finch. "'Whoever
sups with the devil ought to have a long spoon.' I short-
ened my spoon by drinking, and you see the consequences.
It might have been different had I not met that man Bailey. He and a companion of his were on the point of
death, when, as ill-luck would have it, we picked them up
and took them to Chili. I was afraid he would recognize
me; and hence I fled from city to city and became a—
drunkard. But I am going to reform, and make another
fortune."

By this time the beefsteak and onions, the champagne
and brandy, were before this precious pair. Quin, like the
majority of his class, was temperate from sheer selfishness,
and ate little and drank less. Finch did not eat much, but
drank greedily. Liquor might deprive him of his power
of locomotion, but could not wholly deprive him of his native craft and mental power.

"Mr. Quin," said Finch, after a long silence and deep
thought, "what became of those papers which you kindly
showed me the last time we had the honor of dining to-

gether? Do you know who holds them? Did Grady ever threaten to use them?"

"Come, Finch," said Quin, in an angry tone, "no more of that! I'm now a rich man, an' I want no more schames and thrasons. I'm not agoin' to play wid fire no more. I'm willin' to help ye, but not in that way."

Finch gave Quin one of his old, quick glances of deadly hatred, as he replied,

"I don't want you to join in anything of the kind. I merely desire to know if they can use those papers against me."

"For some rason," said Quin, "Grady does not wish to punish or purshue ye; an' sence his frind Bailey is med all right, an' howlds a good place wid Warrenton, Wilde & Co., I think that no attimpt will be med to harm ye; that is, me boy, if ye keep quiet, and play no more of yer ould thricks."

Finch reflected for a few moments before he asked, "Have you heard of a young woman named Miss Edwards in connection with Grady?"

"Once or twice," replied Quin, "Grady mintioned her name. You remimber you saw her whin I was so dhrugged, ye rascal, that I knew nothin' until the next day."

"Have you ever heard of my wife or her father?" Finch asked, with a peculiar look.

"Not much. I hard that she got a divorce, and that ould Van Hess has gone to the dogs. He does some commission business, but not much. He sold his grand house on Fifth Avenue, an' now lives in simple sthyle on one of the crass-sthreets."

Considerably refreshed, and having obtained the information he sought, Finch, fearful of trespassing on the kindness of his friend, arose to take his leave. He paused, hesitated, and finally managed to say,

"I beg pardon, Mr. Quin; you have treated me very kindly; but I have not a cent in the world. Could you lend me ten dollars?"

Quin, proud of his superiority, and with an air of patronage, replied,

"My dear Finch" (he dropped the Mr.), "you must
promise me to dhrink no more bad liquor: you may dhrink
two or three glasses of good stuff; an' ate, man—ate good
hearty food—three square males a day, an' build yerself up.
Why should ye go to the dogs? Here's the loan of twinty
dollars; an' if ye keep sober, come to me at the ind of a
week an' I'll thry and put a dacent shuit of clo'es on yer
back, an' give ye one more chance to mek yer forthin—but
in an honest way, moind ye—ha! ha! ha!"

This honest way, according to the code of morals pursued by Timothy Quin, was to get all the money he could,
by hook or by crook, without laying himself liable in law.
Finch understood him; pocketed the twenty dollars; promised to keep sober; took his leave with many protestations
of gratitude; ducked into another corner groggery about
one hundred yards from Quin's; called for a glass of brandy;
had his twenty-dollar bill converted into small bills and silver; jumped, under the impetus of liquor, into a Third Avenue car, and took a seat in the corner.

"Blast the impudence and ignorance of this low Irishman!" muttered the grateful Finch. "Patronizing me!
Giving me advice! But wait! I must restrain this horrible thirst for rum; for if I do not, I am a lost man. I must
build myself up, that I may tear others down. Oh, faugh!
How I detest that vulgar Irishman! How I detest them
all! So Jenny Edwards would not let that brute of an un-
cle-in-law publish to the world my forgery. Ah! Jenny,
my dear, you have not yet forgotten your first love—what
woman ever does? Jenny, my sweet lady, you have saved
money, and I need some of it. Let me see! I have two
trump cards to play—the divorce and Jenny. And why
couldn't I marry Jenny? She's clever, and that my late
wife never was." Thus soliloquizing, and planning for the
future, this intellectual fiend, who seemed superior to a
quantity of liquor that would have made three ordinary
men intoxicated, took lodgings in a humble boarding-house
in the Bowery, near its junction with Chatham Street.

Chapter XXIII.

"Blow, blow, thou winter wind,
Thou art not so unkind
As man's ingratitude."—Shakspeare.

The next morning Finch lay wide awake in his filthy bed, thinking deeply. He had to struggle against the thirst for liquor, which increased with tenfold force now that he had the means to gratify it. He resisted the craving with all his might, for he clearly perceived that if he continued his present mode of living his days were numbered. To begin life anew he must have all his wits about him; he must keep sober and improve his general health. Reflecting upon his past career, he discovered the one weak point which had ruined all; and that was, trusting a confidant and having an ally in Timothy Quin. Had he ruined George Bailey without assistance—and surely he should have been able to do so—trouble could not have overtaken him. And how careless it was to drop those torn practice-papers into the waste-basket, and thus give that cunning knave, Quin, a power over him!

Engaged in these reflections, and forming these resolutions, he arose with a fearful headache, and went down to the common eating-room, one of the meanest of its kind, and ordered very strong coffee in lieu of his morning dram of brandy. He then entered a second-hand clothing store in Chatham Street and bought, for ten dollars, a suit of half-worn black. As he passed the flaring grog-shops his appetite for liquor almost overcame him; and at the sight of the bottles in the windows his pale eyes glistened, and his frame shook with the effort to abstain. Once he actually reached the door of a vile "bucket-shop" in Mulberry Street; but by a superhuman effort he tore himself away. Here was a singular phenomenon—a thoroughly wicked man, who never scrupled at any crime to advance his interests, endeavoring, with great force of will, to conquer an insatiable desire for strong drink, and manifesting in the fight a firmness of purpose which would have done honor to a man of noble nature who had unfortunately contracted the bad habit. To assist his will, he plunged several times into the coffee-and-cake cellars, and drank cup after cup of strong coffee—at least, the strongest which was for sale in such places.

The craving for liquor somewhat appeased, he resumed his reflections. He recalled what Quin had told him the evening before; and he remembered that Jenny had saved him from arrest. He had ascertained her address; and, fully convinced that she still loved him, he determined to visit her; and in order to work on her sympathies, he would present himself before her in his dirt and rags. Leaving his bundle of newly-bought second-hand clothes in his lodgings, he went to the hotel in which Jenny was employed, and inquired for Miss Edwards, informing the clerk that her aunt in Williamsburgh was dying, and that he was sent in haste to inform her. Finch well knew that, except in case of life and death, he could gain no admittance, in his present plight, into any decent hotel. Hence, poor Mrs. John Grady was put in a dying condition for the occasion. As Finch stood at the end of a long corridor, greasy hat in hand, waiting for Jenny, his white forehead and white bald head presented such a contrast to the red, pimpled face and broken nose, covered with brandy-blotches, that he looked like a man whose head was made of two separate and distinct halves welded together. The moment Jenny Edwards laid her eyes on him, through dirt and rags, through blotches and pimples, through unkempt hair and unshaven face, she recognized the man who had won her virgin heart. All the dye, all the paint, all the liquor stains in the world could never disguise Myron Finch from Jenny Edwards. Had he been away from her sixty years—were he tottering into the grave, an old man—some trick of eye, or foot, or hand, some little tone of voice, unnoticed by the world at large, would have revealed to her the man who was once dearer to her than her own soul.

"My God! Myron Finch, what brings you here? What

can you want with *me?*" asked Jenny, in a cold, surprised tone, and with an expression of trouble and pain in her eye and over her pale face.

Finch hung his head, and nervously twitched the brim of his old soft hat, as he replied in broken accents, "Jenny—you see—a thoroughly ruined man—before you—without a friend in the—wide world!" And the wretch made the tears flow down his flabby cheeks.

"Whose fault is it, pray, that you have not a friend in the world? But, I repeat, what do you want with *me?* What brings you here?"

"I am sick: I have neither house—nor home—nor a cent to buy a loaf of bread. Oh, Jenny, have some pity for me! I know I have been wicked, and treated you badly; but I am so sorry for it—so—" And Finch burst into tears, and tried to hide them with an old dirty red pocket-handkerchief.

"Enough of this—that will do!" said Jenny, somewhat sharply. "This play cannot go on here! Once more I repeat, what do you want with *me?*"

"Jenny, you are very hard on a poor broken-down fellow who is almost at death's door."

"Hard on you?" replied Jenny, with a look of infinite scorn not unmingled with pity. "Were I hard on you, I would—well, no matter what. Myron Finch, we cannot stand talking here in this corridor, attracting the attention of the servants."

"We can take a walk outside, if you please," said Finch, in an insinuating tone; "for I told the clerk that your aunt was very ill, and desired to see you. We need not go out together. I will meet you at the junction of Chatham Street and the Bowery."

"At your lies again!"

"Without this harmless lie I could not have seen you."

"Harmless lie? there's no such thing! But go; I'll follow you in five minutes."

While Jenny was putting on her hat and shawl, she reflected that Finch, being freed by the divorce, could now marry her and satisfy her conscience. If the wedding cer-

emony were once performed a load would be lifted from
her heart. Of course, the wealth of the universe could not
have bribed her to live with Finch one hour as his wife;
but she was resolved that the sin of thirteen years ago
must be washed out by a marriage ceremony, performed
by a minister of the Gospel. Jenny thoroughly believed
in the Ten Commandments—every one of them without ex-
ception—and had a clear, practical, New England way of
calling things by their right names.

When she had overtaken Finch at the appointed place
she said, "Come, be brief; tell me what you want, for I
shall leave you at the ferry."

"You know what I want—I want a loan of a little
money. If I had not been so horribly sick and reduced
I would not have troubled you. I am now sorry that I
called, for you are very hard on me—very hard!" And
Finch sobbed.

"Why don't you reform, and go to work like a man?
See what your crimes have brought you to!"

"I know—I know it," said Finch, "and I shall reform; I
shall indeed; and make atonement to you for the wrong I
did you."

"No, no, no! Myron Finch, you can make no atonement
to me; make an atonement to your God. Repent, and
abandon your evil ways. Ah!" said Jenny, in a tone half
to him and half in soliloquy, "ah! did you but know the
torture, the horrid, horrid torture which I endured when
you abandoned me in this great strange city; how I
writhed in an agony of superlative misery; how my
withered heart slowly turned to stone; how I prayed for
death; how my religion would not permit me to die by
my own hand; how I hoped against hope, day after day,
watching out of the window and listening to every step on
the stair, hoping and cursing and praying—oh, the horror
of those weeks!" and Jenny shut her eyes and shivered at
the very recollection of them. "How I survived I know
not. I think it was owing to the religious instruction
which I had received in youth that, when basely abandoned by you, I turned to my Saviour and he sent his

Comforter. I arose from a sick bed, resolved to work and do my duty to the best of my ability. No, no, no! Myron Finch, you can make no atonement to me. You might as well try to restore the plucked and trampled rose. Would to God I had died believing in your truth and goodness—died in that New England village where I worshipped you, Myron Finch, as the embodiment of all that was noble and intellectual!" The tone of sadness in which this was uttered would have melted a heart of stone. It did not melt Finch's, for the simple reason that he had none to melt. He was calculating how fast Jenny's reminiscences were causing her heart to melt toward him, and how many dollars this melting mood would put in his pocket. He, therefore, thought it wiser not to interrupt her. "Man, man," continued Jenny, "you never knew what you threw away! What was Grace Van Hess's love to mine?—a rush-light to the sun! I could have lifted you to heights of honor that that poor creature never dreamed of. Bah! you deserve it all. You married a poor weak thing, who had not the courage or the decency to stand by her true and noble lover, whom your villany sent to State-prison. And as for you, she never cared a fig for you. You had hardly fled, Bailey had hardly obtained a good situation, when she hurried through her divorce in the hope that he would marry her. Marry her? He would marry first the lowest strumpet who prowls the back slums of the city. But, Heaven help me, I am the last who have the right to speak in this way!"

Finch was sharp enough to read Jenny's heart in this outburst against his late wife, and to profit by the knowledge.

"Jenny, as God is my judge, I never loved that woman. I only married her for her father's money."

"So much the worse for you!" Although Jenny said this, in her secret heart she was glad to hear that he had never loved his wife.

"I have been a very bad man, I admit," said Finch. "I know how wickedly I have treated you. Away down in strange lands, when I was sick and thought myself dying, I had time to reflect. Oh, Jenny, you are the only woman whom I ever loved! can you not be a little less harsh with me? One of my reasons for coming back to New York, and running the risk of imprisonment for life, was to seek you and ask your forgiveness. But you are very harsh with me."

In spite of herself, in spite of her knowledge of his character, she was considerably softened. The man was poor, ragged, dirty, and sick; she had once loved him. Her woman's pity surged up in her heart at the sight of his wretchedness.

"Harsh! harsh!" said Jenny, "why, if I had been harsh, did I not permit John Grady to have you arrested when we had the evidence of your forgery in our hands? Myron Finch, I once loved you; that love has turned to disgust, and I despise you; and yet, because of this former feeling, I would save you, if I could, from eternal perdition."

Finch, instead of recoiling from the woman who reviled him in such terms, wriggled up closer and closer until he touched her hand, and said, "Jenny Edwards, I love you still. I love you only in all the earth. In my misery and loneliness I seek you out. Forgive me; forgive me! Can we not be happy, in spite of the past?"

"Myron Finch," said Jenny, in a stern tone, "hands off! Touch me not! Your touch is contamination!"

Finch slunk back, giving her a sidelong glance full of malice and vindictiveness.

"Well, well; I see you dislike me—hate me—will not forgive me. This is my last attempt. I'll now try my late wife; perhaps she will not be so obdurate. At any rate, she can treat me no worse than you."

Finch eyed her closely and furtively to see the effect of this last shot, but it entirely failed of its mark; for Jenny was too well aware of Mrs. Finch's passion for George Bailey, and knew full well that while he lived Finch had no chance in that quarter. How Jenny Edwards learned everything concerning Grace Finch, and how Grace Finch learned everything about Edith Wilde, is a female mystery which we shall not try to fathom at present.

"Go to your late wife," said Jenny, "and see if she will treat you any better than I have done. But why talk in this way about your late wife? I understand you—I am no child. Go to work, as I said before, like a man: reform, repent! All I have in the world I would give freely to make you a good, honest man."

"What would you have a fellow to do, I repeat, who is sick, houseless, homeless, hungry, without a stitch of decent clothing to his back, without a cent in his pocket to buy his dinner? Good God! woman, have mercy on a fellow!"

Disgusted, and yet full of compassion, Jenny drew out her pocket-book and handed him fifty dollars.

"Here," said she, "go and buy yourself a decent suit of clothes in which you can look for employment. When you are reformed come and see me again, but not before. Go, go!"

The mean hound grabbed the money, and actually counted it in her presence. His watery eyes gloated over it, before he hid it away with what remained of Quin's twenty dollars. The vulture-like avidity with which he had seized her hard-earned money was extremely painful to Jenny Edwards. As she walked away from him, the tears fell thick and fast as she soliloquized:

"Poor wretch! poor wretch! How fallen! how low! And this is all that remains of my *hero?* And yet I would give my heart's blood to make him such a man as George Bailey!"

Finch soliloquized too: "Work be hanged! How can I work? She has plenty of money saved, and I must have my share of it. This is a mine, and I'll work it."

Ah, Jenny, Jenny! by what strange circumstances do heroic women like you fall into the hands of such ghouls as Myron Finch, and frivolous wax-dolls become the idols of the most chivalrous men?

14

Chapter XXIV.

"Vice stings us, even in our pleasures."—Colton.

It was seven o'clock in the evening of the day that My-ron Finch had wheedled out of Jenny Edwards fifty dollars of her hard-earned money, and Mr. Jacob Van Hess, his daughter, and his two grandchildren were seated after din-ner in the dining-room. The old gentleman was trying to read, amidst the clamor and squabbling of the two children, the condition of the stock-market, as recorded in the *Even-ing Post.* Mrs. Finch was vainly endeavoring to prevail upon her son, a boy of twelve years of age, to study his lessons for the morrow. Myron Finch, Jr., was a faithful copy of his sire in form, in color, and in disposition, but not in intellect, for in this he had caught his mother's weakness.

"What's the use of them books?" he petulantly asked his mother, tossing his head from side to side with a strong expression of disapproval. "You won't let a fellow read 'The Boy Robber of the Red River.' That's a bully book! He shot his dad in the knee for lickin' him when he was only thirteen—one year older than me."

"Hush, hush, Myron! your grandfather will hear you, and be angry. Take your books this instant and study your lessons, or I'll whip you and send you to bed."

"Well, wait until I am a few years older," replied the amiable lad, "and I'd like to see any one—"

"Ma! ma! won't you make Myron stop pinching me?" screamed the little sister. "I do believe he has pinched a piece out of my arm!"

"Children, keep quiet," said the grandfather, over his spectacles. "Grace, if those children cannot keep quiet, send them directly to bed. They disturb me—annoy me; they are always quarrelling."

At this the young Myron stuck his tongue in his cheek and winked villanously at his little sister.

"Ma! ma! won't you make Myron stop?"

But Myron simply made a grimace more wicked than the one that preceded it. Ah, verily, "Their fathers have eaten sour grapes, and the children's teeth are on edge!"

In the mean time the father of this hopeful student of "The Boy Robber of the Red River," having refrained all day from drinking strong liquor, and having now in his possession what appeared to him a very large sum of money (for everything in this world is relative), and excellent prospects of making more in a like easy fashion, resolved, "just this once," to treat resolution, and indulge himself in one or two glasses of brandy, for the purpose of steadying his nerves for another pecuniary raid.

He plunged into one of the low dens near the ferry and drank twice in succession. Like the tiger's taste for blood, the taste of the drunkard is only whetted by a little liquor. There never was a better maxim for the dipsomaniac than, "Touch not, taste not, handle not;" and Finch knew it as well as any man living. But this "just once" was his ruin. For half an hour, while walking toward Broadway, he fought against the craving for more liquor; but the insatiable desire overcame his resolution. Again he entered a low groggery and drank a large glass of Jamaica rum, that being, in his estimation, the most fiery liquor in the market. Although his limbs trembled and his hands shook, his brain was untouched; and he entered Broadway making most heroic efforts to steady himself, and wondering why he always became drunk in his legs, and not in his head, like most men.

In Broadway he saw a sight which nearly sobered him; he saw George Bailey and Walter Wilde walking up that fashionable street arm-in-arm, and chatting pleasantly on the affairs of the day. Of course, neither recognized in the dirty, ragged wretch before them their fellow-passenger, Alexander Brown. As they overtook him, Walter Wilde remarked to his companion,

"What a wretched creature! Just see what rum will bring a man to!"

"Yes, yes," replied Bailey; "but who knows the trials

and temptations that led him to such a state? God help us all! I was once sorely tempted myself. My sufferings have taught me one good lesson—charity for the fallen."

Finch overheard the conversation, and instead of feeling grateful for the compassionate language, and still more compassionate tone of voice, he cursed Bailey again and again, and hated the man most intensely because he had injured him.

When Bailey and Wilde were lost in the crowd, Finch plunged into another basement groggery near Broadway, and, uttering internal imprecations, drank off two more glasses of Jamaica rum to console himself for the sight he had just witnessed. "Now," said he to himself, "I am in fit condition to see my late wife and father-in-law, and make them 'bleed.' It will be no paltry fifty dollars this time."

A remarkable feature in this man's character was that he never once thought of his children; and in this respect he was below the brute. When a man once abandons principle, and thinks of nothing but the gratification of his selfish appetites, the very reason which, rightly directed, elevates him to an equality with the angels, enables him to think thoughts and do deeds that would shame the very lowest of the brute creation.

There was a ring at the door-bell of Jacob Van Hess's house. Susie O'Neil, the only servant of all work, answered it. She saw by the dim light of the hall a dirty, ragged man, with a strong odor of bad liquor on his breath, standing in the vestibule, and surveying him for an instant she exclaimed, "No-o-o!"

"I wish to see your master," said the tramp.

"You can't see him. Go 'way; we never gives anything to tramps nor beggars."

"I am neither a tramp nor a beggar, you impertinent flunkey!"

In the mean time the tramp had insinuated his body so far inside the door that Susie could not shut it; she was, therefore, obliged to call out, "Mr. Van Hess! there's a tramp in the hall that won't go 'way! Please come here an' put him out!"

Mrs. Finch went up-stairs with the two children; and the husband and father saw them as they passed. Mr. Van Hess accosted the tramp in an angry tone,

"Well, sir, what do you want here? Leave my premises, or I'll call a policeman."

"Mr. Jacob Van Hess, I warn you that you had better not," said the tramp, in an insolent voice.

"Why not? why not? Susie, call a police-officer this instant! Do you mean to rob me—murder me? Begone, sir!"

While Susie was looking for an officer, the tramp whispered,

"Jacob Van Hess, you had better dismiss the policeman; for if I am arrested there will be a scene. You don't know me, eh? You don't know your son-in-law, *Myron Finch?*"

Had a thunderbolt dropped at the feet of the old man he could not have been more astounded. He was obliged to lean against the hat-rack for support. The color left his face, and the lines about his mouth deepened. He feared Finch with an exceeding fear: he feared him more than he did Satan. Here was his evil genius come back to torment him; here was the fiendish hypocrite whose wiles, tricks, lies, and villany had blasted his life, and whose cruelty had destroyed the happiness of his only child; here was his ruthless enemy, who had destroyed his business and reduced him from affluence to respectable poverty. Jacob Van Hess remained for a minute or two speechless, and almost unconscious, dazed, and horror-stricken by the blow.

"I say, old man, do you desire a scene? Do you want me arrested? Do you want that divorce business ripped up from stem to stern? If you don't, be quick, for here comes the policeman. Just tell him it is all a mistake. Do you hear, old man?"

Words would fail to describe the insolence of Finch's language, tone, and manner. There was a threat in every syllable, a threat in every inflection of his cracked voice, and a threat in every gesture of his bloated body.

The policeman was told that it was a mistake, and that he was not needed. The officer eyed Finch and Van Hess with a knowing look, shrugged his shoulders, and returned to his "beat," muttering, "'A skeleton in every house!' but it's none of my funeral."

"Susie," whispered Mr. Van Hess, "tell your mistress that I have a private engagement with this—this—man; and you need not tell her what sort of man he is. Do you understand?"

Far better for you, Mr. Jacob Van Hess, had you seen your late son-in-law in your daughter's presence. But it was otherwise ordered; for

> "There is a divinity that shapes our ends,
> Rough-hew them as we may."

Myron Finch chuckled at his success; for he had not failed to note that the old man, weak and timid, had taken pains to let neither his daughter nor his servant know that the tramp was no other than Myron Finch. He felt that Mr. Van Hess was simply a goose to be plucked of his last feather and bled to his last drop of blood.

"Well, old man, can't you invite a fellow into your parlor or dining-room?"

As they entered the room, Finch cast his eyes around and observed the shabbiness of the furniture. "I perceive," he continued, "that your Fifth Avenue grandeur has gone, like my money. You may see, Mr. Van Hess—you may see for yourself that I am very poor and very sick, and have not a cent in the world with which to buy my supper or my bed."

"Go on, sir; proceed," said poor Mr. Van Hess, in a tone of weak despair.

"Mr. Van Hess, you and I were partners, and the partnership was never dissolved with my consent. True, I went on a little tour to South America—rather abruptly, I admit—for my health; but that is no crime in law. Now I have come back for a settlement—a settlement, do you hear?"

"Yes, I hear."

"Very well, I want you to heed. I had two purposes in coming back to New York; one I have just told you, the other is to contest that illegal divorce, obtained during my absence by fraud and false swearing. I know why Mrs. Finch was in such haste to obtain the divorce."

For a drunken man, his case was very clearly stated; and he had the subtlety to wind it up with an implied threat.

Jacob Van Hess made one desperate effort to shake off the toils that Finch was casting around him.

"Finch, you committed forgery; you absconded with much of the assets of our house: my daughter obtained her divorce in a legal way. We desire to have nothing further to do with you."

"Ah! that's your game, is it? Old man, age begins to tell on you. I committed no forgery. Where's your proof? I committed no adultery. You have no proof. A divorce obtained for anything else is null and void — at least in New York. Don't repeat these charges before witnesses, for if you do, I may sue you for defamation of character. Come, come, old gentleman; had not George Bailey, your daughter's old lover, returned from State-prison, and so imposed upon Mr. Wilde as to obtain a good situation, my wife would never have sought a divorce. How would all this sound in a court of justice? How would it appear in print that your daughter obtained a divorce by fraud to gratify a passion for a returned convict?"

"Silence, you fiend! Not another word about my daughter, whose life you have blighted."

Finch perceived that he must not irritate Mr. Van Hess too much, and therefore changed his tone:

"Mr. Van Hess, I will not be hard on you. I am very poor. Give me one hundred dollars to-night, and nine hundred one week from to-night, and we will call it square."

"Will you promise me to disturb neither my daughter nor me? But what is the use? I cannot rely on your promise."

"Old gentleman, I'll do better than that; I'll give you my solemn affidavit. I only want to get on my feet again, and then I shall leave you forever."

Finch's plan was to make himself appear as vile and filthy as possible—and it must be admitted that it required little effort on his part—in order to strike terror into Mr. Van

Hess's heart; for Finch thoroughly understood that the
great aim in life of both father and daughter had always
been to stand well with the world, and to be considered very
"respectable." For this cause, chiefly, Grace Van Hess had
abandoned Bailey on the first rumor of his fall; and for
this cause, too, her father was anxious to see her married
to that young paragon of a Christian, Myron Finch, so that
people would cease to talk of Grace's engagement to a convict. Seeing that Mr. Van Hess hesitated, Finch said,

"Mr. Van Hess, I don't want to be hard on you, but if
you don't consent to my terms, I shall go to-morrow and
employ a lawyer—yes, without a retainer—to commence
two suits, one for twenty thousand dollars, as my share of
the business of Van Hess, Finch & Co., and another to set
aside the divorce as illegal."

It is needless to say that Finch intended nothing of the
kind; for the last place which he desired to enter was a
court of justice. He simply desired to work on the fears
of Mr. Van Hess, and this he did most thoroughly. The
last little speech brought the old gentleman to terms. He
counted one hundred dollars into the greedy hands of
Finch, and told him to call in a week for nine hundred
more. Finch, elated at his success, withdrew, and treated
himself to a supper of raw oysters and raw brandy. While
sipping his second glass with intense satisfaction, he reflected on his day's work. One hundred and fifty dollars since
morning, not speaking of the twenty dollars which he had
obtained from Quin, was not a bad beginning; and then
nine hundred dollars one week from to-day! why, it was
better than a gold-mine. Ha! ha! ha! "And I heard
Grace wrangling with the brats. The first time I've
thought of them in three years, I do believe."

CHAPTER XXV.

"He that studieth revenge keepeth his own wounds green."
BACON.
"Soft is the memory of buried love."—BYRON.

THE next evening there were assembled at the tea-table of Mrs. John Grady, in addition to her husband, George Bailey, Washington Scroggs, and Jenny Edwards. Mr. Grady was aggressive and belligerent as ever, and as ready to use the "carnal weapon;" George Bailey was sadly out of sorts, owing to his jealousy of Henry Fawcett, aggravated by the anonymous note which he had received about ten days previously; Jenny Edwards was abstracted, and paid little attention to anything except her own sad reflections; and the little quack prattled away about his panacea for all ailments both of body and mind. In vain the "doctor" expatiated in Johnsonian English upon the afflux and efflux of the sanguineous fluids from the centre to the periphery, from the seat of congestion in the vital organs to the cuticle, which is the grand emunctory of the system. Neither Bailey nor Jenny Edwards paid the slightest attention to what he said; and it is doubtful if Mrs. or Mr. John Grady knew the meanings of half the words that the little man used in ordinary conversation. Though the little quack had the sweetest of tempers, and the most forgiving of dispositions, he could not fail to notice that no one of the party seemed to pay the least attention to his learned disquisition upon "capillary attraction and the specific gravity of atmospheric air."

"Jenny, my dear, I hope you are not afflicted with hypochondriacism (from two Greek words meaning cartilage) or melancholia (which means bile, *id est*, disease or congestion of the liver); for if you are, my dear, I must prescribe for you a melanogogue (likewise from the Greek); or better still, the propulsion of one thousand pounds avoirdupois of air from the surface of the body. The vulgar of the present day call this particular condition of the organs of digestion and assimilation, which is simply congestion, 'the blues.' But why 'the blues,' no man knoweth. Peradventure, it may be because the congested blood assumes a bluish tinge, like the asphyxia (also from the Greek) caused by strangulation. In the olden time melancholia was known by the somewhat singular cognomen of 'vapors.' And why 'vapors?' Because it was supposed by the ignorant that in hypochondriacism the diseased liver gave forth vapors (or, if you will pardon the expression, wind) which ascended to the brain, and played extraordinary freaks with the imagination."

The fact is, the little quack was not under the necessity of asking pardon from any one, for not one of the party heard a syllable of the latter part of his discourse.

"Jenny, my dear, are you ill?" asked the doctor in plain English, which he could speak very well when he pleased.

"I have a slight headache, doctor, but it does not amount to much. I shall be all right in the morning, thank you."

"I sincerely hope so," replied the doctor, with a look of solicitude, for he was very much attached to Jenny; then turning to Bailey, he was about to open his batteries on him, when he (Bailey) knowing what was likely to come, arose, and was about to leave the room, when Jenny Edwards also arose, and, while a deep blush overspread her pale face, said,

"Mr. Bailey, I would like a few minutes' private conversation with you, if you have no objection."

"None in the world," replied Bailey, glad to escape the harangue of Dr. Scroggs.

They retired to the little parlor, and sat for a moment in silence. Bailey was patiently waiting for Jenny to begin, and she was evidently thinking of the proper way to introduce the subject. At length she said,

"Mr. Bailey, you know me well enough to know that I would scorn to flatter you."

"Certainly," said Bailey, with a laugh at the bare idea that this sharp, curt, practical New England woman could condescend to flatter any one.

"Very well, sir; I believe you to be a good man."

"Thank you, Miss Edwards, for your good opinion."

"I believe, too, that you have suffered terribly: so have I."

Bailey did not laugh nor even smile at this; he simply knit his brows, and his eyes asked as plainly as eyes could ask,

"What do you mean?"

"I mean," said she, replying to his look, "that we who have suffered can sympathize with suffering."

"Truly, Miss Edwards, I believe we can."

"Can we forgive, Mr. Bailey?"

"Perhaps we can, perhaps we cannot. It may depend upon the nature of the offence," replied Bailey.

"Mr. Bailey, I know a lady who suffered a worse fate than yours; worse, because her injury, like cancer, is incurable; and she has forgiven the man who wronged her."

Bailey began to suspect the drift of her speech, and as he did so his eye began to dilate and a hectic spot appeared on his cheek-bone.

"Mr. Bailey, you love and are beloved by as good a woman as ever lived. I saw it in her face on the day that the letter came from Mr. Walter Wilde telling of your wonderful escape out of the jaws of death. In such matters you men are idiots; we women read the heart like an open book. Your imprisonment, foul and wrong as it was, has made you strong, and given you the heart of a woman worth double the amount of suffering."

Instinctively Jenny had struck the right chord, and the face of Bailey began to soften.

"Miss Edwards, I really do not understand you. Tell me plainly what you desire."

"Very well, then," replied Jenny, in her incisive way, "give me a promise that you will not prosecute Myron Finch."

George Bailey arose from his seat and took the hand of Jenny in his with profound respect, lifted it to his lips, and kissed it.

"Say no more. The promise is granted. Myron Finch shall never be prosecuted by me."

"I thank you—oh, so much! May God reward you! Now that this fear is removed from him, I may reform him and bring him to a knowledge of the Saviour."

Jenny Edwards was in tears, partly out of gratitude, and partly because, without saying so in so many words, she had let Bailey know that Myron Finch had wronged her; and yet he had kissed her hand as though she were a princess. Bailey took his leave on the plea that he had some writing to do, and left Jenny Edwards to her own thoughts.

During the interview between Bailey and Jenny Edwards, Mr. Jacob Van Hess called upon John Grady for the purpose of obtaining, if possible, the proofs of the forgery committed thirteen years before by his late son-in-law. Grady was well aware of Jenny's extreme desire to save Finch from the punishment which he so richly deserved, and to reform him, if possible, into a good Christian. He knew her whole history, and loved her as though she were his own child. Of course, he did not agree with her as regards the scoundrel Finch, but nevertheless he respected her feelings. But three persons knew of Finch's return to New York, and these three had good reasons for not making the fact generally known. Quin feared trouble about the forgery; Jenny, up to this evening, feared that Finch might be sent to State-prison; and Mr. Van Hess feared personal and family disgrace.

"Mr. Grady," said Mr. Van Hess, "I have called to know if you will let me have the practice-forgery papers which you took from Mr. Finch, or rather from Timothy Quin, for I believe they were in his possession."

"May I ask," said John Grady, "for what purpose you desire these papers?"

"I suppose you are aware," replied Mr. Van Hess, "that my daughter has obtained a divorce from Finch; and *if ever he should return* and contest this divorce, I would like to be able to make him cease proceedings by showing him the papers which would consign him to State-prison."

"Yes, yes—I see," said Grady. "I wish the rascal was at the bottom of the Atlantic Ocean!"

"So do I, with all my heart," responded Mr. Van Hess.

"But look here, sir," said Grady, "George Bailey is more interested in this than any one else. I am only the custodian of these papers, and cannot lend them to you without his consent."

"Is Mr. Bailey at home?" inquired Mr. Van Hess.

"He is; shall I call him?"

Bailey entered the room and shook his old master by the hand. His former aversion had disappeared; and he now thought only of the kind employer who had advanced him so rapidly in business. Mr. Van Hess was always uneasy in the presence of Bailey, for, as he looked at this noble man, he thought, "What a staff he would have been to me and my daughter!"

"Mr. Grady," said Mr. Van Hess, speaking slowly and with hesitation, "you are aware that my daughter has obtained a divorce from her late husband,—and—and—you know he may return—and give her and me some trouble. The essential evidence was procured by her lawyer; the other evidence as to cruelty, peculation, and abandonment was sufficient in most of the States, but not in the State of New York. Suppose—and it is not improbable—that this bad man should return and contest this divorce; the papers—I mean those papers which contained the evidence that Finch forged the check—would enable me to checkmate the villain and send him off about his business."

While Mr. Van Hess was speaking to Grady his countenance was turned to Bailey, as if he were the man from whom he expected the favor.

"I cannot part with these papers," said Grady, "without the consent of my friend, Mr. Bailey. For him I captured them, and they are his to do with as he pleases."

"Mr. Van Hess," said Bailey, with calm dignity, "those papers must not be used for the purpose of prosecuting the —the man who wronged me. If you want a copy, however, for your own protection, or for the protection of your daughter, you can have the loan of them until you make such a copy; but they must be returned to me within one month."

"Thank you," replied Mr. Van Hess; "I shall need

them for one week only; and I assure you that while in my custody I shall take the greatest care of them."

Grady and Van Hess both wondered why Bailey insisted that the evidence of the forgery should not be used for the purpose of prosecuting Finch. Neither liked to ask him the reason for his forbearance; and it is not likely that he would have told, had they asked him. In addition to his promise to Jenny Edwards, he was always endeavoring to interpret the wishes of Edith Wilde. Bailey felt that she would consider any act of vindictiveness on his part as ignoble and beneath him; for had she not always counselled him to leave the matter of Finch's chastisement in the hands of God, to whom alone vengeance belongeth?

Mr. Van Hess having received the forgery-practice papers from Grady, repeated his thanks, bowed, and withdrew. The same fatal mistake that had caused him to hide from his daughter the return of Finch, had actuated him to hide it from Bailey and Grady. The man was old and feeble, and feared a scene; and he fancied, too, that the evidence of his crime would drive Finch forever from the city of New York. In his best days Mr. Van Hess was not a brilliant man; he was narrow, bigoted, and easily imposed upon; and hence he found it an easy matter to impose upon himself.

CHAPTER XXVI.

"'Twas his own voice. She could not err;
 Throughout the breathing world's extent
There was but one such voice for her—
 So kind, so soft, so eloquent."—MOORE.

WARRENTON having retired from the business, Walter Wilde and George Bailey were both made partners, and the house was known throughout Europe and America as Wilde, Bailey, & Co., Bankers. The elder Mr. Wilde intended shortly to retire, and only remained for the present for the purpose of giving the young men the benefit of his wise counsel and wide experience.

Notwithstanding his exalted position, Bailey bore himself as humbly as when a simple clerk, and still continued to occupy his one little room in the house of his friend Grady, to read his rare books, to pursue his usual studies, and, above all, to worship at a distance his guardian angel, Edith Wilde. As far as the business of the bank was concerned, he performed the principal part of the work, and was always calm, cool, and self-poised during the weightiest commercial enterprises and transactions. To the minute details of his office he gave the closest care and scrutiny; and in a short time every one connected with the house discovered that the affairs of the bank were in the hands of a man who understood both himself and his business. Money was made rapidly, and George Bailey was becoming a rich man. He was now nearly forty years of age. His health was perfect, and he had the means of purchasing every luxury; but he was abstemious as a hermit. He had completely conquered his thirst for vengeance, and had put his jealousy of Mr. Henry Fawcett under his feet. His love for Edith Wilde he had so etherealized that it was almost divested of earthly passion. The sting of the anonymous note had poisoned his heart for a day or two; but the comforting words of Jenny Edwards, that Edith loved him, had almost removed it. He still retained his old prison habit of talking to himself in the solitude of his own room. This self-communion was good for him; it enabled him to call himself to account for the thoughts and acts of each day. Resolving himself into two persons, *Ego* and *Doppelganger* —the former himself, with his memory and his passion, the latter the man of business in his contact with his fellow-men—the two kept watch and ward, the one over the other. After dinner he smoked his single cigar, and talked pleasantly to Grady, his wife, the little quack—who was now a boarder in Grady's house—and to Jenny Edwards, whenever that lady called to pay her aunt and uncle a visit. Then punctually at eight o'clock he retired to his room to read, to study, and to carry on the dialogue between Ego and Doppelganger. A specimen of this self-communion will show how carefully this solitary man scrutinized his own conduct.

Dop. "Ego, you were a fool to-day. What business had you to feel bitter toward young Fawcett, and permit your worst passions to boil and bubble up as they used to do when you were persecuted by the brutal keepers?"

Ego. "I could not help it. I love her: I love the very ground she walks upon. This love will drive me mad!"

Dop. "Nonsense, old boy! nonsense! You survived the loss of reputation, of position, of liberty, of everything. No, no, Ego, you must be a man, and control your passion. Her happiness is paramount to your own; and if her marriage with Fawcett will make her happy, you must submit."

Ego. "But Jenny Edwards said that she loves me."

Dop. "True, true! But she may have been mistaken. Ah, if Jenny were right!—then, indeed, you might aspire to the hand of an angel. But, Ego, my dear boy, remember that you are almost old enough to be her father, and that you carry around with you the atmosphere of the prison, which no aromatic odor from 'Araby the Blest' could ever blow away. Bury your love down deep in your heart, and let no man see it."

Ego. "Very well, Dop, I shall try; I shall do my best."

In this way George Bailey gained a complete mastery over his strong passions, which he held under control as a skilful rider reins in a fiery steed.

In the mean time, if the truth must be confessed, Edith Wilde wondered that Bailey never once sought her society. Except on Sunday—before or after church—and then for a brief minute only, she rarely saw him. Indeed, he seemed to avoid her, for he frequently but politely declined her father's invitations to dinner. Convinced as she was of his love, why had he shunned her so much of late? She recalled the short angry discussion with Henry Fawcett, and feared that he was the cause; and, woman-like, she disliked Mr. Fawcett accordingly. In fact, she had lately refused to see this elegant youth, even at the risk of offending her father and brother. To George Bailey, from the very first, she had given all the treasures of a pure heart and lofty soul. Her love, which began in pity, ended in admiration for the grandest character she had ever known. Verily,

Bailey was a noble gentleman; but she exaggerated his proportions, until, in moral greatness, he was a perfect Titan. But why did he avoid her? she asked herself again and again. Now he had no excuse of poverty or want of position to plead; for he was socially her equal. Edith Wilde would have married him had she been forced to leave her father's luxurious home, and to dwell with him in absolute poverty in a cellar or garret; she would have married and cherished him when the world believed him guilty of forgery, and it would have constituted her highest pleasure to have been a comfort and a consolation to him in the darkest hour of his misery.

When Edith Wilde received an anonymous letter, evidently written by the same hand that had penned the epistle to Bailey, she flung it into the fire, and never gave it another thought. Yet this note suggested matter for jealousy quite as reasonable as that which had tormented Bailey. The note was as follows:

"MISS WILDE,—A friend takes this method of informing you that Mr. George Bailey is very intimate with a young woman named Jenny Edwards — employed in a down-town hotel—who calls at his boarding-house every Sunday, and whom he escorts at late hours to the Grand Street ferry. Beware of this man: he will play you false. A word to the wise is sufficient. A TRUE FRIEND."

As Edith threw this villanous note on the blazing coals, she simply said to herself, "Poor creature! you can arouse no feelings of jealousy in my heart by so shabby and shallow a trick as this. George Bailey is as much the soul of honor to-day as he was the day that you cast him off for Mr. Myron Finch."

One day Walter Wilde approached George Bailey, while writing at his desk in the inner office, and slapping him cordially on the back, said,

"See here, old man, why do you work so hard? Why don't you seek amusement? You'll kill yourself by such work."

Bailey bestowed on his young friend a sweet and beautiful smile, though full of sadness; for he loved Walter very dearly; he loved him because he had saved his life, and because he resembled his sister, not only in form and feature, but in many of his ways.

"No, no, not at all," replied Bailey, "I like work; it is a panacea for all trials and tribulations. Work, dear Walter, is my amusement."

"But what troubles have you now?" asked Walter. "Surely, in your present position as the real head of a great banking-house, with your reputation restored, beloved and respected by all who know you, your lot is a happy one; or at least it ought to be."

"Yes, I appreciate it fully. Thanks to a kind Providence and your—your sister, I am restored to an honorable position among men."

"That reminds me," said Walter, "that I have a favor to ask of you, which was the cause of my bothering you with my prattle at this unseasonable hour. A great actor is going to play Iago to-night, and Edith requested me to procure tickets to see him; but, alas! I no sooner reached my office this morning than I find on my desk a notice that our college society will meet this evening, and I would not miss this meeting for a great deal. Last year, you know, I was in California; and it was only the summer before my departure for San Francisco that I graduated. I am very anxious to meet the boys. But Edith is particularly anxious to see Mr. Blank play the character of that subtle rascal Iago. Now what am I to do? I would not disappoint my dear 'little grandmother' for the world; and you would not have me do it for half the money in this bank. Say, you dear old boy, won't you do me the favor of being her escort? Knowing what a recluse you are, I would not ask you, only Fawcett is now out of town, and I can't think of any one on whom I can call just at this moment."

Bailey's heart almost leaped into his mouth on hearing this request. The color rose to his cheeks and temples, and he felt the hot blood burning there in spite of all his efforts to hide his feelings. Fortunately Walter did not observe his feelings or his confusion. The suspicion of love which had arisen in young Wilde's mind—cleared by the near approach of death on the raft—had long ago disappeared. Impulsive, generous, frank almost to a fault, Walter saw no reason why George Bailey, had he loved his sister in that way, should not have sought her long ago in marriage.

"Come, George; like a good fellow, take my place. I know you never go to the theatre, but go to-night, and you will oblige me very much."

"I shall only be too delighted," replied Bailey, "to be Miss Wilde's escort. You know that I would do anything in the world to give her a moment's pleasure."

"Then it is all settled, and I am out of a dilemma. Thank you, George:" and away the young man bounded, to make the necessary preparation for the meeting of the college society.

That afternoon, as Bailey left the bank a little earlier than usual to make preparation for the theatre, Ego and Doppelganger had a heated discussion concerning their mutual behavior. Ego argued the propriety of making the best use of the opportunity, for such another might not come in years. His arguments, however, were ejaculatory and incoherent; for he was so beside himself with joy at the very thought of sitting alone with Edith for three mortal hours, that he was in no mood to carry on an intellectual contest with the cool and wary Doppelganger, nor to be coerced or frightened any more by his grave and austere friend. Doppelganger checked Ego—but not as firmly or decidedly as usual—and called him "vain, foolish, frivolous, light-headed dreamer," etc., etc. To which Ego responded by dragging Doppelganger after him to Williamsburgh and back to New York in great haste, for fear he might be late.

Edith Wilde's reception of Bailey was gracious. She looked radiant with happiness; for she, too, like Ego, had reflected upon the three hours alone by themselves—all alone!—for the first time in their lives. Ego, seeing this, and perhaps divining that she would enjoy the three hours very nearly as much as himself, whispered in Dop's ear, "Dop, you are a goose, an owl, too wise and too good to live long. I am a rebel to-night. I will submit to your iron rule no longer. I am going to manage this thing myself."

Edith would have no carriage; and so they walked arm-in-arm to the theatre, which was about half a mile distant. When Bailey felt her hand resting on his arm, a thrill of joy shot through his heart, such as he had never felt before; and when Edith felt her hand resting on his strong arm for the first time, she enjoyed a happiness truly and purely exquisite. What was there in this personal contact that made them both dumb as oysters? Ah! there was no need of words. There is a language of the heart that speaks more eloquently than any silver-tongued orator, from Demosthenes down. Subtle currents flowed to the heart of each—electric currents, which contact set in motion—giving each lover a feast of joy worthy the gods. Truly has the poet said, "Love is heaven, and heaven is love."

The lady, as usual in such circumstances, was the first to recover speech.

"Mr. Bailey, I am sorry that Walter gave you this trouble. You are such a hermit, and are so fond of your books, that I am vexed to think that he should have annoyed you."

Ah! Edith, my sweet little woman, so full of charity and good works, and so fond of truth and integrity, you must not begin, under the influence of the grand passion, to tell "fibs," however innocent they may appear; for you know in your heart that George Bailey is only too happy to be near you, and you now feel his strong arm shake with emotion beneath your gentle touch.

"Annoyed me! Vexed me!" said Bailey, absently. "Pshaw! You must know that my life is at your service. I owe everything to your goodness."

"Mr. Bailey, no more of that, if you please. I am sure the little obligation—and what was it? a word in favor of a badly-used man—would have been done for $x, y,$ or $z,$ or any other unknown human quantity; how much sooner, then, for the son of my particular friend! It was nothing; and whatever it was, you have repaid us a thousand-fold in the preservation of my brother."

"As you say, Miss Wilde, no more of that. Walter afterward did as much for me, so that the benefits were mutual and reciprocal."

There was another interval of silence which brought them all too soon to the doors of the theatre; and when they had taken their seats, they did not speak another word for at least twenty minutes. The lovers were supremely happy together, and it was better that they should enjoy their happiness unalloyed with speech.

"That 'star,' as he is called, dresses superbly," remarked Bailey at the close of the first act. "He gives his Iago a touch of Mephistopheles in that pointed beard and mustache, and in the peculiar cut of his hat, and in his general carriage; but that is not the Iago of Shakspeare. His voice is rich, mellow, sonorous, but singularly lacking in passion. He but mimics the passion of revenge; he feels it not. Ah, Miss Wilde, if that actor had heard me vow vengeance in my dark cell to the bare walls, until my voice grew so husky that it almost frightened my own ear, he would know something of that passion which, next to envy —yes, perhaps even more than envy—makes us truly miserable."

"Can we never comprehend a passion until we have felt it?" asked Edith.

"As a rule we cannot," replied Bailey. "There are a few rare exceptions—men of genius, like the writer of this play—who seem to know all passions by intuition. But this 'star' is simply an artist, or rather, I should say an artificer. He tries to make up by art what he lacks in genius."

"But you must admit," replied Edith, "that it is art of the highest order; so high, indeed, as almost to equal genius."

"Art of the highest order will please the mass of mankind far more than genius, and is therefore in many respects preferable."

"I do not quite understand you, Mr. Bailey."

"I mean to say," continued Bailey, "that true genius cannot be comprehended except by those who possess a little of it themselves. This man who plays Iago never forgets himself for a moment, and therefore is never lost in his work. He poses; he uses the muscles of his face and eyes with great effect. If you should see him to-morrow night in Hamlet or Richelieu, you would see the same man, only in a different dress, and speaking a different piece."

"Why, Mr. Bailey, you are a critic."

"No, no; I have not been to the theatre since I was a boy," hastily replied Bailey. "But in the portraiture of this passion, I can say, with the poet, 'We learn in suffering what we teach in song.' I understand the passion of revenge infinitely better than that actor, because I have groaned under it. Adversity and suffering are excellent school-masters, though their rattans do excoriate one's flesh so dreadfully."

"But, Mr. Bailey," said Edith, with great sympathy in her tone, "all that is past and gone: you have put revenge under your feet. If it be God's will to punish the wrong-doer, let him do it. Vengeance is his, not yours."

"I have tried to follow your advice; and already I have given a promise not to prosecute the fiend who tried to destroy me."

This conversation was carried on in the intervals between the first and second, and between the second and third acts.

"I fear," continued Bailey, "that this actor has been petted and spoiled by young ladies. I noticed many of them smiling admiringly on him; and when he makes his best hits, I perceive that his eyes turn toward them unconsciously for approval. Did you observe the gross exaggeration of his facial expression in the last act? Why he actually made us laugh, and this laughter was the worst possible commentary on his acting."

"Then you think," said Edith, "that it would be better to read Shakspeare, and rest content with our mental pictures? There; see that Othello trying to delineate the passion of love, of which he knows nothing! Look at that Desdemona! Her love seems as if it had caught St. Vitus's dance, and could not keep still to save its life."

"Miss Wilde, you will find that your conceptions of Shakspeare's characters are infinitely better than these on that stage. Just look at that great lumbering fellow roaring and bellowing with love and jealousy; and he feels no more of either passion than do the boards on which he stamps his huge feet."

"I am afraid, Mr. Bailey," said Edith, "that you are hard to please."

"No, no, not at all. I've had a habit of talking to myself, and criticising things, to keep my mind from rusting. These grand tragedies have a special charm for me; for, in fact, my own life has been a sad, sad tragedy; and just as Walter and I, after our own disaster, took a keen pleasure in reading 'shipwrecks at sea,' so I take delight in reading these magnificent plays; for I find all crimes, all virtues, all passions, all joys, and all sorrows delineated in them."

They walked home from the theatre almost in silence, each acknowledging to his or her heart that the evening had been delightfully spent. Their hearts were too full for utterance. There is a rapture of the soul which no language can express; and there is an ecstasy of delight which causes a kind of precious physical pain.

"Won't you come in and rest for a moment?" asked Edith.

"Rest! Rest!" replied Bailey, absently. "After this I must walk fast, or run; I could neither sit nor rest."

"Perhaps you had better come in and wait a few moments, until Walter returns from his meeting. He will desire to thank you for your self-denial in taking his place as my escort."

"Miss Wilde, I told you before—that is, if I really remember what I did say—that this has been the happiest evening of my life!" Bailey's tone of voice was just a shade irritable; and as it fell on her ear, Edith laughed a low musical laugh, and gayly said,

"Politeness, Mr. Bailey! politeness! What else would you say to a lady in whose society you had spent the whole evening? Have you not seemed to shun our house for a long time? Even now you are in such a hurry to be off that you will hardly remain until the servant opens the door." This was uttered in a light, bantering tone on the stoop. Edith knew that but for the fact of his being an ex-convict, he would have declared his love long ago; she knew that he was sad and lonely, and that the fear that he might lose her was making him miserable. She assumed a light tone of raillery, in order to make him feel more at ease in her presence. All that womanly modesty would permit she did to level whatever social distinction yet remained between them. A moody sadness had taken possession of the mind of Bailey, and Edith found it difficult to rally him out of it.

"Very well," said Bailey, rather ungraciously, "I'll walk in and wait until Walter comes home."

No man could have comprehended Bailey's moody irritation; but almost any woman could, and Edith understood it perfectly.

"Perhaps you had better not come in," replied Edith; "your tone of acquiescence is anything but gracious. Mr. Bailey, I am sorry to see that you are getting a little irritable."

"Irritable! Irritable! and with you?" Bailey uttered this like one in a dream.

The expression of Edith Wilde's face would have been a study for a metaphysical painter. The love of such a woman has always something of the self-sacrificing unselfishness of the mother in it. She felt that this great strong man would hide his adoration of her through a sense of profound respect, even if it broke his heart.

"Yes," she continued, "you have been irritated at my nonsense; for since we reached the house your tone has been abstracted and unkind."

"Unkind? Unkind to *you?*"

George Bailey was greatly agitated. Ego and Doppelganger were holding a "battle royal," and for the last few minutes the latter had frightened the former, and both were ready to beat a hasty retreat. Ego longed to take advantage of his present opportunity, and Doppelganger, cool and logical, was warning him against such "nonsense." The touch of her hand was still thrilling his whole frame, and his heart was on fire.

"Unkind? Unkind to *you?*" he repeated. "Edith—I beg pardon — Miss Wilde, I mean;" and Bailey ran his fingers through his hair like a man who was slightly dazed.

"Go on, please; let it be Edith."

They were now sitting face to face on opposite ends of a sofa.

"I—I beg pardon, Miss Wilde, but really my head swims, and I am a little confused. I meant to say that you are the last person in the world to whom I could be unkind in word, thought, or deed."

Bailey looked into her face and into her large gray-blue eyes, wide-open and weird, and saw there, below the fun, the laughter, the raillery, the great fountain of love which welled up for him from the heart of this pure, good woman. In a moment he arose to his feet and seized both her hands. His eye was dark and wild with passion.

"Edith Wilde! Edith Wilde! I love you—I adore you—I worship you! You have been, since the first day I saw you, my thought by day, my dream by night! I saw these eyes on the raft. I saw this smile when death stared me in the face. You succored my mother, you rescued me. You have been my good angel. You have brought me back to my God. Oh, how I love you! Do not be offended—please do not! I struggled hard against avowing my passion; but I cannot help it."

The fun, the laughter left Edith's face. Tears of sympathy, of joy, of love, coursed each other down her cheeks, as she said,

"I am not offended; do you think that I have not seen your love for a long, long time—almost from the first time we met? If it is any pleasure for you to know it, I am not ashamed to confess that my love for you dates very nearly as far back as yours for me. I knew and loved your mother. She had made me familiar with your character and your wrongs long before I saw you. I pitied you; and the poet says that 'pity is akin to love.'"

In some unaccountable way they were no longer at opposite ends of the sofa; on the contrary, they were close together at her end of it, with her head resting on his shoulder and their hands clasped. George! Edith! clasp hands firmly, lovingly; gaze down deep into each other's eyes in a vain endeavor to fathom illimitable love; enjoy this hour while ye may; for if ye both should live ten thousand years, ye will never drink such another ecstatic cup of unalloyed bliss.

The bell rung; and at the sound, for some reason inexplicable, Bailey withdrew to his own end of the sofa. Will some one inform us why love always imparts, even to the most innocent, a cunning, adroit hypocrisy?

Walter came into the parlor hastily, and sung out, in his usual frank manner, "Halloo, George! have you got back? Ha, Edith! how did you enjoy Othello?" As the young man spoke, he looked from one to the other, and saw George confused, and Edith with the bright roses on her cheek. During the desultory conversation that followed his entrance, Walter wondered if, after all, they would make a match of it.

On his way home that night George Bailey walked as if he had wings: he was in a heaven of heavens. Edith loved him! Could it be true? Was he dreaming? He felt his body and pinched his flesh, to be certain that he was awake. He was afraid that he would suddenly awake and find it all a dream. "Ah!" said George to himself, "blessed imprisonment, that made such a love as this possible, and saved me from that ghost of a love—that false, will-o'-the-wisp of a love for Grace Van Hess!"

CHAPTER XXVII.

"Beyond the infinite and boundless reach
Of mercy, if thou didst this deed of death,
Art thou damned."—SHAKSPEARE.

MYRON FINCH, dressed in his greasy and tattered clothes, and looking the picture of sin and misery, went, on the evening of the day appointed, to receive from Mr. Van Hess the nine hundred dollars which he had promised to give him as hush-money. Finch had been drinking a good deal of hard liquor since morning, but he was by no means drunk. His limbs, it is true, shook somewhat, and his hands trembled a little more than usual, but his brain was clear and active as ever. On his way to the house of Mr. Van Hess, he was reflecting what he would do with the money. He concluded that he would demand another thousand dollars, and with the whole amount commence the liquor business, as the one most likely to give a speedy profit on the capital invested. Timothy Quin had grown rich on less, and why should not he, Myron Finch, whose education and talents were vastly superior to Quin's, make a large fortune in the trade?

Finch ascended the stoop, glanced cautiously up and down the street, and then rung the bell. Mr. Van Hess, knowing who it was that rung, opened the door himself, and asked his unwelcome visitor to step quietly into the small library off the back-parlor. He was anxious to hide the fact of the visit from all in the house; and he had already informed his daughter that a man would call in the evening on particular business, and that on no account must he be disturbed. When they had reached the library, Finch introduced the subject by saying, in a cool, cynical tone,

"Well, old gentleman, have you the money which you promised me last week?"

"I don't know whether I shall give you any money or not. That promise was exacted under duress, and is not binding. Besides, you have been drinking; and if I have any money to spare, it will help to support your helpless children."

Finch looked at Mr. Van Hess with a sly, ugly, menacing eye, and measuring the feeble old gentleman, and remembering his dread of losing his "respectability," saw that he must assume the rôle of a disreputable bully, and perform the part of a low ruffian, to the best of his ability.

"See here, old man, I did not come here to listen to a temperance lecture, nor yet a sermon on duty; I came here to get the money you promised me; and if you don't hand it out it will be bad for you. Your last remark will cost you just another thousand dollars. Now listen to me, and pay attention. I'll charge you five hundred dollars for every five minutes' delay."

Finch had learned his lesson from Quin only too well, even to the assumption of that worthy's manner and tone, minus the mellifluous brogue. The effect of this speech was as Finch expected. Mr. Van Hess raised his eyes to heaven and prayed inwardly: "O God! why didst thou permit such a villain, such a heartless villain as this, to destroy my child's happiness and my own peace of mind; to consign the noble George Bailey to State-prison; and to ruin my property and my business? But Thy will be done."

Finch, perceiving by the attitude of Mr. Van Hess, as well as by the movement of his lips, what the old gentleman was doing, said, in the most brutal and irritating tone possible,

"Now look here, I want no praying or preaching; I had enough of that when I was your clerk. Ha! ha! ha! Then I played pretty well the religious dodge—carried religious books and papers to catch your pious old eye, to supplant Bailey as head-clerk, and win the charming Grace for a wife. Religion, like fire, is a good servant but a hard master, and I'll none of it. By-the-way, how is the lovely Grace? Has she set her cap yet for banker Bailey?"

"Silence, fiend! Do your worst. I'll brave public opinion. Better anything than this. Here! behold these papers, the evidence of your forgery, which will consign you to prison for life! Give you money, eh? I'll give you into the hands of the police."

Mr. Van Hess, maddened at the brutal allusion to his beloved daughter, arose from his chair in a towering passion, pulled the practice-forgery papers out of his pocket, and flourished them above his head. Finch, fearing that Mr. Van Hess was about to ring the bell and summon aid, also arose, and confronting the angry man, seized his wrist, and hissed into his ear, "Stir one step, utter one word, and I'll strangle you!" The old gentleman was in the act of stretching out his hand to the bell-cord, when Finch, still

holding the wrist of the hand that held the papers, buried
his right hand in the throat of Mr. Van Hess. The word
help died away on the lips of Van Hess. "Hand me those
papers, blast you!" Finch hissed in a fearful whisper.

Whether from the unusual excitement, or from the chok-
ing, the head of Mr. Van Hess fell over partly toward his
left shoulder, his eyes closed, his face grew livid, and he
became unconscious. While the old man was in this condition Finch gathered up the practice-forgery papers, which
had been scattered over the floor during the struggle; he
also picked his pocket of the nine hundred dollars.

"Ha!" whispered Finch, "if he awakes I am ruined!
But he must never wake!" He listened attentively at the
door; all was still as the grave; he opened the door a few
inches, then a little wider, and stole into the hall on tiptoe;
not a sound could he hear. Re-entering the library, he
stood over Mr. Van Hess until an occasional sigh warned
him of returning consciousness. He placed his fingers at
first gently on the old gentleman's throat, and held his
hand over his mouth and nose; he pressed harder and
harder; he pressed his neck before and behind. Mr. Van
Hess gave a few convulsive struggles, and all was over. He
was strangled to death by his son-in-law, Mr. Myron Finch!

Finch placed his dirty hand on the heart of the murdered
man, felt his wrist for the pulse, and placed his ear against
his bosom; and when he found that he was really dead, a
fear such as he had never felt before shot through every
fibre of his frame; his body shook like an aspen leaf, and
great drops of perspiration stood out like beads on his
brow, and ran in streams down his face. For a minute or
two he stood fascinated over his victim, as if he were paralyzed, and stared at the wide-open, glassy eyes of the dead
man. By a great effort of his will—for Finch was now sobered—he turned away from the horrid sight, thrust the
papers and the money hastily into his pocket, and stepped
stealthily into the hall. He encountered none of the family; for Grace Finch and her children were on the floor
above, and the servant on the floor below. He passed out
of the hall-door, which he softly closed behind him, and

reached the street; but he had not gone three yards before he met the very officer whom Susie, the servant, had brought just one week ago. The policeman eyed him very sharply, and said, "You here again? I must warn Mr. Van Hess." To this remark Finch made no reply, and hurried on as fast as his trembling limbs would permit. As soon as he reached his low lodging he retired to his room by a side-door, unseen by any one, undressed, tied up the greasy, tattered clothes in an old red handkerchief, put on the second-hand suit which he had bought with the money that Quin gave him, stole down the stairs into the yard, and threw the bundle with the tell-tale forgery papers down to the bottom of the sink. He returned to his room as noiselessly as he had left it. He then undressed a second time, and tying an old torn silk handkerchief around his head, got into his bed and shut his eyes, pretending even to himself that he was asleep; but, changing his mind, he began to groan as if in great pain. This groaning, as he had anticipated, brought the landlady to inquire what was the matter.

"Oh! oh! oh! I am suffering fearfully! I have been lying here in agony for two or three hours, and not a soul to help me! Won't you please send for a doctor? Oh! oh! oh! this is torture! It appears an age since tea-time. What time is it?—Nine, eh? Here I have been groaning since six. Oh! oh! oh! this pain is intolerable!"

By-and-by the doctor entered the room, laid his hat and black kid gloves carefully on the single table which the room contained, put his gold-headed cane cautiously in the corner, so that it could not fall and be injured, sat on a chair beside the bed, placed his right leg over his left, lifting it with both hands as though he had a great affection for it. He smiled the blandest smile, and wore the wisest expression of face. He placed his thin, delicate fingers on the patient's wrist and looked at his tongue. All this time Finch was uttering low moans.

"It is nothing, my dear sir," said the little doctor, "but an undue afflux of the sanguineous fluid toward the abdominal (from the Latin abdo, I hide) regions, which has caused congestion. I shall give you a dovers-powder to-night, and to-morrow I shall have you transported (*porto*, I carry) to my office, and place you in my receiver, which is the panacea (from the Greek, meaning all cure) for all the diseases appertaining to the circulation."

The little doctor had got as far as abdominal (from *abdo*, I hide), when Finch, in the middle of his moans, gave a slight and almost imperceptible start (which might have been one of pain), as he recognized in the person of the speaker his old friend and former teacher, Washington Scroggs. Of course, our amiable little quack had not the faintest idea that the degraded wretch, groaning and moaning with pretended pain, for whom he was prescribing, was no other than the subtle youth who had supplanted him nearly twenty years ago.

The doctor carefully lifted his right leg with both his hands, as before, and laid it on the floor, arose from his chair, took his gloves and put them on with great circumspection, placed his hat on his head and his cane in his right hand, looked supremely wise and philanthropic, smiled his blandest toward Finch, and remarked, as he bowed himself out of the room, "My receiver is the grand panacea."

When he was once more alone, Finch muttered to himself, "What in the name of the foul fiend brought that little school-master here, of all men in the world, when I shall want, perhaps, his evidence to enable me to prove an *alibi?* He would naturally be very unfriendly to me." Finch sat up in bed and leaned his head against his hand, and brought all the powers of his mind to bear on his case. He reflected that from the time of the murder until he was found groaning by his landlady not more than twenty minutes had elapsed. In the midst of his sufferings he had informed the woman that it was nine o'clock, when he knew that it was at least half-past nine. Mr. Van Hess had been strangled to death at ten minutes past nine o'clock; for Finch distinctly remembered looking at the beautiful clock which had once ornamented the mantel-piece of his own luxurious bedroom, and noticing that, in the altercation, he and the old gentleman were wasting time. Myron Finch

knew that a human life often depended upon so small a
matter as accounting for twenty minutes; and he consoled
himself that his pretended sickness would settle, in a court
of justice, a satisfactory *alibi*. Mr. Van Hess, he thought,
might not be discovered until morning; certainly not until
his usual hour of retiring, which could not be before ten
o'clock, and might be as late as eleven. He was more
afraid of the policeman. Well, he would simply deny that
he was the man. But yet the words, " You here again?"
filled him with fear; for this evidence would certainly bring
in the servant-girl as a witness, who had seen him on the
occasion of his first visit to the house of Mr. Van Hess.
Finch arose, and walked backward and forward through the
limits of his narrow room: sometimes he stood still and
tapped his forehead, as if to summon all his powers of intellect; and at other times he sat on the side of his bed in
a state of mind bordering on distraction, as his vivid imagination pictured himself dangling from a rope. Then he
thought of the practice-forgery papers. Evidently Mr. Van
Hess had obtained them from John Grady; but still he may
not have told why he wanted them, for the old gentleman
was anxious to hide the fact of his, Finch's, return to the
city. But Finch realized that his safety hinged on a *motive;* and if ever those papers were found the motive for
the murder was apparent. What if Bailey had given up
the papers to Van Hess? The very thought of this caused
the cold perspiration to break out afresh, and run in streams
down his flabby, brick-colored face. Again he arose and
peered into the yard, as if to be certain that the detectives
were not fishing up the fatal papers; then he cursed himself for a fool for not finding the means of burning these
papers, and so put an end to all his doubts and fears. He
had almost made up his mind to steal down stairs and fish
up the bundle and burn them—but where and how? He
might burn the papers but not the clothes. He had started
for the door, but some noise, perhaps the creaking of the
old floor, frightened and deterred him. He lay down again,
weak and livid with fear. "Fool! fool! why did I kill him?
Anything but this. Murder will out; I know it will. I'll

be hanged! I know I'll be hanged! I see a chain of circumstantial evidence that would hang a man twice over.
Fool! fool! why did I kill him?" And still the burden of
his thoughts was, "Fool! fool! why did I kill him?" He
now imagined that every step which he heard in the street
was an officer of the law coming to arrest him. His hearing became preternaturally acute; his nerves were completely unstrung; he tumbled and tossed on his bed like the
wreck of some ship in the trough of the sea; he heaped
imprecations on the heads of all whom he had ever known;
and he kept muttering, in an agony of fear, "Fool! fool!
why did I kill him?"

Finch then threw himself on his face and wept—wept as
he had not done since he was a baby in his mother's arms;
that is to say, if such babies as he was ever do weep or
smile. No tear did this man shed for his many crimes;
his tears were all for his own cowardly self. Not one
touch of pity had he for the weak old man lying dead up-
town, whom he had foully murdered, without giving him
so much as one minute to utter a single prayer for the salvation of his immortal soul. No, no, all Myron Finch's
pity was for Myron Finch's self.

A thought struck him: he sprung to his feet, put on his
clothes, and stole stealthily down the stairs and out on the
street. He sought a drug-store. He was now respectably
dressed in the second-hand suit of half-worn black which
he had purchased about a week ago. "I want some strychnine to kill rats." The clerk at first demurred, but finally
gave it. He hurried back to his room, undressed, and went
to bed. He then carefully counted his money and hid it
between the cloth and the lining of his coat; the poison
he bound up in a piece of paper and pinned in the centre
of a black silk handkerchief, which he tied around his
neck.

These acts had given him a short respite from his worst
fears. An intense desire to run away, to fly from the city,
and to put as many miles of land and sea as he possibly
could between himself and the murdered man, seized him;
and it required all his power of will to force himself to re-

16

main where he was, as the best place to escape detection. Yet the little room seemed to suffocate him. He wondered if all men in his condition wanted to run. He could not rest or sleep: he went to the window and raised the sash, though the night was intensely cold; he looked out and upward, and it seemed to him that the very stars had a knowledge of his crime, for they appeared to him, in their steely hardness, to look cruelly at him. Then he thought that some invisible power was causing the dingy walls of his room to close in upon and destroy him; and he actually shuddered as he fancied that the apartment was becoming smaller and smaller. He sat on the side of the bed, like a frightened animal, with his lips apart and his teeth chattering, his thin hair almost on end, and the great drops of agony standing out on his pale forehead; and still he kept muttering, "Fool! fool! why did I kill him?"

Yes, Myron Finch, if the truth were known, every murderer, from Cain down to yourself, has given himself this very epithet of "fool," and has asked that very question in an agony of fear, "Why did I kill him?"

CHAPTER XXVIII.

"Go, prick thy face and over-red thy fear.
*   *   *   *   *   *   *
Death of thy soul! Those linen cheeks of thine are counsellors of fear."—SHAKSPEARE.

"Women, ever in extremes, are always either better or worse than men."—LA BRUYERE.

THE next morning the newspapers teemed with accounts of the murder of Jacob Van Hess. He was found dead in his library, at half-past ten o'clock, by his daughter, who, wondering at the cause of his delay in bolting the doors and fastening the windows, and thinking that perhaps he had fallen asleep, went down-stairs to see for herself; and found her father, half reclining and half sitting, stiff and stark in his chair. The opinion of the physician who had

been sent for, was that Mr. Van Hess had been dead two
hours. Black-and-blue finger-marks were found on his
throat; and his shirt, his collar, his cravat, and his clothing
all showed evidence of a severe struggle. His watch, jewellery, and pocket-book, containing between ninety and a
hundred dollars, were found on his person; conclusively
proving that robbery was not the cause or the motive that
led to the murder. Susie O'Neil, the servant, told a confused story about a tramp who had tried to force an entrance into the house about a week ago. The policeman
who patrols the street where the murder was committed
corroborated the girl's story, and stated that he had been
sent for to expel the tramp, but that when he reached the
house Mr. Van Hess informed him that it was all right—
that he had made a mistake. Last night the same officer
met the same man coming out of the house about the hour
that the murder was supposed to be committed. That the
officer recognized him is certain, for he accosted the tramp
—"You here again? I must warn Mr. Van Hess." From
all the facts, it seems that this tramp was the murderer;
but what his motive could have been is a mystery. It is
hinted that Mr. Van Hess has had domestic troubles and
business difficulties; but the person who was the cause of
these is supposed to be wandering in South America.
Such were a few of the extracts culled from the leading
morning journals. An evening paper announced that the
investigation was in the hands of the detectives; that a
highly important and curious slip of paper has been found
beneath a book-case in the library, as if wafted there during the struggle that preceded the murder, and that this
paper consists of irregular fragments of common letter-paper pasted on red blotting-paper. But the most singular
thing of all is the writing itself, which contains the words,
" *William Wilde* "—" *fifteen hundred dollars* "—"*Dec.* 20,
18—," and " *Jacob Van Hess.*" Perhaps the name and
date will enable Mr. Wilde to throw some light on this
mysterious murder. Later accounts stated that there was
no doubt in the minds of the detectives that the tramp
committed the deed, and that he would be arrested within

twenty-four hours. The detectives had interviews to-day
with Messrs. William Wilde and George Bailey, bankers,
and with a man named Grady, who resides in Williamsburgh. They also called upon an up-town liquor-dealer,
named Timothy Quin, once a porter in the employ of Van
Hess & Co. The police, as usual, are quite reticent, and
look very knowing; but they assure us that they are on
the right scent. If rumor be correct, certain family secrets
will be made public in this trial which will once again en-
force the truth of the old adage, that "Truth is stranger
than fiction."

Myron Finch, in murdering Mr. Van Hess, had also
"murdered sleep." The miserable coward died ten thousand deaths during the night, which to him seemed inter-
minable. Long before daylight he arose and dressed himself, but feared to leave his room during the darkness. He
waited and listened; and the first intelligible words which
fell distinctly on his ear were the words of the newsboy,
"Mornin' 'Erald. Murder of Mr. Van Hess in his own
house," etc., etc. These words sent a fresh chill through
his heart like cold lead, and caused his knees to smite each
other. The newsboy was gone, and Finch was hungry for
the details. He mustered up all his resolution and slipped
cautiously into the street; he went to the nearest news-
stand and bought the *Herald*. In the gray dawn of a winter's morning the following headings, in enormous capitals,
told the story:

ATROCIOUS MURDER OF JACOB VAN HESS!

MURDERED BY A TRAMP!

THE POLICE ON HIS TRAIL. THE MURDERER CANNOT
ESCAPE.

A SLIP OF PAPER WHICH WILL UNRAVEL THE MYSTERY.

There was half a column of these terrible black headings,
and they looked as if they were Myron Finch's death-war-
rant. As he read the paper, or rather as his eyes and brain
devoured the reporter's graphic description, and particular-

ly the part relating to the fragments of letter-paper pasted on the blotting-paper, he almost fainted, and would have fallen into the gutter had he not clasped a lamp-post. His worst fears were now realized. His *alibi*, so skilfully planned and executed, would avail him nothing; for the most damning evidence of all was found—evidence which would bring as witnesses against him Wilde, Bailey, Grady, and Quin, and prove an excellent motive for the murder. He slunk back to his little dingy bedroom, undressed, and went to bed, a prey to terrors which really sickened him; so that when the little doctor called to see his patient, there was no sham, as there had been the evening before.

After Washington Scroggs, M.D., had put down his hat and gloves and placed his cane where it could receive no injury, just as he had done last evening, and just as he had done every evening since he commenced the practice of medicine; and after he had placed his right leg lovingly, with both his hands, above his left; and after he had felt Finch's pulse and examined Finch's tongue; and after he had looked very wise and very profound, smiling blandly and wagging his head knowingly, as if that head contained all the combined medical lore of the world from the time of Galen to the present day, he simply muttered, "Congestion tending toward the abdominals (from *abdo*, I hide)." After a few more sagacious waggings of his learned head, he said, "Nothing will effect a cure but my panacea (from the Greek, meaning cure all)."

Finch was tired of the little quack and of his pedantic jargon, and desired to see how far his evidence might be used to prove an *alibi* in case he was arrested and tried for his life. Very soon Scroggs took out the morning paper and commenced to read the account of the murder, giving sundry learned comments upon death by asphyxia (not forgetting the root of the word), and seeming to lose all idea of its atrocity in a scientific explanation how his "receiver" would have restored the murdered man to life twenty minutes after the ordinary physicians had pronounced him dead.

"What time do you say that the murder was perpetrated?" asked Finch.

"Between the hours of half-past eight and half-past ten," replied Scroggs.

"Ah!" said Finch, carelessly, "that was just the time when I was suffering most with this bilious colic."

"Yes," replied Scroggs; "I remember, I was here about ten, and you said you had been in bed since six."

"Did you know this Jacob Van Hess?" asked Finch.

"No, I had not the honor of his acquaintance, though I once knew his son-in-law, one Myron Finch, the worst rascal on this side of the Atlantic Ocean."

"Ah!" groaned Finch.

"Another attack? Here is a powder which will give you relief until you are well enough to come to my office to be completely cured by my 'receiver.' Good-morning, Mr. Brown; I shall call again to-morrow."

When Scroggs had retired, Finch took out the *Herald* and read over and over again the details of the murder. He closed his eyes to think the better; but he clearly perceived that if he were arrested, he would assuredly be convicted and hanged. Already, in imagination, Finch felt the pressure of the rope around his neck. The thought of swallowing the strychnine flashed across his mind; but he was too great a coward, and too fond of his miserable life to end it in this way. Then he thought it would be safest to remain sick in bed for a week or two in a darkened room; and, just as soon as the excitement about the murder died out, steal off to Boston, from Boston to Portland, thence to Halifax, and so on to Liverpool.

Jenny Edwards read the account of the murder of Jacob Van Hess, and never doubted for one moment who had done the deed, and why. She had previously learned from John Grady that Mr. Van Hess had called for the practice-forgery papers, and she readily surmised the rest. As she sat in her room, after reading all the details of the horrid crime, the tears falling silently on the newspaper which lay in her lap, she said to herself, "So this is the end of Myron Finch!" She took up the newspaper and reread the horrid details. She sat with her hands clasped on her knees, weeping bitterly, and hoping that now he would repent and turn to his Saviour. To die in his sins, and to suffer through all the ages of eternity, seemed to her mind something too terrible to contemplate. She thought that if he would now seek pardon from an offended God, they might yet meet, and be forever happy in heaven. Jenny went to her own room and kneeled by her bedside, and prayed long and fervently for the conversion of Myron Finch. She arose, put on her hat and cloak, and went out to seek her uncle John Grady, in order to obtain information concerning the practice-forgery papers. As she ascended the hill leading toward Grady's house, she perceived Mr. Bailey and Mr. Grady walking, arm-in-arm, in earnest conversation. She overtook them, and after the ordinary salutations had been exchanged, Mr. Bailey asked her if she had read the account in the papers of the atrocious murder of Mr. Jacob Van Hess.

"I have read the account," Jenny replied, "and it is dreadful, dreadful!"

"I have been summoned to attend the coroner's inquest, and give evidence concerning the slip of paper found under the bookcase in the library. Mr. William Wilde, Timothy Quin, and your uncle have also been summoned to attend. We shall of course be compelled to state all we know." In making this statement Bailey gave Jenny Edwards a significant look, as much as to say, "You cannot consider this a violation of my promise not to prosecute Myron Finch?"

Jenny Edwards understood Bailey's look, and replied, "Of course you must state the truth, the whole truth, and nothing but the truth."

Finally Jenny accomplished her purpose, and found her uncle alone.

"Uncle, uncle, you have been more than a father to me," pleaded Jenny; "for God's sake, help me to save him! He must not die a felon's death, with all his sins on his head. We must not permit soul and body to perish together."

"Jenny, Jenny, my dear," replied Grady, "you are mad—mad as a March hare! Nothing can now save him—nothing ought to save him! He would murder you, or me, or any one, for a few dollars, or to gratify his meanest passion. Hold your tongue, Jenny! Keep quiet! Never go near him; never pretend that you have known him. Bailey knows nothing of your former relations with him, neither does Quin, neither does Mr. Wilde; so you must keep still and say nothing, for your own sake. If he escapes, let him; but you must do nothing to aid him. You know, Jenny, that I have always stood by you; but if Myron Finch has done this deed, and if you do anything to save him, even to the lifting of your little finger, I shall cast you off forever and disown you!"

Jenny Edwards wrung her hands in a kind of speechless misery pitiable to behold. At last she spoke in a low, broken, and agonized tone: "John Grady, would you let a fellow-creature die in his sins and suffer eternal punishment? The man is wicked, I know, but the teaching of Christ inculcates forgiveness and charity."

"What time did the murderer give Mr. Van Hess for repentance?" asked Grady. "But hush! Here is Bailey coming down-stairs. Remember, Jenny, what I have told you; if you lift your finger to help this man, I'll disown you. If caught and convicted, he will have far more time to repent than he allowed his victim."

After the departure of Bailey and Grady to attend the coroner's inquest, poor Jenny sat like one distracted. If she could only discover his lodgings, she might be able, she thought, to assist him, at least with money. It was truly a sad sight to see this pious woman, with her sensitive conscience and her sound intellect, with her excellent common-sense in all the affairs of life, and with her temper true but hard as steel, willing to aid with her last dollar the man who had so cruelly wronged her, and who had so recently perpetrated the highest crime known to the law. It seemed as if the very dregs of the passion she had once felt for him had the power to turn her moral nature awry. She sat and pondered for a few minutes, then arose and spoke a few words to her aunt, and hastily left the house. She had made up her mind to seek Timothy Quin, if possible, before the inquest, and ascertain from him how far the practice-forgery papers would compromise Finch in a trial for his life. Jenny had another purpose, which will presently appear.

She found Timothy Quin's address in the directory, and hurried up to his residence. Fortunately the worthy " wine-merchant " was at home.

" Mr. Quin, do you remember me ?" asked Jenny, in her short, direct, New England way.

" Throth, ma'am, I remimber yer face, but, for the life o' me, I can't place ye."

" Mr. Quin, do you recollect the night that John Grady and a lady saved your life when you were almost dead with liquor and opium ?"

" It's meself that does, ma'am. Shure you and he tuck good care o' me, and sint me home in a carridge."

" Very well, Mr. Quin, I am the lady who saved your life that morning. Are you now willing to do me a favor?"

" Throth an' I am, ma'am, if ye don't ax too much."

Jenny paused, as if anxious to put her thoughts in the best shape, and then said,

" I want you to retire to the country for a few weeks. I shall pay you double the amount that your business may suffer in your absence. If you would care to visit your friends in Ireland, I shall pay your passage there and back."

Notwithstanding the fact that Timothy Quin was a " wine-merchant," and a chief among small politicians, truth compels us to state that he had no pleasure in reading, for the reason that, being obliged to spell out more than half the words, he usually lost the thread of the subject ; and that, as for writing, he had simply learned to draw—as a child might draw Chinese characters from tea-boxes—certain marks which stood for Timothy Quin.

He had not yet heard of the murder, because there had been no meeting yet in the little gambling-room off the bar, in which Timothy, with spectacles on nose, and newspaper in hand, pretending to read, carefully gleaned the information that he desired, and all the news of the day, from the conversation of men superior to himself. For, unfortunately, in places like Quin's there is not unfrequently to be found an able but besotted lawyer or a ruined physician.

Hence it was not at all astonishing that Quin was still ignorant of the atrocious crime perpetrated the night before. The summons to attend the coroner's inquest had not yet reached him. And so he was puzzled to know what Miss Edwards was driving at, and why she was anxious to get him out of the country. But Timothy was too shrewd a man to express his feelings, or, as he himself said, "to give himself away." So he wisely awaited further developments.

"Miss Edwards," said Quin, "me health is excellent, thank God, an' I niver was betther in me *life*; thin why should I go to the counthry or to the ould sod?"

"How much money," asked Jenny, "will you take for keeping out of the way, and giving no evidence concerning the practice-forgery papers?"

"Why should I give evidence?" asked Quin—"evidence in what?"

Miss Edwards handed him the newspaper; but Quin handed it back to her, as he said,

"By yer lave, ma'am, I broke me 'specs' this mornin,' an' me sight is very wake; wud ye be plased to read it aloud?"

While she was reading, the changes in the expression of Quin's face were a study. They reminded one of the changes on the surface of a smooth lake caused by the fitful sunshine of a partly-clouded April day. When Miss Edwards had finished reading the account of the murder, Timothy Quin's commentary was unique and peculiar: it was simply a long, low whistle, and "So, Misther Myron Finch, ye've done it at last!"

"Now listen to me, ma'am: upon me wor-rd an' honor I'd do anything in rason for ye. But this is sarious: it's murdther, an' forgery beyant it. It must all come out now, ma'am: ye can't smother murdther as ye can forgery an' thim things; an' to go 'way an' hide wud be a mighty bad business for Timothy Quin. No, no; I'll tell the whole blessed thruth whin I'm called to the stan'."

"Mr. Quin," said Jenny, in a tone of entreaty, "Mr. Finch's life depends on your evidence. I will give you one thousand dollars if you will leave the country or disappear for three months."

" No, no, ma'am ; there isn't money enough in New Yark
to bribe me aginst me dhuty."

Jenny Edwards, perceiving that there was no hope in this
quarter, rode home with a heavy heart, and dreading every
moment to hear the newsboys cry out, " Arrest of Myron
Finch, the murderer !"

CHAPTER XXIX.

" Poise the cause in justice' equal scales,
Whose beam stands sure, whose rightful cause prevails."
SHAKSPEARE.

IN the back-parlor of the residence of the late Jacob
Van Hess was assembled the usual crowd to be found at
a coroner's inquest. The coroner, a fat, puffy, pompous
man, with an apoplectic face and neck, and dressed in a
badly-fitting suit of shiny black, and linen that ought to
have been at the washerwoman's, presided with an air of
official and officious importance, and with an attempt at
dignity which was ludicrous in spite of the gravity of the
occasion. He pushed up his coat-sleeves with something
of the action of a prize-fighter; and he settled and reset-
tled his fat chin and jaws within his huge shirt-collar with
the air of an owl adjusting the ruffled feathers of its fat
neck. The jury, composed of men of all nationalities and
of every station in life, sat on either side of this digni-
tary of the law. Near the coroner sat an assistant district attorney—a young man of intelligence and education.
Lawyers, physicians, mechanics, men, women, and even
children had forced their way into the two parlors. Police-
men located or stationed here and there from the door of
the library, where the corpse lay, to the stoop and the sidewalk, were vainly endeavoring to keep back the crowd.
The street was half filled with that miscellaneous gather-
ing always ready to congregate upon the slightest provocation—to whom a military band, a target excursion, or an
atrocious murder, is equally an object of curiosity and
pleasure.

The first witness called was Mrs. Grace Finch, who appeared dressed in deep mourning and heavily veiled. When she raised her veil in order to answer the questions put to her by the coroner, her face bore traces of the shock and grief which the sudden and terrible death of her father had caused. After stating what is already known concerning the finding of the dead body at the hour of eleven in the evening, and concerning her father's interview with a stranger, and his expressed wish not to be disturbed, the coroner asked her if she had any idea who this stranger was; and she replied that she had not.

"Had your father any enemy?" asked the assistant district attorney.

"None that I knew of."

"Pardon me, Mrs. Finch, I would not ask you this question did not the ends of justice demand it. Did you not a few months ago receive a divorce from Myron Finch?"

"I did," replied Mrs. Finch, in a very low tone.

"On what grounds, may I ask?"

"Cruelty, desertion, and—and—adultery."

"Was your late husband a partner of your father?"

"He was."

"Did not your father and he part in anger?"

"No, not in anger. Mr. Finch absconded — and — and robbed my father."

"Where did your late husband abscond to?" asked the coroner.

"I think we heard that he went to South America."

"Have you heard of his return?"

"No, sir; I have not."

"That will do, Mrs. Finch. But wait a moment; one question more. Did your father seem depressed in spirits before his death?"

"I know he did; and, now that I think of it, I am sure he had been trying to hide something from me for one week previous to his death." At this point Mrs. Finch utterly broke down, and was led out of the room sobbing by one of her female friends.

The next witness was the girl Susie O'Neil, who described, as far as she was able, the tramp with the tattered clothes and broken nose, and told the story about seeking a policeman, and of Mr. Van Hess's refusal to accept his services when found. The evidence of the officer corroborated that of the servant, and showed further how he had met the same tramp leaving the house of Mr. Van Hess the evening of the murder. He was sure it was the same man, because he had used the words, " You here again ? I must warn Mr. Van Hess."

" Would you know the man if you saw him again ?" asked the coroner.

" I would recognize him among ten thousand," replied the officer.

" Is John Grady present ? Mr. Grady, do you recognize that piece of paper ?"

" I do."

" When did you last see that paper ?" asked the coroner.

" When I gave it, or one exactly like it, into the hands of Mr. Jacob Van Hess, in my house in Williamsburgh."

" Mr. Grady," said the young attorney, " this is a peculiar piece of paper, as you see—torn irregularly into four fragments, which have been matched and pasted on this thick blotting-paper. The ink has turned yellow with age, and the paper is soiled with much handling. Can you give the jury the history of the papers which you handed to Mr. Van Hess one week ago, of which this is evidently one, and tell us the meaning of these words—of this writing ?"

" Well, sir, this is a long story, and I must be allowed to tell it in my own way."

Grady then narrated the story of the forgery; the trial of Bailey; his conviction and long imprisonment; the unmitigated villany of Finch; his capture of the practice-forgery papers in the hotel; and all the other facts of this story with which he was connected, or of which he had a personal knowledge. John Grady waxed eloquent as he portrayed the virtues of Bailey or denounced the fraud and treachery of Finch and Quin. His manner was inimitable, and his speech had just enough of the brogue to impart a raciness to his flow of language. The reporters for the great dailies, always favored by the politicians with the best positions for hearing on such occasions, took down every syllable that dropped from the lips of the speaker.

"Mr. Grady," said the assistant district attorney, "this is a strange story—stranger than fiction. I would like to ask you how you came to be in such a position in the hotel as to overhear and see what occurred in the room in which Finch and Quin were dining?"

"I was in the next room, with the door slightly ajar. Finch's back was toward me, and my worthy friend the 'wine-merchant' was so intoxicated that he was blind—blind drunk."

"Who was with you, and how came you there?"

"I decline to answer that question unless it becomes necessary to further the ends of justice," replied Grady.

"You need not answer, Mr. Grady. Is Timothy Quin in the room?" asked the coroner.

"I am, yer honor."

As the burly form of Quin shouldered its way right and left to the front, every eye was turned to get a closer view of the man whose character and antecedents had been laid bare by the story just told. The first unfavorable sign of the man was his dress, which was loud; the next was his jewellery, which was weighty, particularly his watch-chain; and last, was his face—his hang-dog face—with beetling brow and sunken, unsteady eye.

"Quin," said the young attorney, "look at that curious piece of paper and tell us if you ever saw it before."

Quin took it in his hand, turned it over, and examined even the back of it, and scrutinized it most carefully, evidently thinking of his answer. At length he said, in slow and measured words,

"Have—I—seen—it—before? I—think—I—have, or at laste a piece of paper very loike it;" and Timothy continued to inspect it as though it were the face of a long-lost friend.

"Did you ever have a paper like that, and others of a similar kind, in your possession?"

"I—think—I—had," replied Quin, in a slow, hesitating way.

"You think!" said the assistant district attorney—"you think! Don't you know? You heard the evidence of Mr. John Grady. Did you pick the torn fragments out of the waste-basket, and paste them on pieces of red blotting-paper?"

"I—think—I—did."

"Think! think!" impatiently ejaculated the attorney. You know whether you did or not. Come, sir, did you, or did you not?"

"I—did."

"Why did you do so?" asked the coroner.

"Bekase — bekase, I wondthered what Misther Finch meant by so much writin' afther business-hours. He wud remain afther the other clerks were gone, an' he wud sit at his desk in a kind ov absent-moinded way, writin' an' writin'. Thin he wud tear up the paper an' throw it into the basket. Knowin' that Finch was a cute kind ov a chap, an' playin' the pious dodge on ould Van Hess, it sthruck me wan night that I would collect these torn papers, match thim, an' paste thim on the blottin'-paper, bekase it was stiff an' handy."

"Why did you do this?" asked the coroner.

"Well—well—ye see, I knew Finch was a deep sort ov chap, and intinded to play some kind ov game, an' I med up me mind to have an oye on him."

"Did you suspect what he was about?"

"I didn't know exactly what he was up to, but I guessed it was nothin' good."

"Quin," said the attorney, "what led you to suspect Finch?"

"Well, yer honor, he wud never read wan ov his pious books or papers until he saw Mr. Van Hess near him; thin he wud pull it out an' lay it an his desk, where the ould gintleman wud be sure to see it. In the evenin's, whin he an' me was alone, he wud never read a word ov his pious stuff."

"Pretty keen observation, Mr. Quin;" said the public prosecutor. "You saw that Finch was an arrant hypocrite, and you knew that a pious hypocrite would commit any crime in the calendar, if he thought he could escape the meshes of the law."

"Exactly, yer honor."

"Why did you not inform Mr. Van Hess?"

"An' lose me place! Do you think I was a fool?"

"Tell us," said the assistant district attorney, "in your own way, what followed."

"Wan day in Novimber, about dusk, Finch med me put on Bailey's light summer business-coat an' go to the bankin'-house of Warrenton, Wilde & Co., an' hand Mr. Wilde a check an' wait for a receipt. Ye see, I was the porther, the messinger, an' man-of-all-work about the store, an' whin Misther Finch sint me it was me dhuty to obey ordhers an' ax no questions."

"When you put on Bailey's coat," asked the attorney, "did you not suspect something wrong? Did you not suspect that you were personating Mr. Bailey when you were sent a little before dark?"

"Wrong? Why should I suspect somethin' wrong? I wint to banks almost every day."

"Ask no questions, Quin, but answer mine. On your oath, did you not suspect something wrong?"

"Wrong? Why should I?"

"Come, come, sir—yes or no: did you not suspect something wrong?"

"Well, if I did, it was none ov me business. It was me dhuty to go errands, an' I wint errands."

"Will you answer my question?" said the public prosecutor, with considerable asperity.

Timothy scratched his head and reflected; and at length he boldly lied, and said,

"No—at laste not at that time."

The young assistant district attorney gave Quin a most formidable look, as he asked,

"How much money did Mr. Finch pay you for that errand? Come now, you are on your oath, and beware!"

"I—I—don't know."

"What do you mean by 'you don't know?' Did Finch, or did he not, pay you for that errand to Mr. Wilde?"

"Am I obleeged to answer that question, yer honor?"
said Quin, turning to the coroner, who was his political
friend.

"I believe you are."

"Did Mr. Finch ever give you any money?" demanded
the attorney—"Yes or no."

"Yes; he ped me wages."

"That will not do, Mr. Timothy Quin. I repeat, you are
under oath, and had better be careful. You know the consequences of perjury. I demand an answer to my question: 'Did Myron Finch ever give you money for carrying
that check to Mr. William Wilde?'"

"I don't know," replied Quin, in a sulky tone.

"Did Mr. Finch ever give you money other than your
wages?"

"Yis."

"How much?"

"Wan thousand dollars."

"For what work did Finch give you so large a sum of
money?"

"To hold me tongue—to keep mum."

"To hold your tongue about what?"

"About the check and the practisin'."

"So you heard Mr. Bailey accused; you saw him tried
and convicted; you knew that he was sent to State-prison
for ten years on a false charge of forgery; and for a paltry
bribe of a thousand dollars you stood by and saw all this
and held your tongue? Bah! you were every whit as bad
as Finch; and you were, if possible, meaner; for he played
for a higher stake—a partnership and the old gentleman's
daughter."

Quin asked his friend the coroner to protect him from
the assaults of the irate attorney; but that gentleman continued: "Protect you! If the law would permit it, I would
send you to prison for life; nay, I would hang you!"

"You'd betther be quiet, Misther Attorney? I kin meet
ye at the polls whin yer masther comes up for re-election?"
whispered Quin, giving the gentlemanly law-officer a most
villanous look.

"A fig for your influence! Do your worst! It is you and the like of you who bring disgrace on republican institutions, and keep gentlemen from the polls."

At this point the coroner called the assistant district attorney to order, and asked if he had done with the witness.

"No, I have not. Quin, did you use these practice-forgery papers, as described by Mr. Grady, to levy black-mail from Mr. Finch about three years ago?"

"I asked Mr. Finch for money," doggedly replied Quin.

"For how much did you ask?"

"How much? How much?—Let me see. At first for fifty thousand, but kem down to twinty-five."

"How did you expect to compel Finch to pay you so large a sum?"

"Bekase—bekase I had his writin', an' he was afeared ov it."

"Did you get drunk and insensible, and did Mr. Grady send you home the next morning more dead than alive?"

"Yis."

"Did you ever see any of those papers since that night, until you saw this one that I hold in my hand?"

"No."

"Have you seen Finch since that night?"

"Yis."

"Where?"

"In me own store up town."

"When?"

"Within ten days. I gev him twinty dollars."

"Mr. Timothy Quin, 'wine-merchant' and ward politician, that will do; step one side. You are a beautiful witness, as you are a worthy citizen. Take care, however, that we do not yet punish you. Somehow my fingers itch to put a rope around your neck."

When the coroner called Mr. George Bailey, every eye in the two parlors was turned with a look of intense curiosity on the grave gentleman who quietly took his place as a witness. There was that indescribable something in his calm, introspective air which told of patient suffering and resolute self-control.

"Mr. Bailey," said the assistant district attorney, "what is your present business?"

"Banker, of the firm of Wilde, Bailey & Co.," replied Bailey, in a low, grave, sonorous tone, which penetrated to every corner of the three rooms, and caused Mrs. Myron Finch, sitting beside the coffin of her murdered father, to involuntarily start and turn her head to see the man who had once been her betrothed husband, and whom she now passionately but vainly loved.

"Is it correct, the story told by Mr. Grady, that you were unjustly imprisoned for ten years on evidence procured by fraud and forgery?" asked the attorney.

"Yes, perfectly correct—true in every particular."

"Does that look like your handwriting, or like what it was thirteen or fourteen years ago?"

"It is so like what my handwriting was, that when the forged check was first presented to me I frankly owned that the writing was mine—a confession which told heavily against me on my trial."

"Does the signature look like the writing of the late Jacob Van Hess?"

"Exactly like it."

"Your fate was simply terrible," said the sympathetic attorney—"condemned to be the associate, for ten long, weary years, of brutal criminals!"

"Worse than that—worse than that, sir!" replied Bailey; "the petty, galling tyranny and unmitigated brutality of the keepers; the indifference of the higher officers; the heartlessness of all the officials; the severe punishments for slight offences—nay, for no other offence than the effort to preserve one's manhood and self-respect—these things, sir, were infinitely worse than association with criminals. The ignorant keepers seem to have a special spite against the poor convict who has the misfortune to be better educated than themselves, and they take a malicious pleasure in torturing him. But excuse me; I did not mean to say so much;" and Bailey drew his hand across his brow, as if to wipe out the memory of those horrible ten years, and heaved a sigh which sounded like a sob.

"Did you never seek to punish Finch?" asked the coroner.

"Ah! for years and years the hope of revenge kept me alive in all my misery; and during my first year of freedom I was sustained by the burning desire to wreak a terrible vengeance on the man who had done me such dreadful injury without the least provocation on my part. But —but I learned that revenge was a mean passion; that God did all for the best; that in his own good time he would mete out to Finch the proper punishment for his crimes. For the personal injury to me I have already forgiven him."

"Mr. Bailey," asked the coroner, "did you see all the papers taken from Finch that night when Quin was drugged? Did Grady show them to you? And, to the best of your knowledge and belief, is this one of them?"

"Mr. Grady showed me all those practice-forgery papers, and you may be sure that I examined them very closely, and to the best of my belief this is one of them."

"It was mainly on the strength of a check like this that you were convicted?"

"Yes, so I believe."

Mr. William Wilde's evidence corroborated that of Bailey. Susie O'Neil, the policeman, and Quin testified to Finch's appearance, even to his broken nose.

The chain of circumstantial evidence was so strong that the jury immediately brought in a verdict that "Jacob Van Hess had been murdered in his library on the evening of the twenty-first of November, between the hours of nine and ten o'clock, by Myron Finch, late his partner and son-in-law, and that the mayor of the city be requested to offer a reward of five hundred dollars for his apprehension."

CHAPTER XXX.

"I am constant as the Northern star,
Of whose true-fixed and resting quality
There is no fellow in the firmament."—SHAKSPEARE.

MYRON FINCH, tortured with abject fear, did not dare to leave his dingy room in his obscure lodging. The second morning after the murder he requested his landlady to lend him a newspaper, and, trembling in every joint, he read the verdict of the coroner's jury. The very headings in the morning paper were appalling. There he read the evidence of Quin, Grady, and Bailey, and the offer of five hundred dollars reward for his apprehension. His teeth chattered, his lips were drawn back until his very gums were exposed, and his pale eyes almost started out of their sockets. Up to this time he had had a faint gleam of hope that he might escape, but the copy of the practice-forgery papers extinguished even that. When he came to the part descriptive of his own personal appearance, evidently obtained from Quin, the newspaper dropped from his nerveless hand, and the wretch sunk in his chair, his chin fell on his breast, and his arms dropped at full length by his sides, utterly overcome by the force of his fears. Once or twice, as if fascinated, he essayed to read, but the paper fell from his fingers; finally, by a great effort of will, he read the following description :

"Myron Finch is a man about thirty-five years old, but, owing to habits of vice and dissipation, looking much older; he is of medium height, with light hair and light-blue eyes, which are uneasy and furtive in their expression; his face is puffy, bloated, and discolored with drink; he is inclined to corpulency, is bald, and has well-formed hands and feet. He may be easily recognized by his broken nose."

"D—n that Spaniard! what disguise will hide this broken nose?" This was uttered as he rose to darken his room. He wondered if Scroggs had noticed his nose. He crept into bed as if to find protection, like a frightened child, below the bedclothes. Then he thought of the strychnine, but again the desire to cling to his wretched life overcame the longing to be out of his misery. A new thought struck him. Actors, he said to himself, can change their appearance in five minutes so that their most intimate friends fail to recognize them, and why could not he? Help—he must have help, or perish! But who was to help him? Another thought struck him. He rapped for his landlady.

"Landlady, be kind enough to bring me paper, pen, and ink;" and when they were brought to him he reflected for a moment, and said in a low tone to himself, "No, no, she would never betray me; I must trust her." He then wrote the following note, with his address:

"Jenny,—For God's sake come to me! I am sick almost to death.   Yours ever,   M."

This note he paid the landlady to post, and then lay down to wait for night, and the woman he had so basely abandoned fifteen years ago.

About dusk the great-hearted Jenny made her way fearlessly through the back slums of Mott and Mulberry Streets to the miserable lodging of the murderer. It is wonderful how little fear for ordinary danger is felt by those who have suffered the agony of a great wrong. One look from Jenny's steady eye and stern face could abash the basest ruffian who prowled about the whiskey-shops of the disreputable neighborhood through which she was now passing. She reached Finch's room, and spoke to him in a voice hard as steel:

"Myron Finch, what do you want with me? I have come at your call. What do you want?"

"I knew you would come—I knew you would come! Jenny, you are a good girl. Read this; read this."

Jenny, who had remained standing, shook her head, and told him that she had read it all, and read it in every paper, with all the variations.

"Myron Finch," she said, slowly and mournfully, "was it not enough that you destroyed my happiness, ruined poor Mr. Scroggs, sent an innocent man to prison, committed forgery, ill-treated your wife and family, robbed your benefactor, but you must, in addition to all these crimes, murder this very benefactor in his own house? Myron Finch, you are a very wicked man, and I don't know why it is that I come near you." Poor Jenny, with all her strength of character, covered her face with her hands and wept. The skeleton of her old love was tugging at her heart-strings.

"Jenny, Jenny, as God is my judge, I did not mean to kill the old man! He had those papers which would send me to State-prison; and in the struggle to obtain them I choked him, but did not mean to kill him. He was old and weak, and I did not think that so slight a pressure would cause death."

"Myron Finch," replied Jenny, lifting her head from her hands, "I do not believe one word you say. You wanted the practice-forgery papers, and you needed money, and in taking them by force you took the man's life, which, in the eye of the law, is murder in the first degree."

"I tell you," said Finch, "that the newspapers show that neither his watch nor his money was touched, and that robbery was therefore not the intention of the man who—killed Mr. Van Hess."

This fact, which Jenny Edwards remembered, partly corroborated the statement of the murderer that robbery was not his object. But Finch took good care to say nothing of the nine hundred dollars which he stole from Mr. Van Hess, and had hidden at this moment between the cloth and the lining of his coat.

"It may be as you say: I trust it is so. I hope that you had no intention of committing murder. But—but, Myron Finch, why did you send for me? What do you want?"

"You read that graphic description of my personal appearance. You know that, with this nose, the moment that I stepped out into the streets I would be arrested."

"Well, what can I do?" asked Jenny.

"Actors, Jenny, can make all kinds of disguises. I have seen the fair-haired, bald-headed, shaven man, like me, change himself in five minutes into a black-bearded pirate. I want the dyes; I want the paint; I want the material; I want a pair of gold spectacles; I want a black wig; I want putty and glue; and see if I don't make a fine Roman nose, and a learned medical doctor, at one and the same time;" and the ruffian actually smiled, for the first time since the murder, at his own ingenuity. The smile was a strange compound of fear, craft, and hope, and caused Jenny Edwards to shudder with a sort of terror which was indescribable.

"Myron Finch," said Jenny, sadly, "the talents which God gave you, you have used all your life to accomplish wicked ends; because your heart is as bad as your head is good — nay, much worse; you have been a vile sinner all your days. Why should I aid you to escape, when perhaps you will use your freedom to destroy another victim? And yet—and yet I cannot bear to think of his dying in his sins, and being consigned to eternal punishment!" The last sentence was spoken more to herself than to him.

"I wish I could be certain that you did not premeditate the old gentleman's death; but how can I? You have never scrupled at any lie that would serve your purpose."

"Never mind, never mind," said Finch, in a desponding tone; "I sent for you as the last friend I had in the world. I know I treated you badly in times gone by—for which, as I told you the other day, I am truly sorry; but I see you don't forgive me; you bear malice against me; so let me be hanged! Now that you have cast me off, I would rather die than not, and so end my misery. Never mind."

This piece of acting was not without its effect on Jenny; for she was a pious woman, and loved the hideous skeleton of her old love. She would have done almost anything to save the soul of her former lover from eternal perdition. The cold-blooded, selfish villain lay there and read her thoughts, and knew that even now he had more influence over her heart than any other man living. Jenny reflected deeply. At length she raised her head and said, "Myron

Finch, my own heart and my own conscience have troubled me for many years."

"What do you mean?" said Finch.

"I mean that though our early relation is unknown to all the world, except perhaps three, and those three love and respect me, I would like to hold in my possession, solely for my own satisfaction, a marriage certificate. Now hear me. I will go for a minister, and after he has made me your wife—and Jenny winced grievously at the word wife—I shall be in duty bound to aid your escape. Do you agree?"

"Why, of course I agree! I am a free man. When my disguise is complete we shall travel to Europe together, and begin a new life in London."

"Hold, sir!" said Jenny, in a tone of command: "were you young and handsome as you were the day I first saw you, and had you all the wealth of the world, I would not live with you one minute as your wife. No, no," and Jenny shuddered at the thought, "your touch would be contamination. You evidently mistake me. I repeat that I desire a marriage certificate, that is all."

The villain was baffled. He had calculated on Jenny's ready wit, her practical New England sense, her rare energy of character, her hard-earned savings, which would help him to establish a tavern in London, and her superior skill as a nurse, which would make her so useful to him in his present state of health.

"Well, well, you need not insult me. Bring your minister. You can have the certificate, and I can have the disguise."

"Myron Finch," said Jenny, sadly, "you mistake me in more ways than one. Every penny I possess in this world I would give—ay, I would give this right hand—to know that you had repented, and turned to your Saviour. Would to God I had died believing in your truth and goodness!"

"Jenny, we waste time. Go for the minister."

Jenny Edwards went immediately to the house of her own minister, with whom she had considerable influence. Fortunately she found him at home. She explained her case in a few simple and direct phrases, without revealing anything in regard to the recent crime or the criminal. The good man was old, infirm, and slightly deaf. Jenny was aware that the marriage ceremony could be hastily performed without arousing suspicion; and she reflected, as she hurried through the streets, that even if the name should attract attention, she had skill enough to protect Finch until she had placed him in safety beyond the reach of the police. The minister accompanied Jenny to the shop of a jeweller, from whom she purchased a plain gold ring, and thence to the dingy, dimly-lighted room of Myron Finch.

"The man is sick abed," said Jenny, "and he desires to marry me before he dies. I will call the landlady and her daughter to act as witnesses to the ceremony."

During the brief ceremony Finch hid his face as best he could, by turning it away from the light, and seemed extremely anxious to have it over. Neither of the witnesses to this strange wedding expressed the least surprise, for doubtless such occurrences are only too common among their class. They evidently looked upon the affair as a death-bed repentance.

How such a woman as Jenny Edwards could reason herself into the belief that a few words spoken by any man could make her "an honest woman"—her, the very personification of truth and integrity—passes all comprehension. We can only explain it by the fact that the same early training which caused her to place implicit faith in the most rigid precepts of Puritanism, caused her to believe that marriage was a very sacred thing; and that a marriage now, even with the vilest of criminals, was necessary to her spiritual rehabilitation. Jenny Edwards had never lost faith in the binding force of the Ten Commandments; and the strictest Pharisee could not have condemned a sin in other people more severely than she condemned herself.

"Now I must fulfil my part of the contract," she said; and, with a business tact peculiar to her race, she pulled out of her pocket a small memorandum-book and a lead-pencil, and proceeded to write down the items which Finch required in order to effect his escape. The minister and the witnesses, in the mean time, had retired and left them alone.

When Finch had given the name of every article necessary to his complete disguise, he said,

"Jenny, my dear, I have great confidence in your tact and ability, and I know that I can thoroughly trust and rely on you. I have not slept in forty-eight hours, and you have so relieved me by your presence that I think I may now sleep in safety."

While the murderer slept, his wife entered an omnibus and rode up town as far as Broome Street, and entered the medical office of her friend and admirer, Washington Scroggs, M.D. She found the little man alone, nursing one limb above the other, supporting the upper limb with both his hands, as was his usual attitude when engaged in profound meditation on the merits of his wonderful discovery.

"Jenny, my dear, how do you do?" said the little quack, shaking her cordially by the hand and leading her to a seat near the fire, for the evening was intensely cold. "Jenny, my dear, I hope you are not sick. You look pale, wearied, and worried. Can I not do something for you? I trust you are not fretting about that bad man who, I see, has murdered poor old Mr. Van Hess."

Outside his sciences and his "panacea," the quiet little quack could talk as simple Anglo-Saxon as any one; and the more his heart was moved, as in the present instance, the better he spoke.

"I am not sick, doctor; I am worried a little."

"I wish that I could bring my vacuum treatment to bear upon Finch. I was just meditating, when you arrived, that all crime, like all disease, is in the blood, and that both must be subjected to like treatment. We must change the currents, my dear, and withdraw the superabundant fluid from the unduly-developed organ."

Jenny, perceiving that if he were allowed to continue talking about disease and crime and their cure, Scroggs would not cease till morning, and as time to her was very precious, she was reluctantly compelled to interrupt him, by saying, in her quick, abrupt way,

"Doctor, I have come to ask you a great favor. Will you do it, and ask no questions?"

"Certainly, my dear, most willingly. You could ask nothing wrong; for you are a good woman and a pious. My belief in you is unbounded as the ocean. What is the favor?"

"Doctor Scroggs," replied Jenny, "time presses. Will you purchase a few articles for me and ask no questions?"

"Certainly, my dear; explain what you want."

"You will be astonished, but I have your promise. The articles I desire can be purchased near the Bowery Theatre." Jenny pulled out her memorandum-book and read: "A black wig, a black beard, black paint, black hair-dye, flesh-colored paint, a pair of gold spectacles, a small piece of putty, a piece of glue, and a suit of black clothes for a man five feet seven inches and rather stout—say weighing one hundred and ninety pounds; and I was nearly forgetting a broad-brimmed black felt hat. Here is a hundred-dollar bill, which will cover the cost."

"Jenny, my dear, keep your money, and allow an old friend, who esteems you very much, to make you a present of these strange articles."

"No, not for the world, doctor—not for the world!"

"Well, just as you please; but you are welcome as the flowers of May."

"Dr. Scroggs, will you purchase these things for me as quickly as you can? for time, I repeat, presses."

"Certainly, my dear, certainly; you remain here and take care of the place until I return."

Jenny Edwards sat gazing into the fire, wrapped in profound but melancholy thought. She reflected on the wedding ceremony just completed, and compared it with the one her young imagination had painted fifteen years ago, when she fancied Myron Finch the embodiment of all that was good and noble. She had persuaded herself that Finch had not intentionally taken the life of Mr. Van Hess; but it is quite probable that had he been a convicted murderer, about to mount the scaffold to expiate his crime, she would have married him at the foot of the gallows. She was fully resolved at all hazards to save his life, and, if possible, his soul. It would have been very difficult for Jenny herself, or any other human being, to analyze her motives. They may be explained, perhaps, by the fact that Myron Finch was her first and only love. While engaged in these unpleasant ruminations, Dr. Scroggs returned with all the articles which Jenny required.

"Dr. Scroggs," said Jenny, "I need not thank you. You know the gratitude that words would fail to express. Doctor, I have another favor to request, and I am almost ashamed to ask it. Will you give me the key of your office for this night, and ask no questions? I will hand it back to you in the morning."

"Jenny, my dear," said the little quack, looking at her sadly and affectionately over his spectacles, "Jenny, my dear, this is a strange request; and I don't know whether I should grant it or not; that is," continued he, kindly, "I do not know whether or not it would be for your own good. But you are a good girl and a pious, and it goes hard with me to refuse you anything. Were it for your good, my dear, this office and all it contains I would freely give you." The little quack, perceiving an expression of extreme disappointment on Jenny's face, and fully convinced of her purpose to save Finch at all hazards, began to think that, after all, it might be the wisest thing to let her have the use of the office, or she might try elsewhere and run a greater risk. After a long pause, Scroggs said, "Jenny, my dear, you can have the key until morning. Tell me nothing about it. I must know nothing about it. There is the key: you have the use of this office and all it contains until to-morrow morning at eight o'clock. I shall go over to your uncle's and stay all night. Good-night, my dear."

As the little doctor rose to depart, Jenny rose too, and caught one of his thin white hands in both of hers and squeezed it, while the tears of gratitude flowed silently down her cheeks. All she could utter was, "Dr. Scroggs, may God bless and reward you!"

As soon as the little quack was gone Jenny left the office, locked the door, and put the key in her pocket; and, without waiting for an omnibus, hurried off to the lodgings of Myron Finch. She had placed the broad-brimmed hat under her cloak.

She found Finch fast asleep, snoring heavily like a man troubled with bad dreams or bad digestion, and, without a moment's hesitation, she roused him out of his uneasy slumber, and said,

"Myron Finch, I give you just five minutes to dress yourself while I step into the other room and pay your landlady whatever you may owe her." Jenny informed that portly hostess that she and her husband were going on a little wedding trip to the country, particularly for the good of his health.

Finch, dressed in his suit of second-hand clothes, with his broad-brimmed hat pulled down over his eyes, and leaning on the arm of his wife, passed out and on to Broome Street without attracting the least notice. They entered the office of Washington Scroggs, M.D. Jenny pulled down the shades, lighted the gas, stirred the fire, opened the bundle, and displayed to Finch's astonished gaze every article, even to the suit of new black clothes, that he had asked for not two hours before.

"Come," said Jenny, in a tone somewhat stern and commanding, like that of a mother giving orders to a bad, refractory son—"come, draw on these clothes over the others; they will increase your size and help to disguise you. Hurry! I have no time to lose, for I must be back before eleven o'clock." Finch made all the haste he was capable of making; he adjusted the wig and the beard; he dyed his eyelashes and eyebrows; he converted his broken nose into a Roman nose; and he so placed the spectacles as to conceal the patch and the paint. His disguise was absolutely perfect, and his chance of escape excellent, thanks to the two persons whom he had grossly injured; but at the critical moment the man's perversity was his worst enemy.

"Jenny," said Finch, with what he meant to be a loving look, but what was in reality a cunning leer, "Jenny, I always feel so safe when you are near me! Now that you are my wife, now that I have a claim on you, will you not come away with me, and we will begin the world anew in some other country, where we shall both be unknown?"

"You are already endeavoring to break the contract.

Remember, I promised to aid you on condition that after our marriage you should assert no claim over me. Besides, were I weak enough to consent, and even if we prospered, you would again abandon me, as you did before, the moment it became your interest to do so. No, no, no, Myron Finch, I could never, never trust you!"

Finch felt so secure in the presence of this able and quick-witted woman, he felt so convinced of her marvellous power, that the craven cowardice which for the previous forty-eight hours had swallowed up every other emotion of his mind had fled, and left him once more free to plan and scheme for his future earthly happiness: as for his future spiritual happiness, he had no faith in it.

"Jenny," replied Finch, "you judge me by the past. I was only an ill-conditioned boy when I, eaten up with vanity and ambition, left you—and—and—"

"Don't repeat, sir, what you did! don't recall the past! I tell you, beware! if you revive the memory of those days when life was a burden—when minutes seemed hours, hours weeks, and weeks years, expecting you to come back; listening, watching, hoping, trusting, doubting, fearing, despairing; starting at every step, eagerly catching at every sound. Oh! oh! oh! the long, bitter agony of those days and nights, when I prayed for death and it came not! And, Myron Finch, you never came back to me until, standing in the shadow of the scaffold, you call on me to save your life!" Jenny covered her face with both her hands, and rocked her body to and fro, and wept. To see this strong woman weep was as pitiful as to see a strong man weep.

Finch approached her and said, "Jenny, darling, can't you forgive me? Can't you come with me and be my wife in reality, as you are in law?" As he spoke he endeavored to take her hand; but Jenny drew back as though she had been stung by an adder.

"Hands off, sir!" she said, rising from her chair, and looking at Finch with an expression of wrath hitherto a stranger to her face. "Touch me in that way again, and, as God is my judge, I shall hand you over to the police!

You mistake me. For the sake of your immortal soul; to give you time for repentance—not a death-bed repentance —I have consented to save your worthless life. But know this, Myron Finch: if you could make me empress of the universe on condition that you could exercise any of the rights of a husband, I would reject you with scorn and loathing. You but waste valuable time. It grows late, and you ought by this time to have been on your journey to Boston. Here is the key of this door; when you leave, put it under the door-mat outside. You have to thank your old teacher, whom you so basely supplanted, for buying the articles for your disguise, and for the use of this office for your security. When he and I forgive you, can you not see the hand of God working for your salvation? Good-night;" and without another word Jenny left him alone in the office of the mild little quack.

"She's a trump!" soliloquized Finch, "she's a fortune! What quickness, what clearness of perception, what promptitude of action! With that woman as my wife—why, she *is* my wife—I could make two fortunes, a dozen fortunes, in London! Who would have thought that the little, unsophisticated, rosy-cheeked Vermont girl would have grown into such a splendid woman? What a jewel I flung away! But I'll recover this pearl. She loves me still—I see it, I know it; her anger proves it—and her tears! By Jove, she was lovely in her tears! She is worth a ship-load of namby-pamby Grace Van Hesses! And Scroggs, too— ha! ha! ha!—the poor little scientist! To think that he should have been called in to see me when I was—manufacturing an *alibi:* and this is his room, his office? Well, as Jenny says, the hand of God seems in this; that is, if there be a God, which I very much doubt. And this— what's this?" Finch was curiously inspecting the vacuum instrument, the very "panacea," as Scroggs termed it, for Finch's own moral cure. The murderer had recovered from his fright. Jenny's influence had given him a kind of courage a good deal like that imparted by a free indulgence in ardent spirits. "I'll stay till morning, and make one more effort to induce *my wife* to accompany me on my travels.

This travelling alone, as I know by experience, is not very pleasant; and Jenny would relieve the monotony wonderfully, for she is a very clever woman. Yes, she loves me; and when a woman loves—" He then flung himself on the lounge and was soon fast asleep. Ah, Myron Finch, perhaps you may discover to your cost that it would have been much wiser for you to have taken Jenny Edwards's advice, and gone straightway to the renowned city of Boston.

CHAPTER XXXI.

"O great man-eater!
Whose every day is carnival, not yet sated:
Unheard of epicure!"—BLAIR.

"O damned despair! to shun the living light,
And plunge the guilty soul in endless night."—LUCRETIUS.

JOHN GRADY felt very uneasy about his niece. He had called at the hotel twice—once in the afternoon, and again during the evening—and on both occasions had been informed that she had left about four o'clock, and had not yet returned. Thinking that she might have gone over to her aunt's, and that he had just missed her, he hurried back to his own house, but to no purpose. He advised with George Bailey as to the course he ought to pursue, for he feared that Finch had found means to communicate with her.

"I am very anxious," said Mr. Grady, "very anxious about my niece, ever since the murder of Mr. Van Hess. Mr. Bailey, I cannot give you my reasons, for that would be revealing the secrets of another."

"I want no reasons and no secrets. You are welcome to my advice and aid in this matter, for I entertain feelings of respect and friendship for Miss Edwards for her own sake; and, of course, anything that concerns you concerns me also."

"Thank you," replied Grady, "you are very kind. I may tell you, however, that my niece and that villain Finch

18

were well acquainted in Vermont, and I am afraid that he can work on her sympathies. What had I best do? I have called twice at her employer's, and she has not been there since four o'clock."

"I am aware of the interest that Miss Edwards takes in Finch," said Bailey, "for she begged me not to use the practice-forgery papers against him."

"Did she tell you her story?" asked Grady.

"No, she did not; but I readily surmised it."

"Very well; you see the necessity of preventing the murderer from communicating with her. I am very anxious. Will you accompany me once more to the hotel to see if she has yet returned?"

"With pleasure," replied Bailey.

Arriving at the hotel about ten o'clock, they learned that Miss Edwards was still absent. Grady then suggested the employment of a detective, to which Bailey at first demurred, but finally yielded, agreeing with Grady that in this way they had the best chance of doing Jenny a great service. The two gentlemen went directly to the office of a private detective, and secured his services for the next twenty-four hours. Grady gave him instructions to watch both the south and east doors of the hotel, to ascertain the exact minute when she returned; and if she should leave, to note the time and follow her. He also gave the detective a minute description of her personal appearance, and requested him to communicate by telegram directed to the house of Wilde, Bailey & Co., where they would remain until they heard from him.

Bailey and Grady had scarcely left, when the detective noticed a muffled form hastily enter the hotel by the south or lady's entrance. The clock struck eleven. "That's her, I fancy," muttered the detective, disguised like a rough country farmer. "I'll have her man before the clock strikes eleven to-morrow morning." The expert in human crime and misery had caught a glimpse of Jenny's face as she entered the hotel, and he read in it agitation and trouble of no ordinary kind. The recent murder, the names Grady and Bailey, dropped carelessly in conversation, and remem-

bering that these two names were most prominent at the
coroner's inquest — the evident anxiety about the woman,
old enough to be employed in a very important position—
these things led the detective to suspect that he might be
earning not only his fee for twenty-four hours' work, but
the five hundred dollars reward offered for the apprehension
of Myron Finch.

All night long the tireless detective walked up and down,
avoiding observation, but never once taking his eyes off
either entrance to the hotel. The same person, he took
care, never saw him twice. Sometimes on one side of the
street, sometimes on the other, sometimes leaning against a
tree, puffing at a cigar, he appeared the most innocent and
unconcerned of country bumpkins.

> " His was the spying eye
> Which, spying all, seemed not to spy."

About half-past five he saw the same lady whom he had
seen the night before, muffled in the same large shawl,
emerge from the south entrance, and pass rapidly up Broadway. " That 'ere lady, it occurs to me, didn't sleep much
last night. I caught a glimpse of her face under the gas-
light and it was mighty white, I tell ye. There's somethin'
in the wind." The detective rolled along on the opposite
side of Broadway, with the uneven, unsteady, but rapid gait
of a man accustomed to walk over ploughed fields. Then
for amusement he would imitate the walk of a sailor who
imagined that the sidewalk was the deck of a ship rolling
in the trough of the sea. But his little cunning gray eye
never for an instant lost sight of the lady muffled in the
large shawl. When she reached Broome Street she paused
and looked all around her. At this moment the awkward
countryman found it convenient to stand stock-still behind
a lamp-post. The woman, thinking the coast clear, walked
rapidly toward the east. As soon as she was out of Broadway the detective ran like a race-horse, for fear she might
enter one of the many alley-ways that abound in this neighborhood, and as soon as he turned the corner he had the
satisfaction of seeing her ascend the steps leading to the

door of a two-story and attic brick house, on the front wall of which gleamed in the gas-light the flaring sign, in largest of block letters, of " WASHINGTON SCROGGS, M.D., WORLD-RENOWNED INVENTOR OF THE VACUUM CURE." " Surely," thought the detective, " the gentle little doctor is not her man." He saw the lady stoop as if looking for something, but apparently unable to find it, she arose and knocked soft-ly on the door, which was opened by a man with dark hair and beard, and gold spectacles on his nose. " That hair and beard never growed on that feller's face," muttered the de-tective; " they are too nice and too black by half. Why don't these chaps disguise theirselves in a nat'ral way?— Here, boy," continued the detective, " Take this note to John Grady, at the office of Wilde, Bailey, & Co., and here's a quarter. Bring me their answer, and I'll give you a half-dollar to boot—d'ye hear? Off with you like lightning!" The newsboy ran like the wind, anxious to earn his seventy-five cents so easily.

*   *   *   *   *   *

" You here yet?" were the words with which Jenny ac-costed Myron Finch, in a tone of voice by no means re-markable for its softness. " You will destroy yourself. You ought to have been a couple of hundred miles out of New York by this time."

" Yes, dear, I know it," replied Finch, in a low, wheed-ling tone; " but I could not leave without seeing you once more before we are parted forever; and besides, I feel so safe and secure when you are near me that I have no fears. O Jenny! Jenny! won't you believe me this once? Won't you trust me? Won't you accompany me? You can—I know you can—reform me, and no one else can. You can make me repent: you can save my soul and bring me to Jesus. O Jenny, my wife! God has joined us together; let no man put us asunder. Won't you save my soul from eternal perdition?"

The lying hypocrite had studied out this appeal during the night; and he well knew that it would weigh more with her than all else combined. Nor was it entirely lost on this noble woman. She had to rouse up all her moral feelings, she had to summon all her forces of will and intellect, to withstand an appeal like this from the man she had once idolized, and who, while living, could never be indifferent to her.

"Myron Finch, don't tempt me. I am, God knows, but a poor weak woman. If you believe not Moses and the prophets, if you believe not the Gospels, you would not believe though one rose from the dead. No, no; if God does not change your heart, I cannot. If I have done you a service, show your gratitude by going away at once, for you are wasting precious time."

Finch was commencing another appeal, and had got as far as, "Jenny, my love, I fear nothing when you are near me—"

At the word "me" they were startled by a loud knock at the door which almost frightened the life out of Myron Finch, and caused Jenny Edwards to tremble from head to foot.

"Open the door immediately, or I shall hammer it in!" said a loud voice outside.

Jenny turned off the gas, and turning to Finch said, "Drop from that back window to the yard, scale the fence, enter another yard, and make your way through the basement to the street, while these men are searching the house. Hurry, man, or you are lost! Good heavens! why do you hesitate?"

"Open the door, Miss Edwards—open it immediately!" roared the voice outside.

"Yes, yes; I'm looking for the key. Why don't you fly? Good gracious! why don't you fly?" she said in a whisper to Finch, who stood irresolute and almost paralyzed with fear.

The knocking at the door became fierce and threatening. Evidently the officers were endeavoring to burst it open.

Jenny took hold of Finch by the lapel of his coat and led him to the window, which she opened.

"Now," said she, "climb out and drop into the yard. I will hold the police at bay until you climb the fences and reach Grand Street. Hurry, man! hurry for your life!"

She actually assisted him out of the window. She flung the key into the yard, shut down the window and fastened it. She had scarcely done so, when the front-door fell into the hall with a loud crash; and the detective, John Grady, and two or three officers, who had been hastily summoned, entered the parlors which Dr. Scroggs used as an office, and turned their eyes in every direction in search of Myron Finch.

Even now, Jenny, with indomitable pluck and presence of mind, said, "Search, search away! Perhaps he is under the lounge or up the chimney. Perhaps he is up-stairs or in the basement." For a minute the officers were distracted, and one of them actually did look under the lounge, and another into the little quack's "receiver" or "panacea." But the detective, cooler and more experienced, said, "One of you hold the front-door, another the basement-door, and you, Mr. Grady, remain here while I search the yard."

Had Finch been half a man, he had ample time to escape; but fear, disease, and flabby flesh, caused by his intemperate use of ardent spirits, had prevented his scaling a low fence which an ordinary boy of ten years of age could have accomplished with ease. He had made two or three attempts, and after his last effort he fell heavily to the ground. He then crawled close under the window and lay perfectly still, in the hope that the officers, not finding him in the house, might leave without searching the yard.

The detective quietly but firmly shoved Jenny Edwards away from the window, and sprung lightly to the flags beneath. In a moment his quick eye caught sight of Finch crouched close to the wall; and, almost in a twinkling, he removed his false hair and beard, and gave him, instead, a pair of handcuffs. Myron Finch was a prisoner at last, in the hands of that law whose majesty he had so frequently offended.

When Jenny Edwards saw him arrested and handcuffed, she sat down on the floor and wept—wept as if her very heart would break. John Grady approached her with the intention of consoling and soothing her, and taking her to his home in Williamsburgh.

"Jenny, my child," said the tender-hearted Grady, "come away with me. No one here knows you but the detective. We can keep your name out of the newspapers."

"I care nothing for the newspapers. Myron Finch is now my husband, and I shall stand by him to the end."

"Your husband? Good heavens, Jenny, you are mad—mad as a March hare! No, no; surely you are not married to that wretched murderer?"

"Not a bit mad, uncle; I married him last night; and in his misery I shall defend him with my last dollar."

"You are insane, woman!" said Grady, with asperity. "If this villain were free to-morrow, he'd cast you off like an old shoe. Jenny, you must come home to your aunt."

"Uncle, I thank you for all your kindness, even for this last act, for I know that you intended it for my good." And the poor woman wept sadly and silently.

Grady gently raised her from the floor, placed her arm within his, and led her out of the office, just as the little quack came in to take possession.

In the mean time Myron Finch was imprisoned in the Tombs, to await his trial for the wilful murder of Mr. Jacob Van Hess! No sooner was he alone than he began to heap curses on the head of Jenny Edwards because she had refused to fly with him. He blamed her for his arrest, and felt fiercely vindictive toward her. Now that the worst had come to pass, he commenced to calculate his chances of escape. No one had seen him choke the old gentleman to death; there was certainly no intention—no malice aforethought—to kill him. True, there was a struggle, and in this struggle Van Hess was killed. Finch consoled himself with the thought that he had in his possession nearly one thousand dollars; and if the worst came to the worst, he had also the poison secreted about his person. He was resolved to play the cheat to the very last, and cheat the very gallows.

But at the moment that Finch was making these calculations, the officers of the law were searching his late lodging-house from cellar and garret to yard and sink. The old clothes in which Finch had returned from South America were discovered, and in the breast-pocket of his coat they found the fatal practice-forgery papers. The chain of circumstantial evidence was now complete, and no earthly power could save him from the death he so richly deserved.

Nor was this all. A card appeared in the morning papers, signed by George Bailey, stating that he (Bailey) had loaned Mr. Jacob Van Hess the sum of one thousand dollars on the morning of the day on which he was murdered, and for which he holds Van Hess's promise to pay in sixty days. "Only one hundred dollars of this sum can be accounted for; what became of the other nine hundred?"

Finch had just finished reading these two terrible statements from the columns of a morning journal furnished him by one of the keepers, when the detective who arrested him, accompanied by several officers, entered his cell, and began a thorough search of his clothing. Between the lining and the cloth of his coat they discovered the exact sum of nine hundred dollars, all in twenty-dollar bills, the very denomination of bill in which the paying-teller of the bank had cashed George Bailey's check. The officers failed to find the poison. When again left alone, all his former terrors returned with tenfold force. Robbery and murder were brought home to him, and he saw no possible chance of escape. He groaned, he wept, he cursed his fate; he cursed Jenny Edwards, George Bailey, his wife, his children, the very man whom he had foully murdered; he cursed God, although he did not believe in him. He threw himself on his cot-bed, and rolled his body and tossed his limbs in the agony of despair. His imprecations were too horrible for repetition.

The keeper turned the key in his door and announced a visitor; and the words had hardly been spoken when Jenny Edwards presented herself before him.

"Blast you, you hag of —— ! Go away! Are you come here to torment me? It was all your fault—you were too good to travel in my company. Begone and leave me! It would have been better for me had I never sent for you. Go, go away and leave me! Oh! oh! oh!" and the unmanly hound wept, groaned, and swore.

"Myron Finch," said Jenny, with great dignity, "I deserve all the bad language you can pour upon my head. I knew you only too well; but no matter. I have come here to help you, if I can. All my savings of fifteen years will be freely expended to the last cent to save your life. Try to be a man; try to pluck up some courage; turn to your God and Saviour. What is this world, at the best, but a place of trial and suffering. Heaven knows I would only be too happy to take your place and die this ignominious death by hanging, if in so doing I were assured that my death would make you repent of your sins, and cause you to return to your Father above, who is eager to forgive you."

"Stop preaching, I say, you infernal hag! There is no God, no heaven, no hell, no hereafter! I don't believe in any of these things, invented by cunning priests to frighten women and children."

"Hardened, cruel unbeliever! must I then leave you, and let you go to eternal perdition? Oh, Myron Finch, it is a fearful thing to die in your sins!"

"Look here! If your nice conscience and your sweet religion had permitted you to accompany me last evening, I would not be here to-day. Out of my sight! I hate you —I hate the very sight of you! The money and the papers have been found, and all the counsel in the universe could not save me. I am doomed! I have now the courage of despair. Do you think I am going to die forty thousand deaths between this and hanging-day? To live in a state of torture for six months—worse, far worse, than that I suffered in yon low lodging—is the refinement of cruelty."

As the very diablery of his nature began to assert itself, and to drown his recent terrors, his voice became stronger and his language more cynical. "Jenny, I do not believe I have any soul; I do not believe that you have any; you and I are mere lumps of animated clay, which perish like the dogs. This is the doctrine which the philosophers teach." The fiend well knew that every word of this unbelief would cut Jenny to the quick, and he took a malicious pleasure in inflicting exquisite pain. "Ah, Jenny, you are a good woman, eh? Ha! ha! ha!" (His laugh was even more horrible than his oaths.) Had you gone with me last evening, I would have made you a blessed martyr; wouldn't I, though! Oh, if I could but torture Bailey and that scoundrel Grady as I do you, I would die happy! See here, my darling pious Jenny, my religious better half—ha! ha! ha!—my better half—that's good! This is my panacea for all ills; this converts the able and intellectual Myron Finch—please pardon the egotism, for you are aware that I have seldom exhibited conceit or vanity—the able and intellectual Myron Finch into a mere lump of mother-earth! and before Jenny could realize what he meant, he had swallowed the poison. "Now, observe how the very acme of despair has given me the courage to die."

"Good heavens!" exclaimed Jenny, "what has the man done? Help! Murder! Help, help!"

Several of the keepers rushed into the cell to ascertain the cause of the alarm.

"Gentlemen," said Finch, "you may retire. I have only taken a panacea to cheat the gallows."

"Go! go instantly for a physician and a stomach-pump! Hurry! hurry! he may yet be saved!" continued Jenny.

"It is useless. This poison takes human life in five minutes; and half that time, I fancy, has already expired."

Nevertheless, the keepers ran for aid.

Finch had reserved his worst shot for the last.

"Jenny, my dear," he said, "we were married last night, were we not? Now, my darling, I forgot to tell you that, under the divorce laws of New York, I had no right to marry, and that had you gone with me last evening you would have travelled as my— But he never finished the horrid word. Terrible convulsions seized him; and in a few minutes Myron Finch lay a rigid corpse!

And this noble Christian woman, on whom he had inflicted such wrong, wept for the miserable sinner cut off by his own hand, with all his sins upon his head, and gave him, what he so little deserved, a decent burial in consecrated ground. Can psychology explain the mind of Jenny Edwards.

CHAPTER XXXII.

"Let still the woman take
An elder than herself; so wears she to him,
So sways she level in her husband's heart."
SHAKSPEARE.

SEVERAL months have rolled away since the events recorded in the last chapter. George Bailey and Edith Wilde were engaged to be married in the spring. He was still living quietly in his humble room, under the roof of his friend John Grady, and enjoying to its fullest extent that period of ante-nuptial delight, when the hungry heart seems completely satisfied, and uncertainty and jealousy have fled, never more to come back to torment him. Jenny Edwards had been so prostrated by the ordeal through which she had gone, in her futile efforts to save Myron Finch, that she had been compelled to resign her situation in the hotel, and was now living a quiet, aimless life with her uncle and aunt, who were extremely kind to her, as were George Bailey and the good little quack, who always spent his Sundays with the family. The large-hearted John Grady had abandoned open-air lecturing on "temperance," and writing for the *Weekly Reformer.* His "carnal weapon" wielded no larger implement of destruction than a steel-pen in the banking-house of Wilde, Bailey, & Co., in which he was now employed as a trusted clerk. Timothy Quin had been shot dead in a bar-room brawl in one of his own stores; and it was discovered after his death that, while he had been managing ward politics, his bar-keepers had been growing rich at his expense; so that his family, after the payment of all debts, were reduced to a state of absolute poverty.

George Bailey employed a detective to discover the generous burglar Bill Williams, in whom he had found much that was good mixed with a little that was evil. His troubles had arisen more from evil companions than from a wicked disposition. Bailey employed him as porter in his own bank; and it is only fair to say that in all the city there was not a more honest servant than the returned convict.

One day, early in March, a lady dressed in black and heavily veiled called on Bailey at his office. What was his astonishment to behold in the person of his visitor Mrs. Grace Finch, whose faded and care-worn face too plainly told the story of her trials and sufferings.

It was several minutes before she could command her nerves sufficiently to announce her business. At length she managed to say, in response to Bailey's inquiring glance,

"Mr. Bailey, I could not bear to see you at your lodgings in the presence of those people, and so you will excuse me for calling on you here."

"No apology is necessary. I think you said that you desired to see me on business, and this is my office." The icy coldness of Bailey's words and manner cut Mrs. Finch to the quick.

"Mr. Bailey," said Grace, with a great effort, "on the day when my poor father"—and here her tears began to flow copiously—"was murdered, you loaned him, in his extremity, one thousand dollars. His estate has been settled, and I have called to pay this debt. Here is the principal and the interest; and allow me to thank you for the kindness which he and I so little deserved at your hands."

"Madam"—and Grace Finch noticed the freezing tone—"madam, I cannot accept this money. I meant it as a present to your father in his trouble, and as a small return for the great favors which he showered upon me up to the time that—that—he was imposed upon, and had strong reasons to believe me a—a—forger."

"But I cannot accept this money. Oh, Mr. Bailey, misfortune has made me a wiser and, I hope, a better woman. No, no, I cannot accept this money from you."

"If you cannot," replied Bailey, "I shall hand it over to some charitable society. The money was your father's, and now is yours. I do not need it."

George Bailey, thanks to the influence of Edith Wilde, had long ago overcome his feelings of revenge; but when he saw this woman, Grace Finch—who, not satisfied with abandoning him in his hour of utmost need, when her interposition might have saved him—began to endeavor, by means of anonymous letters, to destroy his and Edith's happiness, an emotion of extreme dislike arose in his heart, which caused the icy coldness of manner already alluded to. He therefore wished to bring the unpleasant interview to an end.

"Mr. Bailey, I must say," said Mrs. Finch, "that you have acted most nobly toward my late father and myself since your return to society."

"Nobly!—nobly! You don't know how wicked and vindictive I was when I left my prison—what an unforgiving and relentless heathen I was, until I was taught that vengeance belonged to God."

"*She taught you*," said Grace Finch, in a tone which indicated that all her misfortunes had not yet eradicated her jealousy of Edith Wilde.

"Yes, *she taught me;*" and, for totally different reasons, neither would mention Edith's name. "She did more— she saved me; she upheld me when I was sinking. Oh, her divine love has far more than compensated me for my ten years of unmitigated misery!"

These words went through the heart of Grace Finch like so many daggers; for it was the misfortune of this woman to love Bailey with a passionate ardor utterly unreasonable and unjustifiable.

"Yes, yes, yes!" said Mrs. Finch, in a tone of great despondency, "that wicked man felled you with a single blow; but you recovered more than all you had lost. With us it was different. Oh, Mr. Bailey, what my father and I suffered for twelve years no tongue could relate, no pen describe!"

"I understand it well: your sufferings were much worse than mine."

"Oh, had we but trusted you!"

"Madam," replied Bailey, "we had better not touch on

that subject." This was spoken in a tone to shut the door against further conversation on this subject.

" Mr. Bailey," continued Grace, in spite of his earnest desire to put an end to the interview, " to show how much I respect you I shall retain the money ; and please tell your —I mean Miss Wilde—that I humbly ask her forgiveness ; she knows for what. Mr. Bailey, I shall try to be a better woman. I shall live to train my children more wisely, I hope, than I was trained." By some strange impulse Grace Finch rose from her seat, seized Bailey's hand, and pressed it to her lips, saying " God bless you, George Bailey, and God bless Edith Wilde, ever and forever !" and, before Bailey had time to recover from the surprise caused by the act, Grace Finch was gone.

One day about this time, when Jenny Edwards had fully recovered from the nervous fever that followed the suicide of Myron Finch, she was sitting alone with Washington Scroggs, M.D., in her uncle's little parlor.

"Jenny, my dear," said he, "you are a good woman and a pious." It may be noted that the good little quack never said she was handsome or pretty, and he might have said both with truth ; but, with rare delicacy, he always called her " a good woman and a pious." "Jenny, my dear, now that our young friend, whose capillary circulation was so imperfect, causing an unfortunate afflux of blood to the destructive propensities, is defunct and decently buried, you might, peradventure, take into consideration my proposition to become my spouse and heiress."

The little quack always thought and spoke of Finch as a mere youth, such as he remembered him when a smooth, quiet, crafty, well-conducted member of his school in Vermont.

"Doctor," replied Jenny, "you know that I am one of those women who, having loved once, can never love again. I loved the youth of whom you speak—oh, with such a love ! I shall think of him as we knew him at home ; and surely, doctor, he was not wicked then. Don't you think it was this wicked city that ruined him ? I shall always remember him as the bright, intellectual boy whom I worshipped. Ah! God certainly punished me for my idolatry. My dear kind friend, I can never, never love again!"

"Well, my dear, suppose you cannot. Peradventure it may be as you say; for there was such an afflux of the sanguineous fluid to the amatory region of the brain that a permanent congestion occurred which has never been removed. We might, even yet, apply my 'panacea,' and by withdrawing the air—by letting it in and out—so work on the capillaries that the bump of amativeness might be restored to its normal condition. You respect me; you esteem me—at least, so you have said."

"Most assuredly I do, doctor."

"Very well, Jenny, my dear, when a good woman and a pious esteems and respects a rich old man—rich, thanks to my 'panacea'—why should we not join hands in holy matrimony? I have no living relatives; and even if you do not marry me, you shall inherit all my money. My will is made out in your favor. So, you see, you cannot be charged with marrying an old man for his money."

The little quack understood Jenny as well as he did the force of simple Saxon English; and he knew that her pride would never allow her to permit people to say that she married a man old enough to be her father for the sake of his wealth.

"Doctor, doctor, if you were sick and poor I would wed you much faster. I really think I could marry you if you were utterly helpless. Doctor, do you remember the night you went out to purchase those things, well knowing for whose escape they were intended, never asking a single question? and do you remember leaving me the key of the office until eight o'clock the next morning?"

"I do, indeed, my dear; I do remember that night right well; for my heart bled for you, seeing you in such sore distress."

"Doctor, I could almost have loved you that night," said Jenny, with a bright smile.

"Let that night go, my dear," said the little quack, with a smile nearly as bright as her own, "and transfer the feeling to this night. Do you know that I always thought that

I was entitled to a reward for my unquestioning obedience that night—the reward of a—kiss;" and the little man arose with great dignity and gravity to take it; but Jenny cruelly shoved him to his seat, saying,

"Fie! doctor, for shame; at our time of life!"

"Jenny, my dear," said Dr. Scroggs, unabashed, "you are a good woman and a pious. I love you very dearly, as I always have. My 'panacea' and you have always divided my affections since I have known you."

"Come, doctor, tell the truth now; which of us do you like best—me or the 'panacea?'"

"What a question to ask! You might as well ask a youth which he loved best, his sweetheart or his mother. He loves them both, but in different ways."

"Very well, I understand you; I am your mother, and the 'panacea' is your sweetheart."

"And I am an old boy," said the quack, with a merry twinkle in his blue eye—"why don't you finish the sentence?"

"Yes, and you are a dear old boy; and your 'good woman and a pious' will marry you. There now, will that do?" And thus ended this strange wooing.

On the second day of May there were two weddings. George Bailey and Edith Wilde were married in the same church in which the poor ex-convict had worshipped his "guardian angel" from afar; and in the parlor of the little house in Williamsburgh, Washington Scroggs, M.D., was united to the "good woman and a pious" whom he had long and truly loved. The latter pair spent their honeymoon among the friends of their early days in Vermont, and the former pair on a steamer bound for Liverpool.

THE END.

www.ingramcontent.com/pod-product-compliance
Lightning Source LLC
Chambersburg PA
CBHW020511270326
41926CB00008B/822